DON'T ASK ME WHERE
I COME FROM

DON'T ASK ME WHERE
I COME FROM

*How a Refugee from Nazi Germany
Became a UN Correspondent*

For Giles Cora
with admiration
and infinite respect

Lili Loebl

Lili. Tode. Loebl

Book Guild Publishing
Sussex, England

First published in Great Britain in 2011 by
The Book Guild Ltd
Pavilion View
19 New Road
Brighton, BN1 1UF

Typesetting in Garamond by
Keyboard Services, Luton, Bedfordshire

Printed and bound in Great Britain by
CPI Antony Rowe

A catalogue record for this book is available from
The British Library

ISBN 978 1 84624 633 3

For Beryl Bainbridge,
my friend

Contents

Prologue

KRISTALLNACHT 1938

My father had one eye. He lost the other when a bullet penetrated his head fighting for the Kaiser in the trenches of the Somme. Its porcelain replacement came out of its socket at night and rested in a watery solution on his bedside table, from where it gazed at us children when we snuggled into the parental bed on Sunday mornings.

It came out, too, when they came to arrest him on Kristallnacht. He must have put it in his pocket when he pinned his medals on the overcoat he wore anticipating the chill November night. Sitting upright in his armchair in the *Herrenzimmer* (his study) he watched in stony silence the SS men in riding breeches, jackboots and peaked hats strutting from one side of the street to the other. They were herding their unresisting prisoners onto the pavement, targeting Jewish homes with well-documented, meticulously planned efficiency.

I was crouching, terrified, on the footstool, my hands clasped around my knees and watching as my father placed a black patch over his right eye and pulled its band over his head. From the other eye the tears were trickling down his cheek.

Now there was a knock on the door and heavy boots clanged on the marble stairs. My father got up, kissed me and said he would be back soon. I heard him exchange words with the SS men. They wore swastika armbands on their black shirtsleeves and said little. My father knew what was expected of him; I think he was explaining the absence of my brother who had fled across the road to his cousin where they both hid in the attic. Then, wordlessly, he followed them into the

1

dusk. I cried and cried as I watched him being led away out of our home down the street to join the flow of all the others.

My mother had taken refuge in her little *Biedermeier* style salon, her hand resting under a cushion that covered the telephone. In the bedroom I shared with my older sister, Anna the maid was combing her waist-long auburn hair in preparation for bedtime, in slow, thoughtful strokes. She was short and wiry and wore a crisp white apron over her black dress. The sister of the Nazi burgomaster Zahneisen who inhabited the villa opposite, she had been planted as a spy in our household to replace our beloved younger servants, dismissed by decree to safeguard the purity of the Aryan race. All adult conversation would end suddenly when she entered a room. I suspected she had some loyalty to the family she served, and had perhaps alerted my parents to the planned mayhem because she seemed agitated. She kept silent, pressing her teeth, which were long and fang-like and had big gaps, into her lips. She had never missed a parade of the Hitler Youth that passed in front of our house. I used to watch her at night standing on our balcony, silhouetted against the sky, right hand held high in fervent Nazi salute as she belted the stirring songs in rhythm with their march. I, too, knew most of them by heart.

That night, they torched the synagogue, burned the sacred Torah scrolls with their precious hand-embroidered covers, and looted the silver vessels revered by the worshippers. We woke to an iridescent glow which lit up the dawn; a billowing cloud of smoke hovered over the clear autumn sky. The parts of the synagogue not set alight were blown up with dynamite, and there was a thunderous roar as the remains of the beautiful Jugendstiel building heaved into rubble. From the sofa next to the cushion-covered telephone, I heard my mother say that the president of our community had tried to intervene in its annihilation, had been intercepted by some thugs and been beaten to death in the street. Two doors from our house, they dragged our neighbour out of his house. He too was beaten. His wife was assaulted with a knife, which was proudly displayed for the Jewish blood smeared on its blade.

Bands of SA together with the good citizens had apparently gone on an orchestrated rampage; they had the blessing of the Nazi high command and Goebbels himself, to kill and smash homes, plundering their content.

2

The smell of burning filled the air and there was a terrible sense of foreboding. The stillness lingering over the street was disturbed only by the dying groans of remaining masonry, the final crumbling into a heap of rubble of our synagogue. In this nightmare, it came as no surprise that my mother heard on the phone that the men arrested last night had been sent away by specially laid-on transport from the city prison to a recently constructed concentration camp at Dachau.

When darkness fell, a great commotion suddenly broke out in the midst of the eerie gloom. Next door to us people were running and shouting. The warehouse which for a generation had housed hops at the back of the large yard was collapsing into itself and presented a doom-laden omen. I heard people among the gathered crowds outside exclaiming in shock. What had caused this large, solid building to suddenly self-destruct? Some extraordinary force seemed at work here. Soon fire engines, their sirens screeching, clattered to a halt outside. Once again a conflagration lit up the night. I tried to understand why, under these circumstances, should the same people who had let a house of God burn try to save a disused warehouse in the backyard of a Jewish residence?

In the midst of the uproar and the confusion there was loud banging on our door downstairs. I was the only one to hear it. 'Don't open it!' my mother said, and we all tried to ignore it. Fearing it was our turn to be taken away, we cowered in the back pretending not to hear. But the banging continued. I peered out of the corridor window overlooking the front steps outside. There stood my father, hands stretched out and clasped together in entreaty. I could not believe my eyes and barely heard his voice over the confusion that reigned next door. He was home and alive begging me to open the door and let him in, and that was really all that mattered.

We never knew why he was spared the torture and humiliation experienced by others who ended up being transported to the notorious concentration camp. Somehow, he and his brother had escaped by a side-door of the local prison, to where they had been herded. But we knew from then on that this was no passing madness, as my father had hoped against the odds, pretending to ignore the ravings waged by a maniac whose time would pass. We had to escape the demented forces that were operating and threatening to engulf us all.

3

Part One

Childhood

1

Hainstrasse 1933–1939

I had moved with my parents, my brother and sister to the house at No. 17 Hainstrasse in Bamberg soon after my third birthday in 1933. With the success of his international manufacturing business, my father had bought it from his father-in-law, who had stopped trading in hops and was planning to move with my grandmother to Nuremberg.

For my mother, it was a return home to the magical years she and her sister had enjoyed in the house. Their tenant in the apartment below was the Archduke Franz-Josef, brother of the crown prince and of Elisabeth, queen of all the Belgians. His retinue and the girls were frequent visitors. At these gatherings, they received their grounding in the protocol and impeccable manners of the court which were strictly adhered to within my mother's family and it became second nature to them. When his carriage rattled through the entrance into the cobbled courtyard of their home, the duke, resplendent in gold-tasselled uniform and gleaming peaked helmet, accompanied by his handsome young aides, was often received at the gate with their curtsy, and he acknowledged it with a gallant salute.

Instead of a formal education which ended with high school, my mother's growing years were spent learning amid cultured and aristocratic society. I was named after the Baroness Lillie von Michel, a member of the Messerschmitt clan, with whom my mother had worked in the Red Cross and whom she unapologetically hero-worshipped. My father was mercifully overruled in his wish for me to be named Ursula. The girls learnt to entertain with the lute, the piano and with song (my mother had singing lessons from a famous teacher) and owned a subscription to a box in the opera in Frankfurt, where they acquired the musical and dramatic repertoire which they had come to know

7

by heart. Their grandfather, a towering personality, overlooked their lives with kindness but strict discipline. On hearing of his first-born grandchild, he was reported as saying 'How did my daughter behave?' He was wary of ostentation and believed in the discreet social and domestic behaviour of young girls. As a Freemason, and Master of the Lodge, a lot of mystery hung around his activities. Apart from domestic, household, managerial and musical skills, they were discouraged from pursuing other ambitions. Despite her obvious artistic talent, my mother was not allowed to go to art school.

When we moved to the Hainstrasse, Lieutenant von Mannteufel and his family moved into the apartment downstairs, following on from previous military tenants. He was to become a general in Hitler's army and his little son my playmate. I heard my parents comment that the lieutenant never paid his rent on time.

My parents' house stood on a tree-lined avenue in the new residential part of Bamberg between two arms of the river that flowed through, and led straight from the central square to the great Dene (*Hain*) by the banks of the Regnitz. It attested, without showiness but with great propriety, to the prosperity of its citizens, many of them Jewish, whose home-grown industries had contributed immeasurably to the wealth of the sleepy mediaeval town. Unrestricted by the requirement of planning permission from the municipality, they decorated the facades of their villas with panache and individual style. There were turrets and little towers, gabled roofs and mansard windows mimicking the style of the Renaissance, baroque and rococo architecture prevalent in the town. No two houses looked alike behind the chestnut trees that shaded them along the avenue. They all spoke of permanence and a belief in the future stability of the community.

Our house, clad in pale lilac, was more sedate and without adornment. An ancient oak tree overhung the driveway and stone steps mounted to a heavy carved wooden front door. It had a large cobbled courtyard and an even larger storehouse where my grandfather had conducted his hop business. Huge iron-ringed vats still filled the floor space and the sour-sweet smell of malt and dried hops from the adjoining processing plant lingered in the darkness. It was a blissful venue for games of hide and seek – but terrifying when we got lost. At the corner of the yard were the disused stalls where geese were once force-fed with yellow corn by the servants to stuff their livers to bursting. Later, the stalls served as cast-iron sanctuary for my friend Melanie and me. She was the daughter of the housekeepers of the von Wassermans, our neighbours next door. Here we played and explored the inaccessible parts of each others' bodies, safely hidden from the prying eyes of grown-ups.

On the garden side of our house, grapes, pears and peaches climbed up the side wall. In the middle of the lawn there was a newly planted apricot tree bearing succulent fruit, but it was forbidden to be harvested before its seventh year by rabbinical law, a rule enforced without question by my father. The dahlias that grew in starbursts of colour filled the flower beds in the autumn, and in springtime a deep purple lilac tree was my mother's pride and joy.

The cellar had many chambers and ran the length of the house. Within its cool white-washed walls apples, pears, plums and potatoes brought in by the servants from the fertile farms in the nearby countryside were heaped high in preparation for the winter months. Large jars of pickles and cabbage, preserved fruit and jams crowded the shelves; mountains of anthracite and wood for the over-sized tiled stove in the dining room filled an entire chamber. Within the soot-covered walls of this dank cellar I lived out my private terrors and rehearsed my pretended death. My father's collection of wines was locked in a windowless cell behind a gated grill. Rows and rows of shiny bottles with mysterious labels were arranged on racks and were listed in an exercise book with columns marking origin, vintage and vineyard. Only he had the key to this hoard except on special occasions, when Sulzbacher the butler was entrusted with bringing a chosen bottle to the kitchen, and then my silence was bought for a pillion ride on his motorbike up and down the Hainstrasse after he deftly altered the spindly markings on the page and slipped a bottle into the large pocket of his striped apron without fear of discovery.

The servants had their bedrooms in the attic. It was large and airy and smelled of the cedar beams that supported the roof. In winter, the washing was hung up here on lines to dry, and here on shelves in large boxes was stored the blue onion Meissen dinner service and the Christofle cutlery used only once a year at Passover. In the alcoves under the eaves, huge trunks were filled with the forgotten spoils and

9

abandoned trophies from world travels, the stored-away hoard of three generations of my family. They contained untold treasures: ballgowns decorated with gossamer, lace and pearl; plumed hats and little tasselled ivory-bound dance cards with names of dancing partners; and mauve silk dancing slippers with diamante buckles and tiny high heels in which I loved to stagger around over the floorboards. My most complex relationship in the attic was with a porcelain-faced doll with golden hair. She remained always much taller than I and had a wardrobe of musty-smelling garments for all occasions – sailor suits and patio pants and innumerable exotic fancy dresses which I yearned to wear myself. She was American and had been a gift from a visiting great-uncle, and she always smiled at me.

It was a happy and orderly household, in which room had to be made to accommodate me. My mother supported my father in all things: his business expansion, his travel overseas and the stylish entertainment of his business associates. My arrival in the family had not been received with much enthusiasm, since Hitler made his appearance soon after I did. Though no one could imagine what cataclysm lay ahead, my parents were much preoccupied with the impact this upstart would have on us all. I believed my role superfluous and that I was in everyone's way. My brother Herbert, pampered first-born son, was adored by all our grandparents and the many uncles and cousins who lavished attention on him. Sometimes, I was allowed to join in playing cowboys and Indians with the boys, but I always ended up as the captive, the enemy, tied to a tree with rope or otherwise sacrificed. My sister Hanna, nearly four years my senior, also had her own coterie of 'sophisticated' friends. But at night, in our bedroom, when the lights were put out and the cigar smoke from the dining room filtered through the cracks in our door, I became a willing participant in yet another episode of the serial fantasy life we lived, in which we transformed ourselves into two very sophisticated girls living a trendy life in a terribly modern flat in Berlin, with fur coats and diamonds and boyfriends. Since neither of us (nor our mother for that matter) had ever been to Berlin, we had to ransack our wildest imagination to inform us how to live out the magical realism of our dreams. We talked the roles of our soap opera out loud, in unscripted dialogue, until someone would come in and tell us to go to sleep.

I was put into the charge of Annie Eineder, the Froebel-trained nursemaid in our employ. She kept us occupied and amused us with her creative skills, making toys and playthings out of any found objects, encouraging our help. She knew how to chisel matchsticks and balsa wood, mould lengths of wire into dwarfs and how to wind coloured wool round pipe cleaners to make their shapes. Snow White was dolled up in the remnants from the dressmaker and a little house was fashioned from plywood for them all to live in.

The kitchen was supervised by Babette and other young girls from farms in the surrounding Bavarian countryside. But on birthdays, which were special celebrations, cream horns and chocolate-glazed cream-filled sponge cakes (Moor heads), meringues and ice cream were delivered from the pastry shop on the Luitpoldstrasse. Great secrecy surrounded the preparation of gifts, and new outfits and dress-up clothes were made for us; my sister and I had matching dresses with smocking at the breast embroidered by our mother, and shirts were made in the same fabric for my brother.

At harvest festival time, the whole family was invited by the staff to feast off the riches of the land at their farm and to share in a slaughtered calf. My father never drove on account of his eye, and my mother had not yet acquired her notoriety at the wheel of her own little navy-blue Opel, so everyone relied on our driver, Arthur, a dashing daredevil in uniform. We would all pile into the brown eight-seater and head off for the farm, where we were treated like the feudal squire and his heirs by the peasant family.

Afterwards I would race in cornflower and poppy-covered fields with the farmer's children, watching the shimmering clear water tumbling over the stones in the trout stream. The hedges on the bank side were weighed down with hazelnuts and blackberries and the fish sliced through the water. We returned home at dusk, laden with goodies and sugar-iced gingerbread hearts on red ribbons around our necks.

On weekends we went for excursions to the deer-haunted woodlands and mini rocks of the blissful Franconian countryside, redolent with the smell of mushrooms, strewn with succulent purple blueberries and lilies of the valley, which carpeted the moss-strewn paths and tree roots. Wild flowers grew everywhere in abundance, the air was sweet and the forests full of magic. If we were lucky, we would pass a stork's nest perched on the chimney top of an old farmhouse, outlined darkly against the fading light as we drove home with armfuls of spoils. In my mind there was a lingering wonderment at how and if the storks had brought me into my family.

Arthur ruled these outings and showed off his prowess with dangerous feats, such as climbing on to rocks, leaping over crevices and swinging on trees. We children gazed in admiration and spurred him on to greater heights while my parents shuddered; since he was the only person capable of driving, they no doubt wondered how we would get out of the wood if Arthur cracked his skull. On the way we would stop at a beer garden, where the local beer and apple juice and sausages with potato salad were brought out on great trays and heaped in front of us by girls in dirndls and men in leather shorts and hats with feathers on them.

After Sunday lunch, on feast days and name days, my father rolled up his shirtsleeves and washed the dishes himself to free up the staff wanting to celebrate mass in the *Dom* (cathedral). I was allowed to go along. Holding the hand of Annie or Kunni or Babette we walked through the town, past shops announcing their merchandise alongside the owner's name (*Uhrenmeier*) and past the central fountain, a scowling Neptune, trident in hand, who spouted out water in the central market square.

There were timbered mediaeval houses built in sandstone, elegant and restrained Renaissance residences and exuberant rococo-style buildings with sumptuous encrusted decoration, pepper-pot turrets and ornamental gabled roofs. Splendid baroque dwellings lined the streets along the way. Most displayed their own madonna medallion on the front. Some had showy coats of arms, a warning to and a protection from a besieging enemy that plundered the town over the centuries.

As we reached the old town, the streets became secret, narrow and winding. They were unchanged in name or description since mediaeval times; for example, the terrifying Hölle – Hell Alley. At every turn and corner there was a glimpse of one of the four spires of the great cathedral which towered over everything like some fantastic scenery enticing the devoted to clamber up the hill for prayer. From the steeples of the churches named after St Peter, St Michael, St Martin, St Jacob and St Otto that crowned five of the seven hills surrounding Bamberg, the bells would summon the worshippers to prayer, their urgent tunes pealing through the cloudless afternoon sky and clanging back and forth in shuddering high-pitched harmony from hilltop to hilltop across the town.

At the top, the large cobbled plaza swept down to the great Renaissance palace built by and to the glory of the prince bishops of Bavaria. Opposite, more ancient and more modest but equally powerful, was the very ornate timbered old court, home of the mediaeval clergy. To enter the cathedral, we had to pass through the portal with its cautionary tale encrypted on the tympan over the Judge of Judges seated in the middle of the arch. On His right were the lucky ones on the way to salvation, grinning little Romanesque figures with dimpled chins and mischievous sideways glances, hands clasped in prayer, gloating impishly, eyes turned heavenwards. There was even a crowned king among them. The damned were depicted on the left of the judge, being dragged into the jaws of hell by the devil, who bore horns and forked tail and trailed a chain of iron. No one, not even the monarch in their midst, was spared judgment. Although limited, in that it is difficult to tell anguish from joy in stone, the message conveyed to worshippers entering the church was awesome: the good are rewarded with eternal bliss, the wicked are condemned to everlasting damnation.

Inside, beneath the miraculous tracery of the arches that lifted the roof, was a marvellous theatre in stone. Apostles and saints, prophets and angels stared and glared and grimaced and gesticulated from their plinths. Their hair had ringlets that curled like icing on a cake. The models of these larger-than-life-size carvings were no doubt the solid burghers and artisans of Bamberg. There was Adam, properly protected by foliage, and Eve, who had pointed nipples like ice cream cones. Here, Abraham half concealed the knife in the folds of his robe while cradling his son Isaac uneasily on his lap. Most beguiling of all was the figure of Synagogue, a young woman draped in a simple shift of stone flowing around a body that seemed alive. Her eyes were bound; she was the symbol of blind justice.

While my companions confessed their sins I would wander around to gaze at the mysterious Rider of the Dom, powerful and arrogant on his steed, a crown on his half-turned head and an elusive smile on his sensuous lips. On a tomb in the nave reposed the eleventh-century emperor of the Holy Roman Empire side by side with his consort Kunigunde, after whom all local servant girls were named. It was carved out of stone four centuries later by Tilman Riemenschneider and vividly told their life story on the four sides of the plinth on which they shared their eternal rest: the departure of the emperor to the wars; the trial by fire of his queen, coyly lifting her dress as she tiptoed over burning rocks to prove her fidelity; the healing of the emperor's kidney stones; and, in the final scene of these life events of centuries ago, the emperor on his deathbed, the compassionate Kunigunde by his side.

Within this catholic enclave, my parents lived a very Jewish life. The calendar of Jewish festivals was quite naturally observed. In September, when the evenings drew in and the leaves turned into a blaze of colour, it was time to clean the house from top to bottom in preparation for the Jewish New Year. At Chanukkah, which often coincided with Christmas, the seven-armed candelabra was polished and the *dreidl* was taken from the drawer. The game was to twirl the little wheel and gamble on the Hebrew letter on which it came to rest. Three sideboard panels were prepared to be laden with gifts for us children. Around Easter time Passover had its own rules and regulations to commemorate the exodus of the Jews from the pharaoh's Egypt. All utensils were changed, all proscribed foods were cleared out of the cupboards and feather-light cakes and biscuits were baked, with innumerable eggs and potato flour replacing our usual diet.

The same respect for their religion was shown the servants, and at Christmas a tall, pungent conifer from the Bavarian forest was placed in the corner of the dining room. We would help to decorate its branches with tinsel and curly candles in holders. On Christmas Eve when the snow was deep outside and the church bells resounded, the staff were invited in with great solemnity and greeted by my father with a handshake. At Easter, Annie used to paint hard-boiled eggs in bright colours and hide them for all of us to find.

To celebrate the beginning of the Sabbath each week, we would gather at my grandmother's home in the Luitpoldstrasse. In her dining room, clustered with memories and warm with the odours of cooking, she served chicken soup and dumplings with a large silver ladle. At least two of her sons and their families, along with some homeless stranger more often than not, gathered around the table set with damask cloth and the best china. The candles had been lit before our arrival, and we children all had a turn at saying the blessing over the bread and wine.

On Saturday mornings, we walked two blocks to the synagogue where my parents had first met in the choir. It was built in 1910 by the Jews as a monument to their belief in their newly acquired acceptance after centuries of exclusion, and to their confidence in the future of their community. My mother and sister sat upstairs with the ladies, but when the solemnities of the service were over, I was allowed to share my father and brother's pew downstairs among the men. They all knew the songs and their response to the prayers in Hebrew was deep-voiced and evocative. Their elegant white prayer shawls draped over their shoulders and their silk top hats reminded me of the illustrations in the bible stories we were given to read.

When my father was not travelling abroad on business, foreign visitors came regularly to us, laden with gifts. Frequent guests were the firm's agents and personal friends – the Jaehnichens from France, the Carlbergs from Sweden, the Litvines from Belgium and many more from Finland and Italy. Favourite of all were the van Santens from Holland. Then the table was set with white damask tablecloth, polished silver, sparkling crystal glasses, sprays of flowers and the flags of the visitors' country placed in little silver holders in the centre next to the candlesticks. My father would consult his exercise book and bring up from the cellar himself the wines chosen to accompany the meal.

My mother, who had never learnt how to cook, decided on the menu and prepared personally the artistic hors d'oeuvres for which she was renowned. If it was an early dinner, entertainment was provided by my mother at the piano or my brother on the violin or any of the other instruments he was encouraged to learn. My sister, her waist-length plaits opened out and secured by ribbon, would recite a fable of La Fontaine, recently learnt with our tutor. If it was a formal evening meal, we were sent to bed and would eavesdrop at the crack in our nursery door to hear the buzz filtering through. We would listen to the bits of conversation and laughter, and mimic the guests in any peculiarities of speech or mannerism, an art at which my brother excelled. The following morning, there would be some tasty bits of dessert next to our beds, put there by my mother to include us in the feast. And the visitors always brought gifts for us children. My favourite was from Bram van Santen, our Dutch representative. It was a green dolls' cradle painted with pink roses which played 'Brahms's Lullaby' when the little brass lever was wound up.

Visits from Aunt Gisa from Katowice, the second wife of father's handsome younger brother Leo, were magic. She came from Vienna, had little honey-coloured ringlets bobbing about her round pink face and smelled of delicious perfume. She would grab me by the arm and waltz me round the dining table until we both collapsed giggling on the red plush chairs. Then there was uncle Walter Loebl from Kampala in the colonies with gifts of wooden carvings and horror tales of serpents invading babies' cradles, and another dapper one from America, bringing presents from the New World.

My uncle Fritz, who lived opposite us with his three sons, had been famously disparaging of my gender when I was born, but as soon as I was big enough and he realized what he had missed, he adopted me as his Sunday daughter. So often on Sunday mornings I skipped across the road to a breakfast of unimaginable indulgence. Aunt Elsa loved to cook and bake; there was no forced abstention here. Both butter and jam were allowed to be spread over the rolls; at home on account of the poor who had neither, it was one or the other. Here fruits, tarts, cakes, cheeses, salamis and freshly baked breads weighed down the glass-covered cane table in the breakfast room and my cousins, who were all older than I and treated me with the importance I did not receive at home, competed for my tiny attentions.

But before we ate, their father, who was a short and thick-set health freak with a military bent, put his three disinclined sons through their weekly exercise. Dressed in white singlets and shorts, he headed them panting and sweating, in single file in descending order of age, as they ran round and round the central flower bed in the garden, laggards not tolerated. He was as insistent as they were reluctant, but they did not want to falter before my admiring eyes. When it was over, the feast began before I returned to the more restrictive eating practices of my own home.

In those early days, when I was deemed too young to be taken on family holidays abroad, I was left with my maternal grandmother Rosalie in Nuremberg. When she and I went to the railway station to see off the family who were abandoning me and cheerily decamping on their holiday, it was a time of great misery for me, and I found a way of accounting for my tears by inventing physical pain. I had heard grown-ups speak of 'rheumatism', and so rheumatism was my affliction. So strong was my feeling of shame at this subterfuge that the pain became very real. It was not the last time I would experience psychosomatic symptoms.

My grandmother Rosalie lived in a large apartment in a part of a turreted house that looked like something out of a Grimm fairy tale. Half of the apartment's interior was shrouded in white ghost-like sheets draped over furniture not in use. Even more terrifying than the ghostly house was the ancient castle across the road that was surrounded by a deep moat. This contained not only the most gruesome mediaeval German inventions for torture, but on its ramparts the giant imprint of the foot of an escaping knight who leaped to freedom across the moat, never to be heard of again. One of the towers of the castle housed the Iron Virgin of Nuremberg, in the form of a large female in full armour with pointed helmet and gauntlets. A dozen spikes attached to the inside of her armour were designed to pierce the body of the offending young woman as it closed on her sins. I had nightmares imagining it was happening to me and I could not wait to get back home to Bamberg.

My grandmother was very strict. Her sense of obedience and propriety extended to the eating habits of her grandchildren. She would buy us lovely gifts of sweetmeats, but was very strict about when we could eat them. As well as having to be obedient and well behaved, everyone had to be beautiful. She herself had been very good looking in her day and had a great passion for the unfortunate queen of France, Marie Antoinette, after whom she named her daughters. The son she gave birth to when her daughters were already in their teens was born with a harelip and died from pneumonia after corrective surgery at the tender age of eight. He was never mentioned in the family.

I was happier when left with my Grandmother Lina, my father's mother. She was kind and sensitive and her large apartment on the Luitpoldstrasse was always warm and welcoming. From a platform by the window behind the heavy plush curtains we would watch the passing traffic on the main road leading to the railway station. Each day the hairdresser would come with curling tongs and a little gas contraption to heat them up. When the irons were hot, she used them to smooth the silken white hair on Grandmother Lina's head, which crowned her short figure, dressed always from neck to toe in black. Sometimes, the irons were too hot and her hair was singed yellow, the smell of burning filling the apartment and mingling with the smell of food. She was very observant and often brought her own food to our non-kosher kitchen. But her charitable works, personal and financial, were inclusive of both religions, and she made no exception in her charity to whoever was needy. She and her husband, a businessman who died before I was born, had been founder patrons of a Christian orphanage, and she was always busy knitting garments for the children it protected. In her home I felt understood and loved.

When I reached the age of five I was finally allowed to join in the bi-annual exodus to the seaside resorts of Holland and Belgium and the mountains in Switzerland, where we often met up with my father's European agents and their children. Away from Germany and the restrictions and insults that had crept into our lives, we were free to stay in fine hotels, eat in restaurants, swim, play and romp unchallenged.

Once, when I developed a very bad cough, Dr Bauchwitz (belly humour) was summoned. He took my temperature and checked my pulse on the gold watch chained to his waistcoat pocket. Whooping cough was diagnosed and mountain air prescribed. In Garmisch, to where I was dispatched with my mother, I was put to bed on a wooden balcony in the shadow of the Zugspitze, where snow covered the tops of the mountains and painted the village white. I was wrapped up in a blissfully warm feather bed with only my nose exposed to the icy air, and the contrast gave me a very exhilarating feeling. I would bare a part of my body to the freezing cold before scuttling back into the soft engulfing downy warmth. When I got better we took a cable car up into the mountains to the eerie land-locked lakes, which are so deep they never freeze over. Here, immortal nymphs inhabit the black, unfathomably deep waters and lure strangers into their depths. It did not strain the imagination to see pale streaks flitting just under the surface and hear their muffled shrieks. We never managed to entice any of these elusive creatures out of the lake, but heard many tales of those who did, only to disappear forever. Legend has it that in his madness King Ludwig raced round these lakes in his carriage in pursuit of some divine immortal female. And it is said that the sound of his horn can be heard echoing at night even now.

In the autumn of my sixth year, my nursemaid Annie accompanied me as I proudly headed to the school by the river carrying the traditional *Schultuete*, the cone stuffed with sweets, pencils, pens, ruler and eraser. But it was an inauspicious start and the content of my *Schultuete* outlasted my schooldays at St Martins Primary School. By 1936 the Jew baiting had filtered to the eager and receptive younger generation of Bambergers, and, encouraged by their parents in the Nazi party, they bombarded me with insults and threw stones at me. After six weeks, and with blood streaming down my face, my learning was terminated when a municipal edict forbade Jewish children to attend Aryan establishments and my parents removed me from the school.

My academic career had finished before it had begun, but was now miraculously supplanted by a far greater passion. In a corner of the cobbled yard opposite the goose pens that abutted the old hop store, a dance teacher was renting what had been my grandfather's offices and had converted them into a studio, complete with red rubber floor and bars around the walls. She was a family friend, Annie Rau, who had studied with a famous dance teacher and was testing her skills in preparation for emigration. I was enrolled in her classes and spent most of my days there. She encouraged us to develop the imaginative use of our small bodies and harness with discipline our unbounded energy and elasticity. Barefoot, we leapt and pirouetted, bent and twisted and fell to the ground in ecstatic abandon to the

19

sound of a gong and drums and other strange percussion instruments from a pile in the corner of the studio. Our teacher urged us to improvise our own choreography and interpret the spirit of the music. Whenever I changed into the uniform sleeveless tunic, the energy flowed from me to merge with the music. I delighted in the movement whose rhythm powerfully galvanized my body and when I returned home across the yard, I could not stop dancing, especially while my mother played Schubert or Mozart on the Blüthner grand piano.

In preparation for a performance in the improvised Jewish cultural centre, the White Dove, now the hub of the Jewish community's social life, our dressmaker made the chosen costume for my class in green satin-backed crepe, with a high collar and mother of pearl buttons on the shoulder and a complete circle of a skirt to swirl around as we danced. I loved my costume so much I wore it all the time and only took it off at night.

My parents engaged a tutor, Fräulein Goeller, who taught me to write in the Gothic script. Then in November, the expulsion and exclusion of all Jewish children from German schools was ordered by the Nazi municipality. With the same systematic precision and meticulous attention to detail that applied itself to the extermination of six million of our people, they ordered the setting up of a Jewish school, where I was forced to attend, imposed the curriculum and appointed a teacher to preside over it.

To house this insult of a school, the conference room of the synagogue appeared to be the only solution. It was furnished with the dilapidated desks collected from the dusty store rooms of local schools and other equipment procured by the authorities. I was assigned my place at one of the ten desks provided for the thirty-eight pupils from ages six to sixteen. At least here no one shouted 'Jew-pig!' at me. The classroom was restricted in space, badly ventilated and with toilet provision not fit for purpose. Attached to the wall were two maps of Germany and one of Palestine; a blackboard on an easel stood in one corner. Since we were given no stationery, the waste paper basket next to it seemed redundant. Three arithmetic books and three teaching manuals (one for each age group) circulated around the room, together with the solitary ruler and the single inkwell that was provided.

Our teacher, Mr Frankel, had his own desk with a hinged lid placed on a wooden platform, behind which he frequently sought cover. From here he tried unsuccessfully to quell the boisterous behaviour of mentally under-stimulated, over-excited adolescents who had no idea why they had been wrenched out of their regular schooling into this situation. Novices like myself, who knew no better, simply joined in the tumult. He was very strange and seemed bewildered by the absence of discipline and we teased him mercilessly about the bristles on his head and the grim smell about his person. After a few months he disappeared mysteriously, arrested by the authorities on some spurious charge. In this spectral setting, with overflowing toilets and no room to play, we interacted among the sexes and age groups with some excitement but learnt little. At least for me there was always dancing when the day was over.

My brother and sister, meanwhile, due to some perverse reckoning of the Nazi regime, were seriously studying mathematics, Greek and Latin – language and mythology – at the prestigious gymnasium. Here, the study of the humanities was rigorous, the standards uncompromising. They were encouraged to pursue some orderly and meaningful curriculum largely unmolested and managed to acquire a sound academic grounding for life.

It was 1938, five years since Hitler came to power and since the first signs of his intent appeared. It had started with the public burning of books by Jewish authors, the first on German soil since Martin Luther's time, and the dismissal of all Jews in public employment. My father's factory, with its thriving export trade, was exempt at that time because the foreign currency he generated was essential to the Nazi plan. With their brand name Hulorit, he and his brothers had pioneered the use of Bakelite for outdoor installations, and his electrical fittings were in demand all over Europe. But other menacing signs appeared and started to affect us all. Non-Jewish friends of long standing started scuttling to the opposite pavement pretending not to see us and no longer visited our house. The penalties of associating with Jewish families had become severe and the good citizens of Bamberg were craven.

Already our activities were restricted. The Nuremberg Decreees had ordered the expulsion of Jews from official occupations, and their exclusion from all civic and cultural life, concert halls, sports clubs and restaurants. For my father, a curt letter terminating his membership of the German Alpine Club was particularly galling. He had come to terms with the loss of his eye after demobilization by walking for three months in the Bavarian Alps and had retained his love of hill-walking, which he had found healing and restoring after his injury. We were banned from the idyllic swimming pool set in lovely countryside in a bend downstream of the river Regnitz; I remember watching all the children having fun inside, splashing and diving from the boards from outside the fence, and the ubiquitous and unequivocal warning placard 'Jews Prohibited!'.

The programme of the destruction of the Jews, the Final Solution, was on its ineluctable progression. The demonic tirades of the Fuehrer roared over the wireless and sounded from the loudspeaker of the Gestapo chief across the road. The violent hatred spilled into the street and into every aspect of life. It was the prohibition from taking part in leisure activities which affected our family most. Somehow, my parents circumvented these by taking the family away and so we were compensated with wonderful holidays abroad.

Our passports, which still allowed free passage in and out of Germany, and which were renewed because of my father's commercial usefulness, now had the compulsory middle name 'Sara' enforced on its pages to mark the females out as Jews, and all males were lumbered with the name of another ancestor, 'Israel'. The accompanying photos had to be taken in profile, with the left ear prominent to give away our racial ancestry, and a great letter J straddled the page. Equipped with these documents, we visited the mountains of St Moritz in winter and the beaches of Belgium and Holland in the summer, and often met up with my father's agents and their children.

It was during one of our last summer holidays, in the one-street alpine ski resort of Champéry on the slopes of the Bernese Oberland, that our rescue was secured.

My father still held the firm belief that, despite the more frequent and increasingly threatening parade of Hitler's ardent followers and the ever growing restrictions to which we were subjected, Hitler and his thugs were a passing disease. In the summer of 1937 he installed the family where he could climb mountains and we could breathe

22

deeply the pure air. At dawn each morning, I would accompany him to the well at the entrance to the little town where he drank draughts of spring water from a metal cup attached to a chain. He believed it to be his guarantee for a long and healthy life.

Sharing this idyll were an English aristocrat, Sir Robert Dunlop, his wife and their two adolescent sons, with whom my sister and I became acquainted as a result of our clumsy attempts to communicate in French. (My brother, with his advanced knowledge of that language, was at some finishing school for the summer and only joined us later.) The excuse was always an invitation to accompany them to the village sweet shop, which made scant demands on the language ('*Voulez-vous acheter des bonbons?*') and was an irresistible destination regardless of the hilarious Anglo-French pronunciation.

Sir Robert, meanwhile, held increasingly animated conversations with my father in the lounge of the hotel, probably alerting him to the stupidity of taking his wife and children back into Germany. Uprooting his family and going into exile with uncertain provision for the five of us must have weighed heavily on my father's judgment. But it was Lady Dunlop who convinced my mother of the oncoming peril and the need for action.

Like my mother, who was a passionate philatelist and had inherited massive tomes from her father, Lady Dunlop was deeply interested in stamps. She was a powerful lady, emphatic and authoritative. She wore her hat indoors and out, and a long, animated three-strand pearl necklace dropped over her ample bosom, clothed in low-cut navy-blue silk dresses. Over tea on the terrace of the hotel in Champéry, the magnificent snow-clad Mont Blanc as witness, they agreed on a remarkable escape ploy. If the inevitable rise of Hitler became irreversible and presented imminent danger, my mother would simply put into an envelope a unique and highly priced philatelic treasure, the renowned Black Bavarian (*Schwarze Bayern*) and post it to the Dunlops at their home in Newbury, Berkshire. The Dunlops would interpret its message and know that they should initiate our rescue immediately.

No longer allowed to leave the country, our final summer holiday took us to a Jewish-owned lakeside hotel in Constance on the Bodensee. It was renowned for a nearby island where subtropical plants and flowers thrived in the balmy air, and there I saw with wonder bananas, lemons and oranges, and all kinds of strange fruit growing on trees. The island of Mainau belonged to the Swedish crown, beyond the reach of Nazi rule, and so we were able to attend unmolested a performance of Mozart's *The Marriage of Figaro* one evening at dusk in the courtyard of the castle. The air was sweet with the scent of lemons and the music spellbinding. It was 1938, my first experience of a performed opera, and I wore my first pair of high-heeled slingback sandals.

Across the lake at Friedrichshafen, we could see huge hangars housing the first Zeppelins. A great deal of hooded reference surrounded their existence and occasionally one of these airships would roar over the lake and everyone would shade their eyes and look up with wonder at these near-mythical flying boats that pierced the clouds in the summer sky with their flimsy, silk-like shells.

That autumn, the assassination of a German diplomat in the German Embassy in Paris on 9 November gave the Nazis the excuse they had been awaiting to unleash their programme leading to the end of Jewish life in Germany, and the domination at last by the Aryan race of the Reich and finally of Europe.

My father's arrest on Kristallnacht and his miraculous escape from being transported to the concentration camp left no doubt what had to be done. My parents now became totally focused on our departure. True to their word, the Dunlops set in motion the tricky process of obtaining visas on their sponsorship for our two families. Orders from the Nazi municipality came fast and furious: all valuables, property and even homes were confiscated or transferred. The magnificent factory on the canal with its innovative solar-powered roof, its staff of hundreds, its patents and its inventory had to be sold. Not surprisingly, a buyer was speedily found and a token amount exchanged hands but without possibility of transfer abroad.

In the centre of town, straddling the banks on an artificial island, is the *Rathaus* (town hall), built as a compromise in the middle of the river by fifteenth century citizens who could not resolve their dispute. It was to this beautiful building one morning in December of 1938 that my mother made her defiant way to surrender her belongings. Clutching a Red-Riding-Hood wicker basket in one hand and my hand in the other, she mounted to the second floor of the building and deposited the basket in front of a little man wearing pince-nez on his desk next to a large swastika banner. It contained all her jewels, gifted or inherited – her engagement ring, her wedding ring, her pearls and earrings and various gifts from birthdays and anniversaries. There was no point in holding back any valuables. In Bamberg, everyone had a mental inventory of our belongings, especially where gain was to be had, and they were quite ready to denounce any attempt to cheat. The penalty was too grim to contemplate.

First to go into exile was my fifteen-year-old brother, who was sent to a boarding school in Kent, England. Accompanied by my father, who travelled with him as far as Cologne, he continued on his perilous journey alone, somehow defying the Gestapo border police who interrogated him endlessly, determined to arrest him. In the end they merely took away his silver cigarette case, an engraved present from his bar mitzvah.

Next, it was my twelve-year-old sister's turn to be prepared to go to England, where she was to join my brother at his school. Word came from him that plaits were too German to wear in England, so Anna the cook cut off my sister's beautiful long hair. It was shocking to see it lying in a heap on the bedroom floor. Her hair never grew again. Whispers and doors closing on me signalled some secrets in which I was not included. I think it had to do with my sister facing her puberty far from home and without help or supervision. She was to meet and accompany an old Jewish gentleman whom she was to deliver to relatives in England. He collapsed on the quayside on the wrong side of the Channel and left my sister to fend for herself and continue her journey to England alone.

The winter months were filled with anxiety and preparations for the unknown. Without my siblings and the many departed friends, I was beginning to feel uncertain about my identity, wondering what kind of a person I would be in England. We had to say goodbye to the staff; only Sulzbacher, the butler, remained. One day, a man arrived at our house and was shown into my mother's salon in a very secretive manner. She handed him a small green leather suitcase with some objects wrapped in various pieces of material. I did not understand where the gold bars it contained had come from or where they were destined to go. Switzerland was mentioned. I was sworn to secrecy because my father had no knowledge of this visit but I knew the perils and punishment for smuggling goods out of the country. My mother's ill-advised attempt to provide for us in exile could have cost him his life. All I know is that the stranger and the green suitcase were never heard of again.

My parents now applied their energy to learning English in earnest, and proper and frequent lessons from a Miss Deutsch replaced the occasional social ones. *The Times* of London newspaper was delivered daily to the house for practice in the language and mores of the English.

I was entrusted with the task of shopping at the apothecary around the corner, to stock up on all our bathroom requirements and to spend as much money as possible since we could take very little with us. This was a favourite errand and, aided by the old pharmacist, I was proud to buy toothpaste and shaving cream, pastes and balms and laxatives. I emptied the shelves of the Houdnot cosmetics in their orange and gold pots and powder boxes, which I used to play with and sniff on my mother's dressing table. The Nivea creams and valerian drops and camomile extract and tubes, jars and lotions which I had seen on the bathroom shelves would be indispensable and unaffordable in our new life in England.

As the snow melted, and the blossoms appeared in the rose garden behind the palace up on the hill, and the almond and pear blossoms spread their scent over the trees, it became clear that our papers must have arrived and our final affairs had been regulated. The dressmaker packed away her sewing machine on which she had rattled non-stop for weeks making dresses for us, and the carpenters finished downsizing the furniture. Restorers brought back my grandmother's antique glass vitrine that had been upturned on Kristallnacht. It smelt of fresh varnish, but the axe marks that had downed it were still visible.

Two large containers arrived in the Hainstrasse, and our belongings were sealed up within their holds. Sulzbacher smuggled the family silver in among the furniture. When they left, only the grand piano remained in the dining room, reflected in the glossy parquet floor that stretched throughout the empty apartment. Finally the time came for us to shut the door of the house on the Hainstrasse and set out on our journey into homelessness. I saw my mother lock the front door and put the key to the house of her ancestors into her handbag. Like with the Jews of Toledo at the time of their expulsion from Spain, that little brass object remained the symbol of ownership and of return from the diaspora.

Arthur arrived for the last time to drive us to the station to catch the noon train. We made two stops on the way. The first was at my aunt's house, to where my maternal grandmother had fled when her house in Nuremberg was ransacked in a dawn raid by the Gestapo; they had slashed the portraits of her ancestors and upturned her glass cabinet containing her precious collection of porcelain along with all her belongings. She came running out in her Tyrolean hat adorned with a perky feather and cheerfully said her goodbye. She had interrupted her touch-typing practice, from which she hoped to make a living as a secretary when she joined us in England.

Our last stop was at my grandmother Lina's house a stone's throw from the railway station. She looked so tiny in her long black dress, her silken hair piled on top of her head like candy floss as she reached up to cover my father's bowed head with both hands. In a whisper, she spoke the timeless words in Hebrew of the blessing and prayer for peace and protection. The four sons she had sent off into battle for Germany had now fled, and when she bent down to kiss me, I knew that she knew she would never see any of us again.

What she did not know then was that she would be subjected to unspeakable deprivation and degradation, every imaginable inhumanity that could be perpetrated against a dignified and charitable old lady. Instead of living out her exemplary life with us in England, this beloved old lady endured hunger, impoverishment and untreated sickness before finally being annihilated in the concentration camp at Treblinka.

My mother's mother was to suffer a similar fate. But because she survived longer, she ended her life naked in the gas chambers of Auschwitz, to where she had been transported in a cattle truck over several days without food, water or sanitation, in conditions devised to reduce her to the level of an animal and justify the slaughter. My hatred of the German people who committed these barbarities remains with me always, and the fate of my grandmothers still haunts my nights.

We boarded the train with one small trunk and a suitcase. We had a compartment to ourselves and my mother busied herself arranging our possessions. The train hooted and steamed off. Suddenly it snorted and ground to a halt. I heard carriage doors being thrown open and the dreadful familiar voices of men in black shirts and boots yelling 'Jews out!'

It was our turn now.

At the precise moment the door flung back and the head of a Gestapo man appeared, my nose started spurting blood in an unstoppable bright red flow, dripping onto my white woollen stockings and lace-up boots. My father's face was ashen; he seemed stapled to his seat. Never had he taken an active risk where his family was concerned, done anything illicit or disobeyed a command. But he didn't move now to obey the order. As my mother fumbled in her bag to find a handkerchief to staunch the flood, the uniform, who had vanished briefly, reappeared at the door, a square white pillow under his swastika-adorned arm. He strode to the window seat where I sat bleeding, pulled my head backwards and cradled my head on the pillow before slamming the door on his way out.

Outside on the platform, there was a commotion as people were being herded into groups. In vain they tried to re-board the train, but it started and made its way out into no-man's-land. And so we crossed the frontier, without them, into Holland.

I never discovered the fate of those families who obeyed the orders to descend from the train. Were they shipped off, the children separated from their parents and lethally injected, starved, bayoneted or thrown into furnaces? The sound of their protesting cries and the destiny I so nearly shared imprinted unassailable feelings of guilt.

But, for the moment, I felt safe in the welcoming embrace of Bram van Santen, who awaited us at the railway station in Amsterdam and drove us home to his waiting family.

2

Stateless 1939

It was early morning when the ferry from Holland approached the white cliffs of Dover over choppy waters. The swell of the sea under the rolling boat had been too much for me and my father. Leaning on the port-side rail next to each other, we had taken turns at being sick over the side. When I looked at his face it was whiter than the cliffs on the English coastline, and I simply wanted the nightmare to be over and for me to be back in my bed in the Hainstrasse.

We had spent three restorative days in a suburb of Amsterdam where the five van Santen children had tried to make me forget what was happening. It seemed so long ago that we had built sandcastles in the seaside resort of Zaandford and posed for photos in descending order of height in front of the upturned wicker bath chair. My father had remained closeted with Bram discussing financial matters. They had driven us to the Hook of Holland with the promise – but little conviction – that we would soon meet again.

I watched as the boat manoeuvred itself to the quayside and sidled up to the pier. We waited for my mother to come from below deck and after the landing steps had been lowered with much clanging we climbed down and set foot on English soil. Awaiting us on the quayside were my brother and sister. Their headmaster had given them the day off school and they accompanied us to a lodging for the night. So little time had passed, yet so much had changed. They greeted us, superior in their Englishness, with pride. My brother wore a jacket with a message in Latin on the pocket, and my sister, a panama hat perched on her truncated hair, wore long black stockings under a box-pleated tunic.

We met their headmaster in Deal, a kindly man who seemed

sympathetic to these bewildered young aliens he was harbouring. In the schoolhouse, by the entrance door, a sculpture onto which everyone tossed their scarves served as a hatstand. It was the work of his brother-in-law, Henry Moore, who seemed to have peopled the garden with his statues. Here, in the grounds of that sprawling Kent estate, we found ourselves homeless, penniless and stateless; but for a while at least, we five were together again.

The next day we boarded the train to London, and took up rooms in a boarding house at 38 Fitzjohn's Avenue. My parents unpacked their few possessions in the front room overlooking the street; my room was in the attic. It overlooked a wide tree-lined avenue whose prosperous red-brick mansions swept up the hill to Hampstead Heath. A Professor Freud, we were told, lived in the next street and we could see a corner of his building through a gap between the houses. I did not see the relevance of this, except that he, too, was a recent arrival here, nor did I recognise the name Marie Curie, who had lent her name to the clinic a few doors away.

Our existence now became tied in with that of the cluster of refugees huddled together in accommodation around Swiss Cottage and Belsize Park. Vital trivia travelled by word of mouth: bureaucratic requirements, how we were expected to conduct our lives as refugees and, more importantly, news of developments in the Europe we had left behind. Female refugee committee members, volunteers in dealing with the mounting crisis, handed out clothes, food and money in Bloomsbury's Tavistock Square. My mother adapted to the frugality and improvisation of this deprived existence without complaint and it seemed not unnatural for her to queue up at Woburn House for cast-offs for her family. Each day we had to report to the police station in Finchley Road opposite the Underground station. We stood waiting in endless queues to prove that we had not absconded with our signature. With no money and little status it seemed difficult to imagine where we could go. At the Cosmo coffee shop anyone who had the price of a cup of coffee and perhaps a slice of apple cake filled the tables and chairs and compared notes. The subject was mainly what news had filtered through from family members left behind.

And so, common ground was found with the lucky little army of displaced and bewildered continentals trying to put on a brave face in exile. On Saturday mornings my father took us to synagogue to attend service, as he had always done. The first one we tried in West Hampstead was approached through a narrow passage and over a wooden footbridge between railway lines. It seemed a long walk but I loved the Underground and the LMS trains rushing past, whistling. The liberal synagogue in St John's Wood seemed to suit my father better and we could stand next to him during the service. So it was there we went to pray, for our future and for our grandmothers.

There wasn't much to say of those weeks when terrible events were happening in the world. The name of Hitler seemed to have followed us across the turbulent stretch of water to this island of safety; they said he was breaking every term of the Versailles Treaty, had defied every international commitment. Only the news bulletins read by the announcer on the radio in the breakfast room told us that one country after another was falling to the armies of the Third Reich like a pack of dominoes.

My parents were preoccupied and had little time for my personal confusion in these strange surroundings. I barely knew the language, and until my sister arrived at the end of term, had no one to talk to. I watched with wonder as heavy-built horses with hairy feet flopping over their hoofs trudged up the hill pulling a cart full of milk bottles that rattled against each other. I learnt to eat hot gluey oats boiled in salt and water and covered with cold milk for breakfast. At home we had eaten them raw with raspberries, hazelnuts and sugar, which I liked better; the marmalade on the toast was bitter in my mouth and held even less allure.

Slowly, as I was getting used to the sounds and strange smells of England, a plan for our future began to emerge. My father and his brother, whose visas were granted on condition that they provided employment in the north where the Depression had taken a huge toll on jobs, prepared to set up a factory in a government-built trading estate on Tyneside. Each day my father departed by Underground to the little office they had rented in the City, to leaf through the Yellow Pages searching for second-hand machinery with which to start their business. These were anxious times, and our survival depended on his success. The small amount of money my father must have smuggled out and retained abroad at great risk through his exports, and the few hundred pounds his agents in Europe had invested in the relocation, would soon have to provide a living for our two families; in the meantime we had to live on tiny resources.

One day in July an invitation to lunch from the Dunlops was delivered to my parents by hand. We took the train to Newbury and were fetched from the little train station by their uniformed driver. Lady Dunlop received us on the doorstep of the red-brick house at the end of the driveway. She explained that her boys were away at boarding school, but that she had engaged a nanny for the day to entertain me. Mary and I were quickly seen off to a wooden play-hut at the bottom of the garden. It had a billiard table in the centre and lots of sticks hanging on the wall, and bats, balls and board games were strewn around. At lunch in the dining room I was allowed to join the grown-ups at the polished table. Instead of a tablecloth, our plates were resting on mats with paintings of hunting scenes. I noticed that Mary was not ushered to sit at the table but had her lunch in the kitchen. We had a main course of roast beef, and a dessert of a multi-coloured wobbly substance which, to my great embarrassment, kept on slithering from my spoon onto my plate where I tried to contain it. There was also a more solid pink sweet which was very easy to eat and called blancmange.

I noticed a stiffness in the conversation between my parents and our hosts, so different from the assured exchanges between social equals taken for granted in Switzerland. We were refugees now, and it must have shrieked out of every intonation and aspect of our beings. Sir Robert, a tall lean man with a pencil-thin moustache, was very kind and tried his best to talk to me. When it was time to leave I ran down the driveway behind my parents to the awaiting car, and shouted 'Bye-bye!' to Lady Dunlop. She summoned me back and, with index finger crooked in reprimand, told me I must only use such familiarity with my little friends – with her ladyship it must be the formal 'goodbye'. I was then released to drive off with my parents.

Things looked up when my sister joined us from boarding school. My brother, too, had come to London after a happy summer spent at Cadet Corps camp leading the band with the drum. My sister and

I shared a bedroom once again and roamed freely around the streets of Hampstead. Together we walked to the library at the bottom of Arkwright Road, took books off the shelves and sat silently pretending to read with other people at the desks. My sister's English was very good now, but I struggled to read the pages in front of me. I loved to look at old illustrated books. It was my first introduction to Charles Dickens, and in the reading rooms at the bottom of that hill I fell in love with words – English words, their sound and the feelings they described. After a while, we were allowed to take the books out of the library, and we returned nearly every day to exchange them for more.

We were learning to talk to each other in a strange new language, and trying to be the English people we had no choice but to become. I sensed that this was how it was going to be from then on, for always. No one had told me how to be English. I just played at it, like I had played at being a young woman in Berlin. I was beginning to realize that, aged nine, this was the end of the person I had been, and that when I landed in Dover and reached the boarding house in London, another person had emerged who had lived a life without history; the shadows of the past had to be suppressed. It was a forced forgetting, and the pain of ruptured life ran deep. We now had to become English, and my sister and I practised from morning to night to accomplish this, in our bedroom and in the street.

This process was abruptly suspended and rendered seemingly pointless one Sunday in September when, in clipped flat tones, Prime Minister Chamberlain announced over the radio that the ultimatum to Hitler to stop invading Poland had failed; this country, he said, had no choice therefore but to go to war with Germany. His voice resounded through the rooms in the boarding house. Somehow it had been expected (my brother had already been filling sandbags outside Belsize Park Underground Station). After months of fear and anticipation it was almost a relief, a strange sort of exhilaration. The sirens began their drawn-out, doom-laden wail. From nowhere and yet everywhere they pierced the autumn sky and made us shudder. Suddenly, we no longer felt safe.

That broadcast turned us from refugees to enemy aliens. The scared, pathetic creatures seeking asylum from tyranny now presented a threat to the population and were to be treated with caution. We dared not speak German anywhere for fear of being attacked, especially in the street, and we resorted to talking in whispers or not saying anything at all. My parents were full of dread and guilt that all possibility of rescuing their mothers was over, that the exit doors for Jews had slammed shut and had stranded them in Germany. I heard my father express the belief that the Nazis would not harm old defenceless people.

A few days later, news came that we were to be evacuated along with all London children to the surrounding countryside. My parents joined in the collective panic and belief that bombs would fall and jackboots would march once again in pursuit of us. We Jews would be the first target for destruction. They must have been relieved, too, to have two less mouths to feed while they set up home in Newcastle. I had no say in the matter, no appeal was allowed, and my sister and I were packed off to the Church of England school behind Swiss Cottage. My mother watched from the window as my sister and I, a few of our possessions stuffed into the rucksacks on our backs, walked off to destination unknown, desperately trying to be brave.

St Paul's Church School was abuzz with a multinational confusion of children of all ages, some excited, some bewildered, some sobbing, from all over Europe. Some could speak a little English, others seemed unable to cope with yet another separation. We joined the queue for our identity tags, on which my name was translated for the first time into English and spelt with a y. Gas masks in square brown cardboard boxes with a string attached were placed around our necks and we were ordered in strict terms never to let go of them. Cadbury's chocolate biscuits, custard creams and huge slabs of milk chocolate were thrust into our arms; I had never seen any of these before. Soon we were marched in double file into the Underground and on our way to Watford, from where we were taken by coach to the church hall in Abbots Langley, Hertfordshire.

With much noise and commotion the children were selected by volunteer villagers. The hall emptied; only my sister and I were left behind. From out of nowhere two women walked over to where we were huddled, one of them young, the other old. They must have been persuaded by the organizer, frantic to finish her task and clear the place. They asked our age and many other questions, then marched us home with them as their evacuees.

It was a short walk from the church to the row of small houses in Breakespeare Road. At No. 27 their first act was to separate us from the comfort food we were clutching. We never saw Cadbury's biscuits again in the hunger-filled weeks that followed.

Our room was at the top of the stairs. It was painted yellow, had a brass bed which we shared and a washstand with a jug and a cracked white china bowl. A chamber pot stood under the bed. The toilet was at the bottom of the narrow strip of scrubby garden bordered on either side by thorn bushes. A well-trodden cinder path led to the wooden hut. Inside, the seat had a round hole in the middle and a foul smell. Squares of cut-up newspapers hung on a nail on the wall. Once a week, in an inescapable ritual, a tin bathtub was set up in the kitchen. It was filled with boiling water from the kettle heated over the fire in the grate. I was the first to be scrubbed in it with coal tar soap, followed by my sister, who was allowed to wash her body by herself. Once, when a lady inspector from the government came, we were permitted to sit in the front parlour of the little house.

Soon we discovered that the Ostlers, our minders, mother and daughter, were not made in the image of the God to whom they prayed in church on Sundays. Indeed, they displayed no semblance of kindness, sensitivity or awareness of the plight of the two small sisters from a strange tribe cast upon their doorstep and forced into their restricted lives out of patriotic duty and for financial gain. They were harsh and subjected us to a regime of great severity.

We were always hungry, especially at night during the long spell between teatime and breakfast next morning. The great treat on Sunday after church was a plate of egg and chips and sometimes a trip to the local sweet shop, where my cousin George would share his farthing toffee stick with us. But it was my bowels that betrayed me. Uncompromising or uncooperative, my bowels would not move to the sadistic satisfaction of our hosts and enemas were enforced. These were conducted with enthusiasm by the older Ostler. She said what I really needed was dynamite. Sometimes, the detested hot soapy fluid burst urgently out of my body before I could run to the hole in the garden hut; then I was forced to use a bucket in the middle of the kitchen floor. My sister's problems were of a menstrual nature and amid a lot of lowered voices and sudden conversation-stopping, matters were sorted without my being allowed to know about it.

My parents, meanwhile, had gone to Newcastle to set up a home and a factory. We wrote them letters in English, but they were heavily censored by the Ostler ladies so they never had a clue as to what was really happening. We learnt to disguise our despair, so that even our parents failed to read between the lines. When, finally, railway tickets were sent for us to rejoin our family in November, a third one was included. Out of gratitude to our hostesses, and oblivious to the tortures we had endured, the younger Ostler was invited to escort us as guest of my parents, to be treated with their accustomed elegance and hospitality. After three gruelling months of misery, we were at last to be rescued. So, accompanied by Miss Ostler, preening herself in a pale blue Sunday suit, a hat adorned with a feather and secured with a pearl pin lodged at an angle on her head, we made our journey to our new home in Newcastle.

3

Newcastle 1940

We arrived in Rectory Terrace in late November. It was dark when we reached the red-brick terraced house at No. 26, set back from the wide road behind a privet hedge. A silver birch tree leaned over the entrance and a stone path next to a flower bed led to the front door. I walked through the open gate, ran up the path and into my mother's embrace.

She had set the table in the kitchen for our welcome, and had baked her hazelnut cake and crunchy jam-topped biscuits. An embroidered cloth covered the cherrywood table and a vase with dahlias stood in the centre. The flames were half-heartedly licking the coals in the grate of the iron stove and a water kettle whistled in the scullery. With a stranger in our midst the conversation was formal. A little later, my father and brother came home from the factory and joined the tea party.

That night, I slept in my own bed. The white-painted iron bedsteads had arrived in the containers with a selection of the rest of our furniture but no treasured possessions, and were set up next to each other in the back bedroom. Our clothes had been piled into the built-in wall cupboard. My sister chose the bed nearest the door.

Miss Ostler was shown the room on the half landing next to the bathroom. She behaved like an old family friend and savoured the courtesies my parents showed her; it was only after she left two days later that I could peel off the layers of pretence and fear which her hypocrisy had made worse. At last we were able to be alone and pour out our experiences to my parents. For them, too, their short stay in their lodging near the factory in Gateshead had been miserable. My mother had wept to see little children running shoeless in the fog and cold through the grim alleyways, their torn clothes strung together with safety pins. They were happy to rent this house in a genteel suburb from a man who moved to the country fleeing the war.

In these new surroundings, we found ourselves as a family suddenly living in a proximity which had always previously been sanitized by the safety valve presence of nannies, governesses and servants, and began to encounter the expected raw arguments and confrontations of such a situation. My brother especially seemed to challenge my father on all subjects, particularly concerning the running of the factory and the leaving behind of our grandmothers. But the events in Europe were only discussed behind closed doors, not in front of the children. As for the war, nothing seemed to have happened; no sirens sounded, no bombs fell and no soldiers marched in the streets of Gosforth. Life had to be lived normally, and normally we attempted to live it, mixing with fellow refugees and getting to grips with our new environment. Only when the rare letters from the Red Cross arrived containing stilted and brave messages from our grandmothers did a deep gloom settle upon the household. My father's struggle and worries were etched on his face when he returned each evening on the electric train behind our house, and I felt he was too weary for the criticisms and demands thrust at him by my brother in his full-blown adolescence.

My mother needed a home. It was the only place in which she knew how to function and be herself. It made her strong in exile. Declassed and alien, she organized her family, supported her husband and with what little money there was used the skills she had learnt as a debutante to maintain her standards.

I began to understand the house and its needs. I noticed a glass-encased panel over the kitchen door with markers that flicked up when bells were rung in the many rooms, to summon servants long since departed. The only bathroom on the landing was there for all of us and depended on the fire in the kitchen to warm the water in the tank. Freezing fog seeped through the windows deep into our bedrooms in the morning; the stove had to be lit before everyone got up so that there would be hot water in the tank and warmth in the house. I soon learnt to get up out of bed early and set the fire in the kitchen grate. I fetched buckets of coal from the bunker in the outhouse which lined the path to the back lane. There was an axe to splinter wood, logs for kindling and paper to crunch and set it all alight. Success was a triumphant red glow, hot water and warmth; failure resulted in thick clouds of eye-scorching smoke billowing into the kitchen.

I explored the former nursery in the attic. Its front room spanned the width of the house and a dormer window looked far into the distance and beyond. It had to be rented out for much needed income to an engineer who worked in my father's factory.

One day, soon after our arrival, a lady in a calico wrap-around pinafore rang the doorbell, in her arms an iced fruitcake for us to put in our larder to mature for Christmas. Her husband worked on the railways and her daughter invited me to play with her and her little gang in the street. They were kind, the people of Newcastle.

On Fridays my mother and I went into town, where the pavements teemed with the miners and steel workers from the surrounding villages spending their wages. The tram that took us to the Haymarket swayed and clanged along the Great North Road.

Cows grazed over the large expanse of moorland where once, I was told, bears, wolves and wild boar had roamed at will. My mother bought her chickens and groceries and vegetables in the huge central-market halls where the raw carcasses of cows, rabbits and fowl were suspended from great hooks under the vaulted arches, smelling of raw blood. The cries of the butchers in red-stained white overalls selling their wares echoed though the hallways. I held my nose and became a vegetarian.

On Friday evenings, I helped set the table in the dining room where, at dusk, my mother lit the Sabbath candles. I would wait in the street for my father to turn the corner from the station with flowers for my mother and a plaited challah bread from the Jewish shop. We all changed for dinner and waited for my father to do the same. At the head of the table he said the Sabbath prayers. After a dinner of roast chicken and potatoes and some fine dessert prepared by my mother, the men spoke the after-dinner prayer and we all went next door to the drawing room to listen to the radio before arguing about whose turn it was to clear up.

A secondary school was found for my sister. It was the best in the area, with vast playing fields, a very high standard of teaching and a nice headmaster who took an interest in my sister and came to our house for dinner. My brother worked night shifts in the factory, which was in full production mode making components for munitions for the war effort. Meanwhile, I was packed off with our neighbour's daughter Doreen to a small council school at the top of an embankment of shops over the footbridge on the other side of the train tracks.

The school was only open part-time, since many of the teachers had been called up. Lessons at this school, my fifth in my short life, passed without my participation. I felt it was not for me, that life had something less boring in store for me and that my destiny was yet to unfold. No bonds of friendship formed during those months, and no intellectual excitement stirred within me in the drab classroom and the drab playground. The only thrill at playtime was to go down the embankment to Daisy Biggar's with my milk money.

Here the door opened to a blast of cat smell, stale smoke and dank decay. Old newspapers were stacked in toppling piles on the floor, the cracked lino on concrete littered with empty lemonade bottles. One bar of an electric fire kept the cat warm. Only Daisy Biggar's head and shoulders, draped in a grimy shawl, were visible. She peered at any activity coming into her shop, her mouth twisted with undisguised dislike every time the bell at the top of the door clanged. But if she liked what she saw, she would reach her bony fingers into one of the cloudy jars that cluttered the counter, wrench loose a few glued-together sweets and present them in a small paper bag, of which she did not let go until the currency had been placed in her outstretched hand. This was the reward for fawning and, what with frequent shortages and rationing, it was well worth it.

We resumed our familiar habits. On Sundays we were corralled into bus excursions to the historic outlying Northumbrian villages, where we would walk in the surrounding woods and meadows. Sometimes, the little electric train took us to the coast, where we would climb over the dunes away from the fairgrounds and, at the waters edge, look out to sea. There, beyond the horizon, was Norway, my father told me, and I was very comforted by this information,

40

for it seemed to me I could reach out and touch the familiar country and all our friends who inhabited it.

But Norway, too, was soon invaded by the armies of the Reich in the Blitzkrieg which followed, and so were Denmark and Holland. War began to feel real now and once again our lives were on a knife-edge. These months were lived in parentheses and we knew it could not last.

That May, the twelfth, on a glorious sun-filled Sunday morning, they came again to arrest my father. This time, instead of jackboots, they wore lace-up boots and grey suits underneath their belted mackintoshes, and they took my brother with them, too. It was a government decree that all male immigrants were a threat to the country and should be put away. They were very polite, but impatient as they stood in the porch between the outer and inner front door. In a gesture of trust, they offered my father an exit through the back door, away from the curiosity of prying neighbours. My father declined and, with a wry look, half of bewilderment and half of despair, left my mother standing on the marble doorstep and followed the officers down the path through the gate and out of our lives. My father's brother was also taken away and the factory had to close down. They were marched off to the local barracks, where soldiers with mounted bayonets guarded them until they were transported to a more permanent prison.

We stayed on until the end of the month, when we too were considered too dangerous to be allowed to live within signalling distance from the coast. Once again, my mother locked the door of her safe house and took the key away in her handbag.

4

War 1940

The villa at 38 Stormont Road in London belonged to my mother's cousin, and after leaving Newcastle we found a temporary home there. The Griessmans had made their escape from Nuremberg early in 1933. Uncle Ernest had been on a train crossing the Swiss border when news arrived of the rounding up and arrests of Jews. He had hidden in the toilet and jumped train in the darkness to join his family, who were vacationing in the mountains. They never returned. After a stay in Paris, they came to London, started a textile business and prospered.

The house had a large garden and a granny flat for their mother, my mother's aunt. After some weeks, a discussion took place between my mother and Aunt Gerd, during which it was agreed that for our self-esteem and their privacy we would be better off living independently. 'Eat an apple less, and spend a little more on decent accommodation,' was my aunt's mantra. My mother looked around and decided to take us back to the familiar rooms at Fitzjohn's Avenue.

Fortunately, the school holidays had begun, and most children had been evacuated anyway, so with no possibility of an education we roamed around the sandbagged streets, went swimming at the lido in Kentish Town, visited the wax works at Madame Tussauds and were taken to the bloody Tower of London by cousin George, who delighted in showing us the cells with the gory history of the most gruesome events. The smell of dried blood and damp stone and their history of torture and murder gave me nightmares.

My mother started a small industry in the front bedroom of the boarding house. She bought squares of coloured felt from the department store John Barnes and made flower posies to wear in lapels. My sister

42

delivered these to customers, mainly fellow refugees or anyone who would pay a small sum to brighten up their appearance, and collected payment, which my mother felt too shy to do.

From my father and brother there came occasional brown envelopes containing heavily censored letters. Thick lines tantalizingly obscured parts of sentences suspected, no doubt, of harbouring secret messages, making us wonder what really was happening to them. For the moment, they were locked up in a prisoner-of-war camp in Huyton, near Liverpool, hemmed in by barbed wire fencing, watch towers and of course armed guards, suspected of being agents of the Nazis from whom they had just escaped with their lives. There was talk of their being shipped to Australia but it seemed their destination would instead be the Isle of Man.

The war had started in earnest; the Germans had thrashed their way through the continent of Europe and captured Paris in June. More terrifyingly, they had trapped the British forces sent to France to halt their progress and a citizens' army had to be sent to rescue the remnants stranded in Dunkirk. Hitler's Luftwaffe had been trounced by the Spitfires of the RAF and he had to find other means of subjugating this country. But the threat of invasion was real. The Air Force, we were told, had saved us for the moment. They downed nearly two thousand German planes over Britain and forced Hitler to unleash the Blitz over London.

At the end of the summer the air-raid sirens signalled the beginning of the relentless attacks from the air. The warnings tuned up in an eerie growl and rumbled on until they scaled to a strident high-pitched whine, which announced unimaginable danger. Slender beams of light lanced the star-filled September skies, searching to entrap enemy planes in their beams and single them out to the anti-aircraft guns primed to shoot them down from the ground. They hummed with a steady purr, so dreamily and peacefully in the night. We learnt after some weeks which aircraft were ours and which were theirs. We knew that when the wailing of the siren aroused us from our sleep, we had no choice but to stumble out of bed in our nighties, grab our gas masks and rush down to the garden, where a grass-covered mound concealed an air-raid shelter intended to protect us from the bombs that were hailing down on the city. Together with the other residents of the boarding house, we sat there night after night, aching with fatigue, slouched on the narrow wooden benches which lined the sides, hardly wide enough to accommodate our sleep-soaked bodies. The searchlights scanned the sky, the anti-aircraft guns stuttered and the enemy planes dived to release their hail of bombs.

We became accustomed to the sudden stop of the throbbing engine, and the deadly silence that followed the release of their bombs; a pause, followed by a mighty explosion, let us know that the crash was nearby and that we had been lucky to escape a direct hit yet again. Not until the all-clear sounded were we allowed out from our hideaway, only to be summoned again just as we had gone back to sleep. I was so exhausted that I thought I would rather be killed by bombs than endure this shattering tiredness. I felt dispensable anyway, since unlike my sister I could not contribute to our upkeep.

And so we lived that end-of-summer in the eye of the storm while a battle of deadly duels raged above us. One night, we were startled by the proximity of a diving plane. We heard the engine stop and a whistling close by. Expecting a direct hit on our bunker, someone ordered us to run out as fast as we could. As we started to cross Fitzjohn's Avenue we heard a loud crash. Behind us, our boarding house had been hit and the shelter demolished. We piled into a brick air-raid shelter on the opposite pavement. Inside, a crowd of frightened, bewildered people and their children were crammed together, but they made room for us. Once again came the sound of a diving bomber. We all rushed to where we thought the entrance was located but came up against a brick wall. Instinctively, we turned to the other end where there was an opening; that saved our lives, because a bomb exploded where we had sought to exit from the shelter.

In the commotion and among the shocked people huddled around on the pavement, air-raid wardens in their tin hats directed us to the designated rescue station. It was the library in Arkwright Road, where we spent the rest of the night on mattresses on the floor. The next day, we retrieved some essential clothing from the wrecked boarding house building and went to stay with a favourite aunt of my mother's in Golders Green, where she lived with her granddaughters, who were waiting to hear the fate of their parents stranded in France.

I forgot what normal was, and felt bewildered and insecure. I wondered why life had become so temporary, why we had to keep wandering from place to place, where we would be tomorrow and when would I see my father again. Though my cousin Lore and I made light of things, playing silly games in the broom cupboard under their stairs which acted as a shelter, I was sure that the next time one of those bombs fell out of the sky it would kill us all. It was little comfort to hear people say with pride that the Battle of Britain had been won.

Meanwhile I accompanied my cousin to yet another primary school in Wessex Gardens – but not for long. My mother's sister-in-law had found a safe place for us to stay and the possibility of a cleaning job for her in the Lake District. And so we boarded a train to the north, escaping from the bombs but journeying into a new kind of purgatory.

5

Keswick 1941

The sky was menacing and thick grey clouds shrouded the little market town when we arrived at the railway station in Keswick, setting the mood for the best forgotten months ahead. My Aunt Elsa and cousin George, who had earlier fled from London, took us to their loft where they had made room on the floor for some makeshift beds for us.

My mother wasted no time in joining her sister-in-law in taking on a cleaning job at the vicarage when a vacancy arose. She was sacked for sitting on the bathtub smoking her cigarette, and when the prohibition against immigrants living near the shore was lifted, she finally gave in to my sister's nagging to be taken back to Newcastle to continue her studies. I was told that it was safer to remain behind in these hills as an evacuee, provided for by the government. Clearly, there was not enough money to support three of us, so I was placed with a postman's family at the edge of the headland on the shore of the lake Derwentwater. Although I understood that I was being left behind for economic reasons, I felt that the circumstances of my abandonment were cruel and unjust. I now prepared to face the most fiercely despairing months of my eleven-year-old life.

The Atkinson family received an important 15 shillings a week from the state for the privilege of having me billeted in their home They lived in a tiny stone house and had three young daughters. I was to share a room with the girls and their mother. Father slept alone in the only other bedroom. I dreaded the nights spent in the brass double bed with Mrs Atkinson; I had clearly displaced one of her daughters, all three of whom now shared the other bed. She was a large woman, her face glistening with sweat, perspiration forever trickling down the side of her cheeks, her matted bobbed steel-grey hair restrained by a clip. I was forced to squeeze myself against the wall away from contact with the wheezy heaving body, and slept little. What revulsion I felt I could only express by edging myself deeper into the groove between the bed and the wall, until the sharp rim of the mesh dug into my side. The chamber pot for the use of all stood under the bed, wafting with increasing flavour its malodour into the airless room at night. After a few weeks of my unexplained sleeplessness, an army camp bed was found for me and it felt like paradise.

Mr Atkinson was the town postman. His frame was thin and his grey hair tapered close to his domed head. He had a sort of amused indulgent detachment, a whimsical grin on his open face when he rested among his family at teatime, his post bag empty next to him, his job well done. He, too, meant well and was kind to me.

I was sent to the parish school at the end of the town with the Atkinson children. My classmates soon discovered that my name sounded similar to that of Hitler's club-footed propaganda chief, regularly derided on the wireless. I ran like the wind on my way to school each morning, trying to elude my tormentors who yelled 'Goebbels! Goebbels!' at me and aimed white mice at my neck. I had no allies and developed a passive defiance, an amnesic non-participation in life, a sort of performance without feeling or responsibility. It was as though some other creature inhabited my body, and I merely guided it to perform the routines required of me.

I avoided the boredom of my existence by imagining things clearly in my mind, so that when it came to actually doing them they were already in the past and I no longer felt involved. This mechanism kept something inside me intact.

Once a week the class played shinty in a field shared with grazing horses. This was a poor man's hockey, played with crudely bent wooden sticks. There were whispers that a girl had died from a blood clot as a result of a collision with a stick I had wielded, and that I was responsible for the accident and clearly to blame. I had no recollection of such contact, but felt very guilty.

Thursdays were spent learning to make knots at the Girl Guides group in the scout hall, for which I won a badge. They had difficulty finding me a uniform because I was so tall. Fridays were market days and the main street of town teemed with refugees, evacuees and army personnel, who had given the town a new sense of self-importance. Pairs of girls from Brighton's Roedean School, temporarily housed in the town's splendid Lodore Falls Hotel, dominated the pavements. They looked so strong, so powerful and self-assured in their flowing capes, spread like wings, which a gust of wind would send soaring. And they did not play shinty. Instead, on sports days, they swung their shiny hockey sticks with an elegance and pride that seemed due their privileged status. On Friday evenings, the Atkinsons sent me to the fish shop in the early autumn darkness to buy supper for us all. A few lights shimmered from the blacked-out windows and were reflected in the inky black water of the lake as, clutching my shillings, I ran to avoid the groups of soldiers from the barracks, smoking and chattering as they reached out to catch the hem of my dress and lift it over my head. Around the headland, the shadow of the fells loomed darkly as I sprinted down the road; I learnt to run faster and faster to avoid their jeering and groping.

As autumn became winter, the green bracken on the bald humped hills turned from amber to the colour of red wine. The wind blew over the lake, raising tiny ripples of light, and the sparse trees by the edge of the water creaked. Skiddaw, the highest of the Lakeland mountains, sprawled high above the rest, and townsfolk and visitors alike spoke with pride of having climbed to the top. It rained remorselessly; the water just came out of the sky and, hemmed in under the low engulfing clouds by the mountains, the little town was grey and dank and claustrophobic.

There was no one I could talk to or discuss my dreams with. No one missed me when I escaped to the bracken at the foot of the fells and did my dreaming alone. Nor was there anything beautiful to look at; no carvings or paintings or sculptures, just outings to the local pencil factory, a proud relic of the region's mining days, when graphite found in the area and developed to supply the world with pencils became its prosperity.

I felt that the scars of those months were deeper than the shelling from bombs would have caused. My despondency went unnoticed by my kindly hosts, or, at least, unchallenged. Only the weather separated the time from itself for me, dividing the days and weeks from each other. At last, Mr Atkinson brought me home a letter at the end of his round, which told me that my brother had been released from internment and that I may go home for Christmas.

Christmas shopping took the Atkinsons and me to Whitehaven. In the local Woolworths, my allowance of a shilling covered all my needs: handkerchiefs for my mother, a pen for my sister. A few days later, laden down with these gifts, I boarded the coach to Newcastle. It was a strange journey across the Kirkston Pass. As we reached the top of the high range through sparse sheep farms, stopping at places forgotten by the world, the bleak Cumberland moors stretched endlessly into the distance below and I could not envisage how we would ever get to industrial Tyneside.

My brief stay in Newcastle was blighted by the knowledge that I would have to return soon to Keswick. Pleas and protest seemed inappropriate, as my mother had endless worries to contend with, so I made none and returned over the now snow-covered pass, back to exile.

In January, I spent my eleventh birthday in Keswick. Presents of toothpaste and toiletries were delivered to me by the son of a friend of my mother's, who had come to visit a hostel for refugee orphans in Windermere that she supported. Soon after, I was confronted by secondary school entrance examination papers testing my skills, my intelligence and my learning. I sat in the classroom where the desks were spaced out to prevent cheating, completely perplexed by the questions and not knowing how to answer them. It remains a mystery to me that no attention whatsoever had been paid to my backwards state and my unfamiliarity with the language. With absolutely no tuition in literature, I was to be examined on the poets and history of England in order to gain a place at a decent school. Naturally, I failed miserably.

I was kept in Keswick another three months. In May, after a whole year of internment and the most unjust of circumstances (his brother had long ago been released), my father was finally allowed home. And so was I.

He was standing on the red velvet carpet at the top of the stairs when I arrived in our house in Rectory Terrace. With that familiar gesture, half in prayer and half triumphal, he clapped his hands together above his head. I dropped my bag and ran upstairs to meet him and feel his arms around me. We were both wounded and his embrace celebrated our rescue – for the moment at least.

6

La Sagesse 1941–1948

The war, forgotten while I was marooned in Keswick, had transformed our house. In the front room, a rectangular iron cage with mesh sides large enough for us all to crawl into during air raids replaced the oak dining table. Brown adhesive tape criss-crossed the window panes to prevent splintering when the bombs fell and opaque black curtain fabric draped the frames. Gas masks hung in the entrance porch next to walking sticks and flower pots. Ration books and identity cards lay on the side table in the kitchen.

The machines in the factory had begun to run at full throttle and were turning out parts for the munitions of war. Each morning, my father took the little train behind our house on his way to the Team Valley Trading Estate; twice a week he drove with a local friend, Dr Freedman, who held his surgery for the employees on the industrial estate. My brother worked long night shifts which sometimes stretched into the day.

Slowly a feeling of normality drifted back and although I had to go back to the school across the bridge, it was only for a few weeks before the summer holidays and there was always the thrill of Daisy Biggar, now empress of the strictly rationed sweets; a trophy of sticky toffees depended on her foul mood in that dank reeking shop.

My mother had closed ranks with the refugee community in the intervening months. They shared the separation from their men; the struggle to survive economically and resume ordinary life was a powerful bond. My father's long confinement behind barbed wire had brought him into contact with Europe's outcast business and cultural elite – scientists and musicians, writers and men of the theatre, who bonded while cleaning latrines and sharing packages from home. They

51

improvised evocative meals and made music together. On their release from internment, they became a new and exciting addition to weekend gatherings in our house, my mother assuming her stylish hospitality. The limited raw materials were compensated by the artistic way she presented them. Large platters of open sandwiches and tarts made from the hand-written recipes she had collected over the decades filled the table for our guests. They were made with dried eggs, imitation sugar and flour and produce from our friends' allotment. These were supplemented with the berries we gathered in the woods in Morpeth on our Sunday outings. The tables were always laden and the company second to none.

Sometimes at the weekend my mother would sit at the piano and accompany my father and my brother, or herself singing a Schubert lied or an aria from some opera she had learnt by heart in happier times. When she was not entertaining visitors, she made her small felt flowers and animals stuffed with kapok from patterns in women's magazines to sell at Bainbridges, Fenwicks and the newly set-up boutiques in town.

My sister had removed herself and her possessions to the attic vacated by the lodger to concentrate on her school work without interruption. If a professor of mathematics or of science happened to be among the guests downstairs in the drawing room, he was sure to be seconded to help her with her homework. The grammar school she attended had exacting standards, but the rude jokes she picked up there and insisted on repeating around the table-shelter at mealtimes were considered highly unsuitable; and so it was determined that my destiny lay elsewhere.

My parents had heard about a convent school, perched high on the ledge of the wildly romantic overgrown and neglected Jesmond Dene. Written in gilt letters on a green board above the entrance gate was the inscription BOARDING AND DAY SCHOOL FOR YOUNG LADIES. Surely, no crude jokes would be brought to the family dinner table from such an establishment and our Jewish way of life was a bastion against intense Catholic influence.

On the Sunday before our interview at the convent my mother nervously asked me to go for a walk with her. As she detested going for walks and avoided these at all times, I suspected something peculiar was on the agenda. We both walked, tongue-tied, as far as the allotments in Rectory Road. She looked straight ahead, took a deep breath, and in German asked me if there was anything I wanted to know from her. And that is how I was officially instructed in and prepared for the facts of life and the monthly discomfort I was about to experience. I knew it all already from the sudden lowered voices and the hurried change of conversation when my sister started her periods. The rest I had studied secretly from the *Duden*, a comprehensive and crudely illustrated German encyclopaedia which had drawings of breasts and penises and their function in procreation. I listened to my mother's nervous account, delivered in a constricted voice, and felt my cooperation was needed. I decided to oblige her with a question to which I already knew the answer. She was palpably relieved, her breathing returned to normal and we turned round and went home.

Next day, I kept close to my mother as we walked along the winding rhododendron-bordered gravel driveway to the Convent of the Sisters of La Sagesse, a grey sprawling Victorian stone mansion set back behind tended lawns. We rang the door bell inside the central porch and were shown into a large salon, where the Mother Superior, Bonne Mère Joseph, was standing to receive us. She came forward, nodded a greeting and waved us to one of the gilded, aristocratic bow-legged chairs that were dotted around the large room, whose bay windows overlooked the extensive grounds. In each corner, painted plaster statues of the Virgin Mary cradling the infant Jesus smiled down at us from gilded plinths.

Bonne Mère Joseph was short in stature but imperious in manner. Her hands were tucked into the folds of the wide cuffs of her grey robe. Her face, with its polished rosy cheeks and button nose, was beaming under the stiff white wimple which framed her head and bounced on her shoulder as she leaned to one side, listening intently. My mother bravely explained that she and my father would like me to be educated here but that they could not afford the high fees. She heard my mother out and then sat down.

She asked a few questions about my past schooling and, smiling with pride, told us that the order liked to help refugee children. She asked what we could afford to pay and agreed a sum, on the understanding that when my father's circumstances changed so would his financial contribution. Then my participation in the religious life of the school was discussed; I would be excused religious instruction but would have to attend chapel with the rest of the children. She said she would confer with the sisters and let us know their decision.

A few days later, the letter confirming my acceptance arrived. For the time being my parents would pay only three of the eleven pound fees each term. A list of the required school uniform was included, along with information on where to buy it.

I relished the thought that I was to receive a proper education at last, along with a real school uniform. At Bainbridges' department store for the first time, I claimed for myself all of my clothes coupons. With these we bought the serge material for my winter tunic, a crisp cream shirt and the pale blue poplin for the summer dress. A blazer and a panama hat with an enamel badge in the form of a shield with 'DS' engraved over a cross completed the equipment for my new life. For the duration of my school days, I would no longer have to wear my sister's outgrown clothes.

Mrs Callman, a refugee dressmaker, set up her Singer machine on the table-shelter. I was thrilled to be asked to try on my tunic as it came into being. It was much too big of course and very unflattering to my developing shape, but at least it was the right disguise for an alien aspiring to be like the rest of humanity at last.

Somehow, an unwieldy iron-framed German bicycle had found its way into the containers alongside our childhood skis, and was now brought down from a shelf in the garage. Perched high on the saddle, I bounced along the bus route by the railway line, barely able to reach the lofty square handlebars or the pedals which, when reversed, acted as brakes. But on a bright autumn day in September of 1941, dressed in every prescribed detail of my oversized uniform, I crossed the railway bridge, swooped down the last stretch of the hill on the other side and entered the school gate. From now on, this would be the arena for acting out the drama of my existence, and I relished both the companionship and acceptance of my classmates and the institutional regime amidst the Sisters of Divine Wisdom, whose linen headgear gave off the smell of starch as they floated around the corridors in their long grey robes, appearing not to touch the ground.

The protocol was spelled out to us and followed with enthusiasm rather than fear of punishment by the three hundred odd pupils. We changed our shoes in the locker room, which smelt of sweaty games shoes, assembled each morning in the gymnasium, curtsied to Bonne Mère and moved silently between the classrooms at the sound of the bell. I entered the social order of this life that seemed to have been awaiting me, obeyed the rules, handed in my homework on time and joined the other new girls in groups divided among houses. The captain of StDavid's chose me, and I now pinned the daffodil badge on my tunic.

Initially, the nuns taught us art and needlework. They were in charge mainly of the boarders who retired to their dormitories above the Chapel Wing each night. They lived a separate existence and I quite envied their secret community. Maths, French, English and Latin were taught by lay staff.

My first classroom exercise, a daft poem by William Blake, was neatly copied out in rounded slanting letters and seemed to echo my situation:

> 'When the green woods laugh with the voice of joy
> And the dimpling stream runs laughing by
> When the air does laugh with our merry wit
> And the green hill laugh with the noise of it
> Come live and be merry, and join with me
> To sing the sweet chorus of "ha, ha, hee!"'

At last, the English language became grounded for me in grammar, spelling and punctuation. I learnt about nouns and adjectives, predicates and prepositions, when to put single or double inverted commas, plural or possessive apostrophes and not to use a squiggle for 'and'. We were encouraged to structure a composition by making a plan of the story, within which the imagination could be given free reign. The excesses of my imagination seemed to unnerve Miss Lee, my English teacher, who gave me high marks for my work but peppered it with red exclamation marks. She voiced disquiet about my sensual descriptions of nature and was quite taken aback by my expressing feelings with an intensity probably unsuited to the set piece or incompatible with her experience of eleven-year-olds. She took me aside after class one day and warned me that if I did not modify my expressions and harness my emotions I would become very neurotic and suffer serious consequences.

Mr Sullivan took the choir in the music room. We learnt to sing our hearts out to songs with a local connection, like 'The Keel Row' ('Oh wha's like my Johnny, sae leish, sae blithe, sae bonnie?') and 'The Road To The Isles' ('A far croonin' is pullin' me away'). I'm not sure where 'Rolling Down To Rio' fitted into the scheme of things. These were rehearsed to perfection for performance at end-of-term assemblies, on feast days and patriotic occasions. They were taught with musicianship and sung with gusto.

In the science lab there were Bunsen burners and, eventually, frogs and worms to dissect on slabs of marble. During needlework class we practised the cross-stitch and the chain stitch on little pieces of muslin stretched over a frame, and were given khaki wool to knit into balaclavas for Stalin's beleaguered armies, who had changed sides and were freezing to death outside Leningrad. My skill at knitting continental style, without the ponderous movement of the whole arm to place the wool over the needle, ensured that a lot of poor Russian soldiers would find a little warmth. I learnt tennis on my mother's ancient gut-strung racquet, but had little encouragement on the hockey field where, although I could outrun most of the team from the right wing, found myself placed unfairly into goal – probably because I was big and reticent after my shinty experience. Once a week, we filed to the Jesmond baths where I learnt the breast stroke, how to dive from the high board and lifesaving skills, for which I received a bronze medal.

There was a lot of catching up to do and my charitable status to justify and I set about it with diligence. Only Sister Augustine, who took us for art, made a point of announcing at all opportunities, for all to hear, that she knew under what circumstances I was tolerated here. With a malicious glare over her steel-rimmed spectacles, she would wag her index finger at me, the hairs on her face bristling with excitement. Art classes became a penance and I never did learn to draw.

Sister Bernadette, on the other hand, was young and sweet and radiated kindness. I wondered what heartbreak had made her give up life, romance and freedom for the love of Jesus and thought, briefly, that this was my destiny, too. But if I was carried away with idealism by the sacrifice and religious devotion of the nuns, the temptation to emulate them and take holy orders was stifled by the bloodied, pale alabaster figure of Christ on a crooked cross, raised daubs of blood dripping from every part of his body, that faced us from the entrance of the chapel. It was a mystery to me how this crude depiction of suffering could represent a divine being or could be part of a divine plan. And anyway, in my Jewish upbringing, God had no body; He lived in my mind, and there He was going to remain.

Inside our uniforms, the personalities and aspirations of my classmates were very different; they planned to be doctors, ballet dancers, Olympic medallists. I wanted to be an actress, but when I announced this to my mother she shredded this ambition to ridicule; my legs, she said, were much too big to go on stage. I never mentioned it again. Meanwhile, I threw myself into any learning on offer with a hunger that had been unsatisfied throughout the year of my abandonment. My escape route was via the books borrowed from the Gosforth library and gifts from my brother and sister, which I devoured late into the night in bed after my homework was done. I nourished my craving for romance by immersing myself in the epics of Hugh Walpole, Mazo de la Roche and *Anne of Green Gables*. I could not bear for them to end.

The end of term ritual of our results being read out in front of the whole school was fronted by Bonne Mère, Sister Ernest, her headmistress, and the combined staff. Even the only two male presences in the school, the altar boys, attended, because the proceedings were followed by a visit to chapel. The ceremony took place in the gymnasium, between the frames that climbed up the wall and the leather vaulting boxes, pushed into a corner like race horses retired from an event. We stood in rows, the lower classes in front, ignorant of our fate until Sister Ernest read out our marks and our resulting place in class. There followed a general shuffling, a ripple through the line, making room at the top until each girl had placed herself in the order of her achievement.

I came third in my class that first winter, and top every term after that until in the upper forms, where places were no longer allocated. I thought it an embarrassing and inhuman procedure and had no pleasure from this academic success; I only wished fervently that my parents would become rich and pay my full fees, which never did happen. But the school had newly gained the lofty status of an efficient secondary school by the Board of Education, under visitation by His Majesty's inspectors, and it was our duty to preserve this ranking.

During the Easter holidays in my twelfth year I developed a high fever. My bedroom was turned into a hospital, but the poultices and other Bavarian remedies failed to cool my overheated body or relieve the burning in my throat. I shivered uncontrollably and kept vomiting. The rash that had appeared behind my ears spread over my whole body and it dawned on my parents this was something rather serious.

Dr Freedman was called, took one look at my face, peered under my armpits, examined the creases in my elbow and diagnosed scarlet fever. Everyone shuddered at the pronouncement, because this carried the danger of blindness, kidney failure, rheumatic fever and heart trouble. I was to be removed instantly to an isolation hospital, while the authorities were advised that I had a communicable disease and was a public menace, threatening the community, my schoolmates and, possibly, the whole of England with contagion. I protested the best I could in my feeble state but was too ill to care about being incarcerated again.

An ambulance came to fetch me and took me on a long, bumpy ride to outlying Prudhoe. I knew we had arrived when I heard the creaking of iron gates clang shut behind us. I felt the jolts of the rickety vehicle and crunching on the cinder path and finally we came to a halt at a red-brick Victorian building. It had a feel of the workhouses I had seen in old books, and now served as isolation hospital which could not quite shed its hideous past. A bustle of figures in white crowded round me, loaded me onto a trolley and wheeled me to a small room. I was lifted onto a narrow iron bedstead and was surrounded by doctors, who told me it was serious and that the only remedy was for me to be injected with sulphur drugs, penicillin not yet being an option. I don't know how long passed before I came to life again. I just know that one day a nurse asked me to go to an iron-barred opening in the wall where my father and sister stood with packages of food, which they handed me through the grille. We spoke a little, and then they left to catch their bus back to Newcastle. My mother never came. She had an aversion to illness and could not handle it easily.

When I was allowed home two weeks later, the war was raging throughout Europe and North Africa and was taking its dreadful course. The news of the deportation to concentration camps of our grandmothers shattered my parents. They read and re-read the rare letters from the Red Cross, but without much hope. Nor was there much optimism for my mother's sister who had fled to Belgium, or for my beloved uncle Leo, last heard of in Katowice. The pain was too great and it was rarely mentioned. At six o'clock every evening we would all gather around the wireless for the news, and thrilled to the reassuring voice of Churchill, who encouraged us to believe in victory. Even so, the fear of invasion loomed large, especially for us German Jews who would top Hitler's hit list when his triumphal armies landed in England. After the 'Day of Infamy', when the Japanese attacked Pearl Harbour in 1941, Americans joined in the war and raised our hopes that we might win after all. Their military vehicles with the white five-pointed star dashing around town were very comforting. The first decisive victory in the North African desert at Tobruk was jubilantly celebrated; church bells pealed out across Newcastle, and we knew that the tide of the war had turned.

We slowly settled into a life which had, until now, always felt temporary and provisional. The tranquillity of our family was often disturbed by moments of high drama, arguments and confrontation between my brother and my father when issues were virulently discussed before being put aside with tears and slamming doors. My parents sometimes quarrelled too, my mother making out it was always about us children. She would then be offended and retire to their bedroom sulking, leaving my father sitting disconsolate by the fireside in the drawing room, looking bleak and puffing on his pipe, which he never learnt to light up properly. When the pipe had gone out several times, he would knock the bowl against the tiled fender to empty out the half-burned tobacco and place it carefully on the ashtray. I sensed his misery and sat on the footstool near him, remaining there without attempting small talk until he got up and went wearily up the stairs. I was sad to hear him knocking on the bedroom door and begging to be let in. I don't know how they made their peace, but next day my mother would be downstairs as usual, setting the breakfast table and seeing him off to work with an embrace. On special occasions, we brought breakfast to their bed, which made us feel good.

My mother objected to my going with my sister to the Royalty cinema on the high street. With the money she earned from the private lessons she gave to Tante Mousie, the diminutive mother of uncle Leo, my sister could go to the pictures whenever she liked. After many disputes I was allowed an occasional Saturday morning serial of *Zorro*. My mother also felt that our finances would not stretch to school outings. I ended up alone in the classroom doing homework while my friends went to see Shakespeare plays at the Theatre Royal.

When the school went potato-picking in Derbyshire, my parents overcame their hesitation to let me go along because it was expected of us to do our bit for the war effort. We stayed in a youth hostel and were ferried each dawn in a great truck to the potato fields, belting out the tunes Mr Sullivan had taught us. I loved being outdoors in the early morning air, under a panoply of orange-pink sky, with the pungent smell of newly ploughed earth, the potatoes hidden in clumps of loam, the handsome, swarthy Italian prisoners of war working alongside us and the weariness at the end of the day when we clambered back into our bunk beds and partied with hot cocoa.

One day I found myself alone in the barn where a bearded man was pitching hay. He came nearer and nearer to me, muttering about the glories of being a Jehovah's Witness, and as the distance between us grew less I realized I was threatened by more than conversion to his religion. As I tried to step back into the haystack, he lunged forward and grabbed me. I managed to wriggle out of his grasp and escape through the barn door, nearly falling into the deep muddy ridges of the path as I ran back to the farmhouse.

My brother decided that I should learn to play the piano and worked overtime at the factory to pay for my lessons with Mrs Wightman. Her studio was on the first floor of Alderson and Brentnall, a large music shop on Northumberland Street, full of glossy Blüthners and Steinways, violins and brass instruments and the smell of varnish. On my way through the building to her studio I would hear a cacophony of clashing sounds from violins tuning up, brass instruments blaring and people in booths sampling records with or without their earphones. My teacher talked with pride of the world-renowned Polish virtuoso Małcużyński, who had been her pupil; he looked beautiful on the sleeve of the record she gave me.

I didn't like practising in the unheated drawing room where, for many months, the fog penetrated deep and thick and my hands were rigid with cold, so that I could barely pick out notes on the keyboard. Sometimes, at the weekend, my brother tried to improve my playing and guided me through parts of a Haydn sonata, and I learnt enough to play a solo, and accompany myself in a song as a present for my father's birthday. There was great musical activity at the city hall to lift the spirit of the people of Newcastle. The London Philharmonic Orchestra came and Yehudi Menuhin was airlifted directly from a concert on a troop ship to perform for us. It was from him I heard live for the first time Mendelssohn's *Violin Concerto* and the *Rondo Capricioso* of Saint-Saëns. The Soviet Army band performed their profoundly melodic tunes, and, not to be outdone, so did the American official army Air Force band, tickets to which we were given us by our Uncle Leo who bought them in aid of the RAF Benevolent Fund.

A miner's daughter from one of the coastal villages was hired to help with domestic chores at home. Millie was a shy sixteen-year-old who wore the ill-fitting adapted uniform of the Bamberg servants and was dreadfully self-conscious about the pus-filled pimples that covered her round face. She was quite ill at ease eating together with us at lunchtime while listening to *Workers' Playtime* on the radio. She would have much preferred having her meal by herself. Once a week I would help her scrub the collars of our shirts on a wavy metal board before boiling them with the sheets and pillows in a copper vat which was pulled into the middle of the scullery and was heated by a gas flame underneath. The clean clothes were hung out on the line in the back garden or on an overhead wooden rack that was raised and lowered by a pulley.

I taught myself to make French onion soup, which delighted my father because it reminded him of his time in Paris. The busiest baking time came in preparation for weekend tea parties. My mother made cakes, sometimes halving an egg to make it go further. We adopted the English way of starting with savoury sandwiches which my mother made into an art form with bits of red and green vegetable decoration, followed by scones (made with flour and lard), cakes and torte, made with whatever ingredients were available.

The guests on those occasions were mainly my father's fellow internees who had become close friends. Uncle Roco from Leipzig was professor of pure mathematics at the university and a fellow of the Royal Society. His great height would have been unnoticeable had it not been for his minuscule wife. The folds of loose flesh wobbled under his receding chin when he spoke in his deep resounding voice. He was the kindest of men and very learned. He gave my brother his first violin from an important maker in Wrocław and helped him get into college when he had difficulties after the long interruption of his studies. There was Professor Hirsch from Berlin, an applied mathematician who was an expert on the theory of knots and had his picture on the cover of *Picture Post*. Dr Wasserman was deep into thought-transmission, published papers on extrasensory perception and entertained us with all kinds of card tricks. The subject of most of our mimicry was Joseph Weiss, because he snorted out his sing-song in a gusty Viennese accent, his body moving forwards and backwards in rhythm with his words. He was a brilliant biochemist and had studied with the famous Dr Heinz Haber. A bachelor in his late forties, he invited me out on a first date early in my teens to the People's Theatre. Surprisingly, my parents had no objections to my going. He shared his lodgings with his mother, whom he called his auntie because she was uneducated and primitive and he was so ashamed of her that he pretended she belonged to his cousin, the extremely talented violinist Peter Schidlof. Within the community, where his secret was well known, she was called 'TanteMutter'. With great patience and kindness, my mother invited her to sit with her while she was doing needlework.

On our return to school that summer, we started to prepare for the School Certificate. Lay teachers replaced the nuns to prepare the curriculum. Into my life now came Mademoiselle Canel, whose timely appearance turned everything around. Teetering on minute feet far too small for her short barrel-shaped body, she dressed all over in clashing shades of green, from mint to moss. Silver hair was knotted at her nape in a bun, from which she would try to catch straying wisps with an impatient hand, and in conversation she constantly brushed imaginary crumbs from her bosom with a flick of her upturned fist. Her rimless spectacles glinted over her watery-blue eyes; her words were sibilantly squeezed out between tight lips, and her assertive statements and ironic asides were always followed by a conspiratorial sideways glance from under lowered lids, as if anticipating the effect of the verbal gauntlet she had thrown down.

Both her strong French accent, entrenched despite forty years' residence in England, and her liberal interpretation of life through her French culture, set her apart from the minority Catholic community. By her own confession, she maintained a healthy scepticism and never missed an opportunity to make her feelings known. With such spirited opposition, she aroused a nervous kind of suspicion in the staffroom, where she remained an outsider. Her descent from an ennobled general in Napoleon's army explained her criticism of everything British. This suited me well, and from the outset we colluded in a sort of conspiracy against the establishment, within the strict boundaries of our alien status. In the classroom, she made no concession to this alliance; she was miserly with her marking, and very demanding as to the standard of my homework. Mademoiselle Canel not only fired within me a love for the sound and elegance of her language, but educated me in words which expressed feelings of refinement and passion. This regime inevitably opened up a world suppressed in my literary experience until then.

Of course, she had to be invited home to meet my parents and indulge my father. But first, her love of meat, which she had made known to me, required a family-wide saving up of our miserable butcher's ration. Since we neither had the opportunity nor the daring to profit from the black market, sacrifices had to be made by all and when she came to visit, she was received in her native tongue with a kiss on the hand along with our combined meat rations. She even managed to persuade my parents to attend, unprecedented, a school performance where, in my father's woollen tailcoat and probably because of it, I headed the cast of *Les Précieuses Ridicules.*

On 8 May 1945, the war in Europe ended. In a voice thick with emotion, and at risk of faltering, Winston Churchill announced our miraculous delivery from tyranny, and England exploded. Throughout the city, the church bells rang out and people gathered to dance and sing in the streets. We moved amidst the cheering crowds to the Haymarket and were hoisted high into the air by American airmen who showered us with real kisses. For us convent girls, this was almost as exciting as the event it celebrated.

With the progress of the triumphal armies came the dreadful news of the massacres and annihilation in the death camps. Reports from Belsen, the first to be liberated, were too unbearable to absorb and the radio accounts burnt in our heads. One after another of the camps revealed the residual humanity and skeletal bundles of limbs. The gas chambers of Auschwitz were the final destination of our grandmothers and millions of others, efficiently, systematically and with the utmost cruelty and degradation sent to extinction. A terrible silence engulfed my parents and filled them with a grief from which there was no recovery. It was to be the death of my father just three years later.

In July 1946, I sat the School Certificate examination. When the results were published in August, I had obtained distinctions in eight of the ten subjects; I obtained a credit in Latin and an unpromising pass in maths. Four months later, one particular event helped to raise the morale of our family and made us all proud: on 9 November, the eighth anniversary of Kristallnacht, my father signed the Oath of Allegiance, swearing by Almighty God that he would 'be faithful and bear true allegiance to His Majesty King George the Sixth, his heirs and successors according to law'. We were stateless no longer. This, and my advanced age of sixteen, propelled me into a new phase of adulthood where I would be able to make up for missed opportunities. I was due to sit my Higher School Certificate the following year, and Mlle Canel managed to persuade my parents that a summer spent in France in a *pension de famille* would improve my French.

So, on 17 July, bearing my newly acquired passport imprinted with the magical exhortation signed by Ernest Bevin 'To all those whom it may concern, to allow the bearer to pass freely without let or hindrance and to afford her every assistance and protection of which she may stand in need in the name of His Majesty', with an allowance of thirty-eight pounds in currency, clutching a suitcase full of utility clothes and a letter of introduction to a Parisian friend of my father's, and heeding a warning not to eat unwashed fruit, I boarded the London train with the little lady in green. After a night spent in the sister convent in Golders Green, we joined the boat train to Dover on my way to Fontainebleau and my personal liberation.

Part Two

Liberation

7

Fontainebleau 1947

Our ferry crossing to Dieppe was uneventful, the sea calm, although in Dover two uniformed customs officials had politely abducted Mlle Canel. To my astonishment, she just shrugged her shoulders and, with a whimsical look, accompanied them, asking me to wait for her. She must have convinced the authorities that she was not trafficking young girls into the white slave trade, merely escorting them abroad with the intention of firing them with an enthusiasm for foreign languages, and returned fairly soon, a free woman. She had clearly experienced this interrogation before and I suspected she enjoyed the attention.

On our arrival into Dieppe, all the familiar scents and noises filling the air in the bustling port told me that I was back on the continent of Europe. The train we boarded whistled and puffed through the green fields and orchards of Picardy and Normandy, gleaming rivers snaking through the blood-drenched countryside that only two years ago had seen the savage battles of the liberating armies. The red-roofed houses and fortified manors scattered around the landscape made little reference to the brutal fighting, but the tens of thousands of crosses marking the warriors were still being erected beyond the view of passing trains.

The large old house in the Boulevard du Marechal Joffre was set back behind tall chestnut trees a short distance from the woodland railway station. Monsieur Duchenois and his daughter, at whose pension I was to spend the summer, received us warmly. In the dining room, the table was set for the evening meal, which was cooking on the stove in the corner.

That evening I was introduced to the dozen or so young fellow boarders from Paris, sent by their parents to escape the polluted summer air of the city. Some were Jewish, all seemed to know too much, had seen too much and seemed older, thrust into adulthood before having been truly young, their growing-up years wasted in hiding from the occupying forces or in protecting their families from them. I learnt, as we spent time together on our outings and at mealtime discussions, how edgy and fiercely addicted they were to risk-taking. Many had been in the Resistance, some in hiding, always in danger from the occupying Wehrmacht and the Gestapo, a gun thrust into their hands, trained to shoot first and ask questions later. As companions, with their irrepressible swagger, they proved to be exciting, loud and inclusive. In my austere clothes and with my occasionally comical French, I had a slight celebrity status with them, and they delighted in mimicking my misuse of their language while improving their English. They were convinced that they had in their midst the typical English girl.

The ten or twelve of us gathered punctually at mealtimes, Monsieur Duchenois presiding over the proceedings. A tall, elegant man with a lean moustache, his slight stoop wrestled with a proud military bearing, which no doubt had some connection with Napoleon. Frequently he would pull out the watch from his waistcoat pocket and consult it to remind us of the importance of attending meals on time. He then ladled out the soup from a large Limoges tureen, the first course in a choreographed menu which included wine and with which I soon become familiar.

Mademoiselle Canel departed next morning; my companions and I saw her off on the train to her home town in Normandy, I set out with them to discover the town. Fontainebleau embraced in its midst the chateau, and the traffic flowed around its entrances, its lakes and canals. Its cobbled courtyard led to the horseshoe staircase where Napoleon had addressed his troops in a farewell eulogy before being arrested and marched away to exile on St Helena. The trimmed box-hedges which bordered the groomed lawns and flower beds exuded a pungent fragrance, especially when the rain moistened the leaves. Ancient carp flicked around the water of the lake created by King Henry II for his beloved mistress, which had a dreamy island gazebo in the middle for their trysts. One wing of the castle was occupied by the American music summer school under Nadia Boulanger, and all day long the combating sounds of scales and arpeggios, sonatas and chamber music filled the air. Their weekly concert in the tennis court of kings compensated the townspeople for the unending din. Inside the palace, the apartments were lavishly furnished with works by Italian artists of the Renaissance brought over by Henry II's bride Catherine de Medici. Sculptures and paintings in gold and silver provided the sumptuous backdrop before which the royal families of France carried out their royal duties, their love affairs and their intrigues. Poor Catherine only came into her own after Henry's death when she reclaimed her territory and sent his mistress, Diane, packing.

The *pension* was at the edge of the great forest of Fontainebleau, which provided a blissful escape from the blistering heat. It was difficult to resist the advances of a group of so very romantic-minded young men, but it never interfered with our enjoyment. I walked barefoot on the sandy undergrowth amid shafts of sunlight slanting through the cover of the tall ancient beech trees, and climbed rocky mounts to explore the stone grottos and caves which were dotted around the forest, providing cool, quiet and secret places for us to picnic and tell our tales. Once, a film crew came to the forest, and we spent afternoons watching in fascination as the glamour and illusion of film-land disappeared over the tedious and nerve-wracking hours. The actors, their make-up hideous in the sunlight, had to repeat their scenes over and over again, until the heroine fell off her horse and had to be taken to the hospital.

This was my world now for the next six weeks, my liberation – and it was pure bliss. I loved the language, the colours and smells and my involvement with others. There was something particular about Fontainebleau; every house seemed to embody the taste and grace of the Renaissance and the townspeople treated the castle in its centre with pride. The memory of Napoleon was still supreme; every morning, the clatter of the hooves of horses being ridden out from the many riding schools, military academies and *écuries* were a reminder of him, and the names of most bars and hotels, streets and avenues, and even pastries, all deferred to the man who once had brought glory to France.

I became attached to the *bande* of *pensionnaires* and moved easily around together with them in agreeable and uncomplicated friendship. We found relief from the heat at the *piscine,* incongruously perched above the railway station with its forest beach. I was aware of my shabby swimsuit amid the glistening bodies of the others in glorious déshabillé playing handball and dancing to the music from the jukebox. I realized for the first time that one could laugh out loud and be teased and enjoy flirting. During the years in Newcastle, there had been so little opportunity for fun. I felt for once that I did not have to try to be good, to be better. In this welcoming, slightly amused and entirely non-competitive facsimile of a family there was an ease of respite, and I felt happy.

Mlle Duchenois was well connected in the town and managed to get us invitations for everything that was happening. She was full of common sense and very wise, providing a disciplined and pleasurable extension of home life. Early each morning, a wicker basket on her arm, she went to the market place in the town square. Accompanying her, I discovered an abundance of fruit and vegetables that I did not know existed. There were artichokes and courgettes from the region, eggs and cheeses, large wheels of Brie from Melun and Meaux, Camemberts from Normandy and fish from a nearby tributary of the Seine. She would push her nose into the melons, squeeze the peaches and pears, and sample the grapes and wild strawberries that were piled high under the awnings. Depending on the quality, the flavour and of course the price, which was written in spindly figures on boards and clearly open to negotiation, she planned her menu for the day. On Sundays, she would tie a kerchief round her head, and climb up the few steps to the church which adjoined the market. Here she lit a candle with her free hand, kneeled through a brief mass, and emerged into the noon sunlight to return home and cook our lunch.

The invitation to visit the Jaehnichens in Paris was for one o'clock. I took the earliest morning train, and stepping off into the steam-hissing, train-whistling Gare de Lyon, I found Paris deserted, shut down for the ritual August exodus and in suspended animation. Restaurants were closed (*fermeture annuelle*), shutters were drawn over kiosks, shops barred and chairs piled up on the *terrasses* of the cafes where waiters, not yet dressed in their long white aprons, were mopping up detritus and vomit from the night before. Only the khaki walk-in urinals were gushing water, inviting a visit, as in the very first such facility described in *Clochemerle*.

Along the *quais*, the booksellers were putting out on display their mini libraries of prints and old tomes. Alongside, rows of tall trees cast their splintered images on the surface of the still-flowing water. Below, on the cobbled river banks, the *clochards*, the down-and-outs – both men and women – were sprawled against the stone foundations of the bridges in raucous alcoholic daze.

In the midst of Ile de la Cité, the island which divides the river in half, Notre Dame loomed out of the mist and as I approached the vast and silent magnificence of the building across the square I could see the gargoyles leaning out from behind the flying buttresses and ogling visitors. Over the entrance, the tympans must have been carved by the same hands and with the same object-lesson as those of the *Dom* in Bamberg. Inside, I gazed at the columns rising uninterrupted to the vaulted roof. They were a more persuasive metaphor for a belief in Heaven than I had ever seen. On either side of the nave the great rose windows threw a kaleidoscope of changing colours onto the people kneeling in morning prayer by the altar; deep violet, indigo, blue and green. It took 100 years to build and cost thousands of lives in the building of it.

In the Latin Quarter behind the splashing fountain of the Place St Michel next to the carved dolphins, there were plaques solemnly inscribed with the names of the men and women who had been gunned down here in the last days before the liberation. Even as de Gaulle was heading his men into the city they lost their lives in hand-to-hand battle, fighting street by street against the occupiers desperate to carry out Hitler's demented order to obliterate Paris rather than let it fall undamaged into the hands of the Allies. His infamous question 'Is Paris burning?' had been his final delusion.

As I crossed and re-crossed the bridges of the Seine my fantasies left my body and ran ahead of me through the quarters of Paris, and wandering through the deserted boulevards and narrow streets I could sense the magnetic forces that had drawn revolutionaries and innovators, philosophers and artists to this city, and understood the nostalgia with which Paris had infused them. Was it the conflicts and rebellions played out in these avenues or the ideas that had made the city a stage on which the history of Europe rotated, to which people had fled, and from which they had escaped? Here, movements in political thought, in art, literature and science were born and sometimes destroyed. I had no doubt that I would be infected with the same nostalgia, and no inoculation would protect me against it.

The mist was lifting and the sun breaking through as I crossed the Alexandre III bridge with its monumental statuary and its magnificent lamp posts, where the adolescent Alain-Fournier had first glimpsed, fallen in love with and stalked the beautiful, blonde young Yvonne de Quiévrecourt, as they were both leaving the Grand Palais. Fugitive and remote, she became the idealized and inaccessible love of his short life, and despite several face-to-face encounters, his passion for her remained unrequited and he could only live with his sense of loss and disappointment by recreating her in the magic realism of *Le Grand Meaulnes*.

Across the river, guarded by an avenue of beech trees in martial formation, the golden dome of Les Invalides rose in great splendour. Entombed under scrolled red granite, commanding a deep bow from me over the railings to glimpse his coffin, Napoleon is surrounded by garlands and laurels encircling the names of his great battles and guarded by warrior-like angels. Here, the little Corsican with the Roman profile, reviled and lampooned and finally beaten on our side of the channel by generals competing for swathes of Europe, was finally accorded peace and respect by his countrymen. I knew from my study of the French Revolution and its aftermath that the official notices and prohibitions posted on most public buildings refer to the laws and governance he introduced.

Past where the river forks and curves round Ile de la Cité, I saw the towers of La Conciergerie. It was from the prison here that Marie Antoinette was taken in a tumbrel to be executed in the Place de la Concorde. Where now cascading fountains rippled into glittering pools of water, blood had dripped from the thousands of severed trunks of the victims of the guillotine.

I could have prowled longer round the boulevards and streets with their tall distinguished old houses and lofty facades, which seemed to preen themselves in awareness of their own history and their beauty, but I had an appointment to keep. So, with a bunch of fiery gladioli purchased from the market outside the Palais de Justice, I took the metro to Montmartre.

They received me with all the affection they felt for my father, who all those years ago had come to them to Paris as a young man to study. Monsieur Jaehnichen, sprightly and jovial, said with a twinkle that he would act as bank if I ran out of money. Under his unpretentious, almost doddery exterior, there was a keen intellect fluent in many languages. They convinced me that they had been uncompromising during the occupation and survived by keeping a low profile. Mr Jaehnichen returned to his nearby office after our meal, and Madame took me through the poky little streets of Montmartre to that Byzantine confection the Sacre Coeur, then along the rue Lepic to the top, passing the studios of Picasso and Matisse, Derain and Braque.

Along the way she told me of their rivalries and passions, and sometimes the duels which occurred when disagreements and jealousies arose amid the coterie of artists and writers who worked there. We descended on the *funiculaire* and were whisked off by taxi to the Marquise de Sévigné a tea room on the Champs-Elysées, where *pâtisseries* that had no bearing to the rationing at home were served on fragile porcelain. The decor was in pink and gold and so were the elegant people at the little tables around us.

Back at the *pension,* a package of home-made biscuits from my mother and letters from all my family awaited me. In the cool of the night Rene, Marcel and Gerard took me to the Select cinema to see the newly released film *Les Enfants du Paradis.* The creaky floor of the smoke-filled hall was aquiver with excitement as the usherette showed us to our seat and demanded her *pourboire.* After a while, there was a stamping of feet until three hammer blows on the floor announced the beginning of the spectacle. The curtain rose on the teeming last-century crowds milling around the Funambules theatre; there were tightrope walkers, jugglers, a monkey on stilts, pickpockets, a public scribe dealing with stolen goods and blind beggars and hoods all pursuing their activities in stunning fashion – and, of course, there was a mesmerizing mime, played by Jean-Louis Barrault. Arletty, Empress of Cool, played a *courtisane* with whom an actor, a murderer, an aristocrat and a mime were all hopelessly in love. She provided the language of courtship with the iconic phrase 'C'est si simple, l'amour.' That was a thought to carry with me and caused no end of trouble in my life.

Around the dinner table at the *pension* the next night, there was a lively discussion about dreams, about love and life, personal freedom, existential despair and nihilism. This was not surprising, since the film's dialogue was scripted by the poet of the Resistance, Jaques Prévert. I returned again, and then again, to the Select, until I knew many lines by heart.

Two more events marked my sentimental education in France. One night at a party for the daughter of the proprietor, in the magnificent second empire Hotel de l'Aigle Noir, I did not see Angeline come into the room where I had retreated, a little drunk and exhausted, for some respite from the noise of the band. She seemed to know that I was somewhere under the pile of clothes on the bed which acted as wardrobe and, without saying a word, bent over me and slid her hand over my face. Before her head could reach mine, I wriggled out and ran as fast as I could and rejoined the party, trying my best to avoid her. There was merriment that night at the *pension*. Did I not know that women could love women?

Then in August, on the feast of Ascension, the celebration began at nightfall throughout the whole town. In the cool of evening crowds swarmed into the market square, where the accordions and guitars were strumming their lilting tunes. Under the coloured paper lanterns strung across the square, couples glided and tapped to the sound of the *musette* (accordion music) arms intertwined around bare necks. It seemed as though the party would never end, with the anniversary of the liberation of Paris and the feast of St Louis providing more excuses for non-stop merry-making over the next three days.

All too soon, it came time to book my return journey, and I took one last trip to visit the beautiful cemetery of Père Lachaise to see the graves of the great people I had studied – Molière and La Fontaine were honoured here, and Sarah Bernhardt, who had placed flowers on her own grave in anticipation of her death, Oscar Wilde, exiled from his country, and the musicians Rossini, Fauré and Bizet. I laid a little bunch of roses on the grave of Chopin.

It marked the last of the holidays and my days in France were numbered. From now on, we all started preparing for the harsh realities and duties of our lives. I knew I would miss the mental athletics and culture of my fellow boarders – and their flirting. When we embraced each other goodbye, we promised to meet again. Although we all knew this was fantasy, it eased the regret of parting and leaving behind the summer idyll. But I knew with certainty that this was where I wanted to live out the rest of my life.

8

St Briac 1948

I returned home that autumn to shroud-like fogs descending on Newcastle and the trees shedding their leaves, the city and life turned inwards. My parents returned from Scandinavia, from my father's first business trip since the war. They had sailed on the Fred Olsen line out of Tynemouth and savoured the luxury and good food on board ship, and had enjoyed meeting up again with old friends. They brought back with them Lars Carlberg, the son of our friend, for a visit to our home. He had a self-deprecating sense of humour, and his Swedish way of talking English was very entertaining. He was the first of many visitors to our house and we became great friends.

My brother, now 25, was finally resuming his interrupted engineering studies at the university, and found academic work hard after his internment and compulsory war work. My father paid for him to move out into a flat on his own to avoid distraction and ensure his success. My sister had finished her degree in biochemistry at King's College, had begun her PhD and had won a post-graduate research grant from the British Council at the Université Libre de Brussels for the following year.

She was greatly assisted by Gaby Stein, a young radiation chemist from Israel, whom her professor, Joseph Weiss, had recently brought to live with us. I idealized this sweet dumpy, husky-voiced Hungarian from the start, not only for his seductive manner, which belied a razor-sharp brain evident in our discussions around the dinner table, but because after escaping from Budapest he had swept the streets around the port of Haifa for a living, rescued his parents and put himself through college at the Hebrew University. I shadowed his comings and goings at home, but failed to make any impression on

78

him at all. It was my sister who attracted him. She, however, was unmoved by his feelings and was merely single-minded in accepting his help to complete her PhD.

Our next visitor was Bram van Santen's daughter, Wiesjie. Her parents and mine thought she would find some renewal after her harsh experiences in the Dutch Resistance, where, like Leda forced against her will by Zeus, she had to succumb to the amorous attentions of the camp commandant to save her from the firing squad. She was slight in build, and at times shudders fleetingly convulsed her body, betraying an indescribable anguish. Although she tried hard to be sociable, I knew she craved to be left alone within our family, though I sometimes sat with her in her room. I sensed that she welcomed my company and we became very close. Her four siblings had all found themselves in various extreme situations, and her parents, concealed in a loft above a factory in Amsterdam not far from Anne Frank's attic, had been saved by an East Indies employee in the factory below. He had kept them alive and provided them with their basic needs. At the end of the war, he was rewarded with the hand in marriage of their eldest daughter, Eline.

One day, browsing through *The Times*, I saw an advertisement for an English tutor for a titled young French girl for next summer, to which I eagerly responded. But first I had to pass my Higher School Certificate. Studying now took me over in earnest. The syllabus required an in-depth understanding of 'modern' history, spanning the fifteenth century to the establishment of the Empire via the French Revolution. It encompassed philosophy, political science and geographical influences. In French, we studied Racine (*Britannicus*) and Molière (*George Dandin*), and in the literature of the twentieth century, Giraudoux's *Ondine* and the novels of Balzac. In English we were introduced to Chaucer and Shakespeare. *A Winter's Tale* appealed to my irrational, absolute and uncompromising sense of unforgiving.

But it was in a performance of a play at the Theatre Royal by Jean-Paul Sartre, starring Roger Livesey, Michael Gough and Joyce Redman, that I recognized a powerful contemporary play, and experienced my first encounter with existential thinking. The play was called *Crime Passionel* (*Les Mains Sales*).

Hoederer, a leader of patriots in a mythical post-war state, is faced with the choice of surrendering to the invading Russian armies and sharing power with them, or remaining obdurately intransigent and dying. He justifies his willingness to compromise, thereby averting bloodshed and saving lives, and encourages his followers, the patriots, to do the same. His secretary, Hugo, adheres to his principles and refuses to dirty his hands. At the point of being persuaded to join them, he almost accidentally and ambiguously kills Hoedere when he discovers he is having an affair with his wife, only to find out that the comrades who had supported him and prodded him to assassinate their leader have been persuaded to succumb to his reasoning and have agreed to surrender. In the end, Hugo is judged and executed not for adherence to his principles, but for the crime of passion committed in the sexual betrayal.

This logical and dramatically satisfying construction made marvellous theatre and started me thinking existentially. These characters were so unlike the heroes of Corneille, Racine and Molière, who were driven by their coruscating personalities which determined their destiny. From the first act of the drama to the blood bath on stage as the curtain fell, their dreadful fate could be anticipated. What this play was saying is that our actions are determined by the sum total of our experiences, not by the fixed boundaries within which we are fettered. To achieve our freedom we must constantly recreate ourselves in a new direction. Sometimes these irreconcilable alternatives demand sacrifice. Circumstances outflanked Hugo's choice gratuitously. Neither his idealism nor his sexual betrayal were served.

My planned return to France as au pair met with strong opposition at first. For my father, it was fine for me to go to a secure establishment protected by my school mistress; but to place myself into a situation of employment at the mercy of some French nobility seemed to him of a different order. As a matter of course, he wrote to the British ambassador in Paris, Sir Owen O'Malley, to request an investigation and a report back. Two weeks later, a reply came from the Foreign Office: Sir Owen St Clair O'Malley KCMG was his Majesty's ambassador in Mexico from October 1937 until May 1938 'when diplomatic relations were suspended with Mexico'. He added that Sir Owen had now retired from the diplomatic service and, to add insult to derision, included his retirement address in County Mayo, Eire.

My mother was showing the stress of the past years and the pain of the fate of her mother, and badly needed a holiday. My father thought it was a good opportunity for him to take her to France and drink the waters at the spa in Vichy. We would travel together as far as Paris and there go our own way. I was glad I could supplement their meagre foreign currency allowance by giving them most of mine, which I would not need. My last exam was on 20 July, and ten days later we three embarked on a slow ferry to Dieppe, my father in a panama hat and a white linen suit which hung loose on his shrinking body and my mother in a polka dot georgette dress and wide-brimmed hat.

In her letter of appointment, Mme la Vicomtesse de Fraguier explained my role that summer. At a villa in St Briac, a small seaside town in Brittany, I was to be in charge of two little girls of eleven and twelve. I was to supervise them on the beach, accompany them on walks and work them hard in English in return for free board and lodging, and conversation and lessons with my French. The cleaning of one room might also be involved, 'but perhaps that's not a good idea' she added. I would have one day off each week. I was to make my way to the home of Madame Grandjean in L'Isle-Adam and travel with her down to the coast.

On 1 August, I left my parents, and took the 13.52 train to L'Isle-Adam, a village situated on a bend in the river Oise and an hour's journey north from Paris. At the station, among the Sunday crowd of picnickers, I saw a tall good-looking young man with a shock of black hair falling over his face making his way towards me. He bowed low over my hand, introduced himself as Eduard Grandjean and said that his mother was expecting me at Les Forgets.

In elegant English, he told me he was studying diplomacy and had travelled widely. He drove me through a beautiful forest and we arrived at the iron gates of the ancestral home. Shaded by arching trees and overgrown bushes, the driveway seemed to go on endlessly, winding deeper and deeper through the dense greenery. Suddenly, out of a clearing in the wilderness, a red-brick fairy-tale house of exquisite symmetry appeared. Mysterious and secluded, I felt it harboured a secret.

This feeling did not leave me; in the vast entrance hall I could hear the echo of my heels clicking on the marble floor. The house felt uninhabited and silent, except for the eerie sustained sound of a siren blowing. Eduard took my suitcase upstairs to my room, which was huge and connected to an ancient bathroom. Through the open windows I could see the vast parklands, with ponds and gardens and fields stretching out to the horizon in the milky haze of early afternoon heat.

I unpacked my suitcase and tried the taps in the immense bathtub. The enamel was chipped and the taps were reluctant to be turned on and then off. But the cool water felt balmy in the heat. I changed into what I deemed was my best dress. Mrs Callman had badly misjudged my needs with her confection; it was severe and formal in black and white houndstooth wool with cuffed elbow-length sleeves and a bias-cut belted skirt. I felt sticky and uncomfortable in it and this did nothing to sustain my fragile confidence. An hour or so passed before I opened my bedroom door in reply to a tentative knock, to a little lady in a black dress and lacy apron. Would I descend to the salon where Madame was expecting me?

Madame Grandjean was sitting with her back to me facing the open French windows. On her lap was a silver tray with rusks and a china cup from which she sipped weak-looking tea. She was large-boned and hard-faced, with blonde hair wrapped around the nape of her neck; her fleshy face was the colour of pale peaches. She scrutinized me with penetrating blue eyes as she buttered the *biscottes* on the plate before her and the effect I had on her did not seem encouraging. Between bites, she asked me to talk about myself. Her expectations were low; a succession of English au pairs had failed to teach her daughter English. She noticed a wart nestling on the knuckle of my right hand of which I was ashamed but which I had forgotten to conceal, and instructed me under no circumstances to touch her daughter.

I was dismissed, and walked in the park at her suggestion. I had one idea; it was to flee. I was busy devising an escape route to my parents in Vichy when I came across a tombstone, half-concealed in untended shrubbery. I stared at the inscription: *Ici gît* Georges Grandjean, *mort pour la République.* No wonder she felt cool about my German origins, which she had prized out of me. I don't know what gave me the courage not to escape; instead, I wrote an enthusiastic letter to my parents and Eduard drove me to the village to post it.

Promptly at 6 a.m. next morning (to avoid the midsummer heat) I went downstairs as instructed. Eduard was there waiting. He apologized for his mother and his relief at her departure was manifest in his body language. He stacked the luggage into the car and waved us goodbye.

The journey was terrifying. Mme Grandjean's large frame hunched over the steering wheel of the massive black Citroën, gripping it fiercely and driving at great speed. I was half paralyzed, not daring to open my mouth. We skirted Paris and headed south. I was reminded of the patronising and superior attitude of the Dunlops, but she added snobbery and arrogance, and I tried to devise a mental strategy to survive the eight-hour drive to Brittany.

Early into the journey, I was cautioned not to distract her with talking and remained silent as she waged a continual battle with the eccentric black Citroën. It wobbled in fits and starts along the narrow, rutted roads. When it stalled, the suspension deflated and it heaved to a standstill with a terrifying moan. Each time seemed terminal, but obviously she was used to it. Despair alternating with fierce invective, she succeeded each time in restarting the motor, which somehow re-inflated itself with a gasp. I was numb with foreboding when we finally arrived at our destination.

The little girls, Isabella Grandjean and Marie Solange de Fraguier, welcomed me with great excitement and warmth. Isabella was the taller of the two and seemed very sweet-tempered. Marie Solange had blonde hair and fine aristocratic features. They were delighted with the little felt thimble hats my mother had made for them because they said they both liked sewing, and they wrote letters telling her so. The vicomtesse, slim and elegant, was gracious and kept her word to the letter. The villa was pink, small, modern, beautifully furnished with every convenience and the food, prepared by a resident *bonne* (maid), was an entirely new experience.

We settled into a comfortable routine. The day started with gymnastics in the garden, followed after breakfast with an hour's English lesson. Then there was an outing to the beach and games on the warm dunes which lined the shore. In the sunshine we watched the little sail boats bobbing on the lift of the waves. Often the sky was dark and threatening, the rain beat down and the spray flew up from the water's edge, lashing the shingles on the shore. But the best part of the day came after the siesta, when we made afternoon excursions to the surrounding towns and villages of Brittany.

We drove to Dinard and across the estuary to St Malo, a port heaving with activity. Formerly a haven for pirates, its rocky promontory faces Cornwall. It is barely attached to the mainland and folklore has it that a shifting undertow of currents is always ready to cut it loose to join other horizons. We clambered around the massive ramparts and wandered round streets littered with the names of famous men of medicine, psychology and natural history, including, most famously, the writer Chateaubriand, who was born there. With their genius and inventions these men helped to write the history of all of France.

In the vast, wild and brooding countryside where the sea seemed to cast a sombre mood over everyone, I saw primitive farms which seemed to employ antiquated agricultural methods unchanged for centuries, but the peasants were sturdy, kind and hospitable wherever we went. Like their feudal masters, they seemed tenacious and strong-willed, resembling, I was told, the granite which is scattered around the landscape. In overwhelming contrast, massive feudal castles dotted the countryside. The round edifices were unlike any castles I had seen; they were crowned with hood-like towers resting on crenelled walls upheld by delicate corbels. They were clustered together, without windows opening to the outside and were unbreachable, secure against the assaults of enemies.

One day we were invited to lunch by the lord of one of those grim turreted fortresses. The bountiful feast he triumphantly served up for us was the exuberant expression of a very jolly man. Lunch consisted of fish, game and poultry from his lands; cheeses and tarts were swilled down with bottle after bottle of vintage wines, cider and home-brewed liqueurs. With impish delight he unlocked the impenetrable secret vaults where his cellar had hoarded the riches he concealed from the marauding Germans.

On my days off, I would sit on one of the sandy capes that jutted out from the coast, watching the waves crashing on the shore before disappearing, and listening to the cry of the sea birds. At times the sea darkened over and the craggy promontories seemed to merge with the land. I learnt the rhythm of the tides and awaited their comings and goings. I read the Celtic legends passed down the generations, especially that of local hero Tristan, joined in death by Yseult, who came too late across the sea and off the boat to claim him, not far from here at Trégastel. At night, with the sea air in my nostrils, I slept as I had never before in my life.

I could only glimpse the life of the high society and the tourists, Belgians and British, who came to the region to race their yachts, play golf in exclusive clubs and compete in bridge circles. The dead body of a young woman dumped in the grounds of the Hotel du Golfe where they all stayed disturbed the local complacence. Lurid headlines screamed from the local press, people huddled in groups and innuendo swirled around dark allegations against local personalities. We did not go to the beach for several days, but the murderer was never found and the victim never identified.

Before Marie Solange and her mother departed to their own castle nearby, I was urgently pressed to accompany them to Madagascar for four months to visit her husband serving in the French colonies. Her invitation was contagious, because no sooner had she departed when Madame Grandjean astonished me with her own proposal, to spend the academic year in Paris with them in their Bois de Boulogne apartment, accompanying Isabella, who had until now been tutored by a governess, to her first *lycée* and supervising her studies. Weekends would be spent at the estate with the family. I would of course join them in visits to the opera and theatre and be included in invitations to visit their influential friends. I would have ample time to attend lectures at the Sorbonne. Her final attempt to lure me was by offering me her many powerful connections, including the publishing house Fayard, which would help me into a career of journalism.

Her proposal offered everything I could have dreamed of. I wrote excited letters to my parents at the Alexandra Hotel in Vichy, spelling out my excessive enthusiasm, weighing it against my feelings of responsibility towards the family and what my absence for many months would mean to them and to me. Then something happened that changed the course of my existence.

On 10 August, a small blue envelope was delivered to the villa. It was a telegram from Bonne Mère informing me that I had been awarded a State Scholarship and asking me to confirm my acceptance. It meant admittance to any university of my choice with tuition fees paid and a means-tested living grant. My disbelief was only turned around when a second telegram arrived from my brother with the same information. I scribbled three ungrammatical lines to my parents who had just landed back in Paris. Back came a letter from them: 'One must feel happy,' my mother wrote, adding, 'I must admit I am very proud.' My father fitted three sparse lines on the bottom of the little letter-card. But his words meant more to me than all the extravagant congratulations that were heaped on me, and have remained with me always.

Even if I had succeeded in containing my excitement, the ladies and my charges could not. Madame de Fraguier returned from her castle to celebrate, and at the bar of the Hotel du Golfe the stately Duc de Montmorency, Madame Grandjean's uncle who was on a visit to us, paraded me to his golf adversaries and his bridge partners while his valet dispensed the Krug. A tall, kindly gruff old man, he bore the history of a long line of Constables of France on his back and was now proudly informing all who would listen that Mademoiselle from England had been honoured by the state and that his niece was proud she was part of her household.

In the manner of my upbringing, I sat down and wrote a letter of excessive gratitude and appreciation to Bonne Mère aided in my impeccable French by my pupil. Her equally fanciful reply arrived by return of post, describing my award as a 'flowering on the crown of La Sagesse, which unlike other flowerings, would never fade'. I believe that the sisters thought it to be a divine gift to the order, as it coincided with the canonization of their founder, St Marie de Montfort.

I entirely savoured my unexpected notoriety, oblivious to the fact that the small matter of my future plans needed my attention. In the last week of August, Madame Grandjean was required by her business in L'Isle-Adam. With her accustomed impetuousness, she bundled Isabella and me into the old Citroën and off we went on an eight-hour jaunt to Les Forgets. How different was this journey, and how wonderful to be close to Paris again. I suddenly felt in a hurry to begin my life and was reluctant to waste more time, and although I savoured my newly acquired standing, I decided not to return to St Briac with them, especially as I learnt that my sister was suffering from depression, probably apprehensive about being away from home for the first time. I also needed to think about my future, which seemed open-ended with unnerving opportunities.

9

The Death of my Father 1949

While I had not the faintest idea what I wanted from the future, I had earned the luxury of my independence and freedom; at least, that was how it felt at the moment. There was scant possibility of discussing my future with any member of my family; the only advice I received was from Uncle Leo, who discouraged my application to Cambridge, saying it would be viewed as taking up the place of an English student and would risk causing unnecessary anti-Semitism. My options were limited anyway; I had never held a slide rule in my hand, the teaching of physics and chemistry had not found its way into the convent laboratory and science presented as dark a mystery as calculus and quantum mechanics. The all-women's colleges at Cambridge held little appeal after my sister's experience, and anyway, I was needed by my parents at home. And somehow, the other option of Durham seemed an extension of our home, with so many of the lecturers frequent weekend visitors and firm friends.

I was admitted to the honours course in French at King's College Newcastle, on the condition that I qualified in the first year general studies exam in Latin. The interview with Professor Girdlestone was as daunting as was his enthusiasm in accepting me into his department. For me, it was a tactical choice to steer me back to Paris in the third intercalary year.

On commencement day, disguised in a hired cap and gown, I was watching the proceedings from the upstairs gallery in King's Hall when a very tall young woman with a haughty manner tapped me on the shoulder and said she liked me and wanted to be my friend. She wore a homespun skirt of many colours and her knitted knee socks were encased in thonged leather sandals. Her hair was piled high on her head and held in place by a tortoiseshell comb, which made her look even loftier. She was Minona McEwan, a first-year medical student from Peru who owed her clansman's name to her Scottish father. Her unintentional flattery was forthright and irresistible and I wondered why she had chosen me from among the crowds of undergraduates. Beguiled by her outlandish persona and her unselfconsciousness in crossing the accepted social boundaries of undergraduates, I was projected into my first adult friendship. We quickly became the magnet for exotic creatures from all departments and all stages in their courses at the university. Even my brother's final-year engineering classmates joined our motley gang. This was very welcome, since most of the students in my class were mature ex-servicemen recovering from their war experiences, making up for lost time and very single-minded in the pursuit of their degree. We all congregated between lectures and tutorials in the basement of the union building – Norwegians and Greeks, Turks and Egyptians, amongst us a descendant of Napoleon from Corsica and the son of the Egyptian foreign minister.

The faculty, too, were dramatic. The professor, Cuthbert Girdlestone, a Renaissance man of formidable learning not only in mediaeval and classical literature, but also in architecture and music, was slim and spry and darted around the lecture-theatre podium, gesticulating with his arms and exhorting us to share his enlightened insights into the heroes, heroines, villains and minor characters of Molière, Racine and Corneille, which he spread before us with conviction and understanding. His other passions were Mistral and the Catholic author Claudel. He integrated into his interpretation of literature his profound erudition in music and had published a learned tome on Rameau, at that time a little-known French composer of the eighteenth century, and a ground-breaking analysis of Mozart's piano concertos. All these preoccupations enriched his lectures, but required uncompromising commitment from his students. When our work was not up to his standard, he did not spare us his ironic verbal reprimand and peppered our essays with caustic and sometimes reproachful corrections in red ink.

Norman Suckling enthusiastically taught me the Romantics. When he had teased a conclusion out of a literary argument in a text of

J.J. Rousseau, he arrived at its climax by stabbing his two middle fingers through the air in circles with such vigour and excitement, that he invariably launched himself off the podium and only landed on his two feet by a miracle, a grin of satisfaction spreading across his sallow face. He, too, was an accomplished musician, with the composer Poulenc as his special area of research. He played the bassoon skilfully and ran the music club and lunchtime concerts in the university union.

In Spanish, my subsidiary subject, I acquired more knowledge of the language from the way Minona constructed her English sentences than from my text books and was soon ready for the literature we studied with Professor Sarmiento. My mother delighted in exploiting my exotic knowledge by showing off to her guests at teatime. 'Speak Spanish, Lili!' she would say with pride, as I edged myself out of the drawing room.

In these first months at King's everything thrilled me; I found all things bigger and more exciting than they really were and every experience a learning one. Besides Minona, a girl called Anne Girdlestone and I became close and we discovered a shared sense of melancholy. She was French and studied economics and we attended extracurricular classes in the art school together. I envied her ability in drawing, which far excelled anything I could produce with the stigmata of Sister Augustine on my artistic soul. She had sparkling black eyes and olive skin to match, was extremely beautiful and wore stylish dresses designed and made by herself. She also had an edgy intellect. Most of the young men in our group competed for her attention but she confused them all with a sort of crypto-naive misunderstanding of the obvious in her heavily French-accented perfect English. Fred Ellegers, who suffered from polio and was as blond and pallid as she was dark, felt territorial because they were classmates in economics and it was funny to see him limping triumphantly down the college road by her side without the slightest chance of conquest.

The only problem was that she was my professor's daughter, and at first I felt constrained in our friendship. As it progressed, she confided in me her difficulties at home with her fiery Corsican mother who only stayed part-time in Newcastle, on account of Anne's disadvantaged sister Madeleine who, older and much bigger than

Anne, needed protection and a different way of life. I think I was the first and only friend invited to her home, in an act of trust and bravery. They lived in one of the only two remaining Tudor houses by the quayside. It was a thrill to climb the sloping staircase to the panelled rooms with the carved chimney pieces, beautifully moulded ceilings and slanting floors. From one of the many-paned windows, Bessie Surtees (like Anne, the belle of the town two centuries earlier) had climbed down a ladder and into the waiting arms of John Scott, the son of a coal fitter who became Earl of Eldon, Chancellor under George III. Madame Girdlestone, a gifted musician who had earned her living playing piano accompaniment in silent movies, hated living in England and never ceased complaining about this to me, which made me feel that I was betraying my professor by intruding in his domestic situation.

Then, one foggy November evening, on his way home from the factory, my father collapsed at the bottom of our street. With the help of a passer-by, he recovered enough to reach home, gasping and vomiting. Doctor Freedman's diagnosis was food poisoning, but my father never really regained his health. His face remained the colour of putty and I felt sure he was ill, though my concern was generally dismissed.

Perhaps because I sensed how precarious my father's life had become, or perhaps because the terrible fog and coal dust began to depress me, I found myself living what I deemed a sort of half existence. By Christmas, I had started to profoundly question the values exposed in the world outside my imagining, and I was overcome by a crisis of despondency. I left the usual round of parties with their stupid games and charades, pretending to have thoroughly enjoyed them but loathing myself for this untruth. None of my friends seemed able to fulfil my demands on human nature and circumstances and people seemed to drag every ideal out of me. It was a simple formula for getting bruised. I felt that in order to safeguard happiness and avoid being hurt one had to be hollow, except then one was left with nothing to hold on to, no standards to apply. The routine which governed my life lost its sparkle and encounters with people, whom I tended to place on a pedestal in my initial enthusiasm, suddenly cracked. The creature I idealized would invariably fall from its plinth

91

in pieces at my feet. I wrote to my sister in Brussels. She was the only one in whom I could confide my dark feelings of depression. I described my disillusion and begged her to come home for the Easter vacation. I suspected she was having her own difficulties.

In the run-up to Christmas, I found a job at the post office. I reported for the night shift at the station sorting office in Orchard Street, where the shift started at eleven o'clock at night and lasted until seven in the morning. I worked next to odd unwashed characters with long hair stuffing envelopes into their slots next to me. Going to work when the town was settling down to sleep was exciting. Outside, the overnight trains puffed through the deserted station and only their whistles could be heard blasting through the muffled sounds of the empty night.

Not long after my parents returned from a visit to my sister at the Université Libre in Brussels, my father departed on a business trip to an international trade fair in Birmingham. Before he left, he walked down to Dr Freedman's surgery to make sure he was fit to go. I accompanied him to the electric train the following morning, and never saw him again.

A few evenings later, I was in the kitchen preparing his tray of hot chocolate and his favourite sandwiches when the phone in the hallway rang. It was my Uncle Fritz. He had difficulty finding his words, but what emerged was that my father had collapsed with a heart attack on the platform awaiting his train home and was dead on arrival at the Birmingham Infirmary.

My mother must have heard me shrieking in disbelief and stumbled down the stairs in her dressing gown, asking 'What is it? What is it?' I watched her as a look of puzzled incomprehension crossed her face and I must have resorted to shorthand in telling her because her face became distorted. We stared at each other speechlessly. There were no tears of grief; we didn't hug each other or fall into each other arms, we just stood there in the corridor, motionless, like pillars of stone, not grasping the situation, while the world seemed to continue spinning on its axis. I suddenly remembered the night in January when I had a premonition: my father had died in a faraway country. I woke up with my heart pounding and not believing it was the sound of him splashing in the bathroom next to my bedroom. I rushed to the door to make sure. I did not tell him about my nightmare because he clearly felt unwell. Now, I would never again wait out in the street, watching out for him to turn the corner from the electric train station and run to meet him.

Next morning, we were in the drawing room when my uncle arrived, accompanied by his son, Ronnie. He was agitated in his grey suit and overcoat, and the remains of his silver hair bristled on his balding head. Having been the bearer of this dreadful news he at first talked calmly of the circumstances of my father's dying. He repeated an account of the events in Birmingham then, suddenly, a long-contained anger boiled up in him and he launched into a tirade of recrimination against my father for having refused to participate in the wedding of his GI son Bill to a titled German woman in Bamberg, a town from where, not long before, my father's mother had been transported to her death in a cattle truck.

He could not overcome his rage at this rejection by the brother he loved, and in his grief at losing him he could not contain himself, the accusations just came pouring out. His face turned a dark purple. My mother sat, silent. As for me, I gasped in blank incredulity and with a terrible howl rushed out of the room. At last the tears came, and they could not be stopped. I leaned against the wall and cried and cried. My cousin Ronnie came out of the drawing room and tried very hard to comfort me.

Afterwards, events unrolled in an unrehearsed but well-orchestrated plan, and I was carried along with them. My brother was despatched to Birmingham to identify the body in the morgue. My sister was on her way back from Brussels. All matters concerning the funeral were removed from our responsibility and, under orthodox Jewish law, women were prohibited from attending the burial. The orthodox Jewish community (there was no other in Newcastle) had special people to undertake all tasks connected with death and, according to biblical law, the funeral had to take place within twenty-four hours.

I propelled myself into automatic mode. There were things to be done; the house had to be arranged for visitors who would come in their numbers. I polished the brasses on the front door and tidied the living spaces. I knew my mother would want the vases filled with flowers and went into the front garden to gather the early springtime amber wallflowers and blue forget-me-nots, just beginning to bloom. By the time my sister arrived on the train with Aunt Gerd, the house was in impeccable order. A white lace tablecloth covered the table, which was set with crystal and silver for the guests, who ate the food my mother had prepared, lemon sorbet and little cakes and sandwiches. And all the while, somewhere out there they were taking my father away.

We sat at home, the women, in the dreadful silence of calamity while they buried him. I never knew who these anonymous women of the orthodox Jewish congregations who bathed him were, nor the men who laid him into a grave unadorned with flowers. But I despised the archaic and inhumane procedures and rules which ordained our mourning and prohibited us from visiting his grave.

I could not reconcile my father's sudden death with any meaningful logic, because, even when everything had been turned upside down in my life, there had always been my father to give it meaning and direction. It made no sense of his struggle to accomplish a longed-for existence for himself and for his family in a new country in which he took pride and to rescue some happiness scaling the hurdles that had been placed in his path. Why, having survived the trenches of the Somme, having eluded the concentration camp at Dachau, having faced penniless exile and having endured another imprisonment in the Isle of Man, should he end up defeated on a station platform? I knew that life as we had known it had come to an end, the constitution of our family was irretrievably altered and nothing would ever be the same again. I wondered what would become now of the perfect glass eye on the night table beside his bed?

My father's death left a deep chasm in the tightly held-together family fortress within which we were beleaguered on alien territory. He was our champion, who shielded us against a new and uncomprehending world, helping us to adapt and survive. With his disappearance we had to face our demons, as a family and individually.

The consequences of the loss of the wage earner had to be confronted and our lives needed to be rearranged without him. Our house was quiet now, all the noise and vibrancy that had filled it disappeared. My mother, in her fifties and a widow deprived of the prospect of a well-deserved, easier and less sparse future, had now to rely on a small pension from my uncle, my father's partner in the re-established firm which apparently could barely sustain two families. I realized she needed looking after and made a promise never to leave her.

The letters of condolence came from the all over the world and from classmates and staff at college. Professor Girdlestone ended his letter expressing his sympathy by saying, 'What a difference this loss is going to make in your lives.' He excused me from classes and added that, 'for the actual examination I leave the decision to you according to your feelings and condition nearer the time. But I hope that however you feel at the present moment you will not think of giving up the studies for which you are so clearly fitted and in which you will certainly meet with success.' But despite their care and sympathy, my tutor, Mme de la Courcelle, told me that academic rules were strict and I would have to present myself at the right time next month for the qualifying exams in order to remain on the MA course at the end of term. From the university high-ups I was granted a deferral until September for my Latin. Three weeks later I tackled on auto-drive the daunting papers in Old French, philology, etymology, philosophy and literature, as well as Spanish. I passed, enabling me to continue with my studies in the coming year.

With my scholarship grant of three pounds a week, I would be able to contribute to the household and there was the possibility in the future of some restitution money from the sale of the house in the Hainstrasse and the now thriving factory on the canal in Bamberg. If my life had a course, I would now have to redirect it into financial independence and responsibility for my widowed mother.

10

King's College 1948–1951

The pain I experienced at my father's dying stalked my second year at college and created an intensity in the way I lived. I immersed myself in French literature and philosophy, where there was much to learn about feeling, style, elegance and depth. But despite my appreciation of the great writers we studied, from mediaeval to modern, it was the discovery of a young communist French Algerian's novel which transcended literature for me and had a profound effect in its depiction of the senselessness of life and the gratuitousness of death. He was Albert Camus, and his short novel *L'Etranger* was a statement about the casualness of death, the absurdity of mortal life, the passion for the absolute and for truth, and a refusal to compromise or submit to artifice. It gave legitimacy to the nihilistic feelings I had about the nonsensical death of my father, and everything that devolved from it, and I felt I could now continue my existence in the light of the absurd, which put me on another plane where nothing really mattered.

My sister vanished into her laboratory and seldom surfaced. In October, her name preceded that of eminent scientists Stein and Weiss on a milestone paper published in the *Journal of the Chemical Society* entitled 'Chemical Actions of Ionising Radiations on Aqueous Solutions'. My brother, newly graduated in engineering, started work with a prominent Tyneside engineering company, away from my father's factory where he was no longer welcome.

My daily academic programme and the prospect of impending exams at the end of the year (I had successfully fulfilled my obligation and passed the compulsory Latin exam) still left time for meeting up with my growing band of friends, absorbing their way of life and the culture they brought to our encounters. I learnt about the Bahai faith from my Persian friend, Minou Sabetian, and about Egyptian food, cooked on an oil stove in his Tynemouth hotel room from Sayed, the son of the foreign minister. From my Norwegian friends I learnt about uncomplicated living and easy, loyal friendships which inevitably crossed over into flirtation. They were studying naval architecture and marine engineering, which is why they had come to Tyneside, and had a biological need to get stone drunk once a month. Their capacity for alcohol on those outings seemed bottomless and astounded even the barman at Marsden Grotto, a bus ride down river in South Shields, which was the watering hole of choice.

Sexual encounters were not apparent in our scheme of things; the Greeks in our crowd took their pleasure with local girls from the surrounding mining villages, whom they met in pubs and seduced with the cars they drove and the money they had to spend. Different from the rest of us, they were privileged and seemed to have unlimited resources, which they spent lavishly. Their sexual enthusiasm was dealt with outside our circle, because any serious attachment to someone not from their island was unthinkable. When, in time, these boundaries were breached, the results proved tragic.

The door to my bedroom at the back of the house had a glass panel at the top and any late night visitors' comings and goings were under careful scrutiny. I could hear my mother open her bedroom door, stand there listening, and after a while call my name. It inevitably sent my visitors scuttling to the exit. It was a relief, therefore, when she sailed to America for a reunion with her sister in Texas.

My date to my first college ball was Tony Kidonievs, a Greek student of naval architecture. I made myself a long dress with swirls of blue bows out of a remnant of white taffeta. He arrived in his Morris Minor, clutching a posy of red roses encircled by lilies of the valley, and when he appeared at the door, he was accosted by my brother who, to my great embarrassment, wanted to know what he wanted. Tony stammered that he had come to take me to the ball. I liked this tall sallow-faced young man who taught me Greek love songs, thick with the scents and warmth of his island.

Anne and I decided to celebrate our birthdays together, though they were a month apart. We received permission from the French Consul, who leased the top floor of Bessie Surtees' house, to have our party there, no doubt with the intercession of the professor. We prepared sandwiches, bought champagne and hired a band, and were thrilled when our friends from everywhere trooped down to the quayside and up the sloping stairs of this historic house, which undoubtedly lent a little magic to my twentieth and Anne's twenty-first birthdays.

Just before Christmas, I was again delivered by ambulance to the casualty department, this time with acute appendicitis. Lying on the examination table, I was dumbfounded to recognize that the medical students eager for clinical experience filing into the cubicle were all my friends, but I was far too shy to make this known to the surgeon poised to expose my body and demonstrate his skill. Finally, a nurse whispered something in his ear and they all filed out sheepishly. They made up for this embarrassment by coming to visit me in the convalescing clinic in their droves, making me feel very loved, but were evicted when my fever recurred.

When she returned after a six-weeks stay in Texas, bringing with her my first pair of blue jeans, my mother resumed her social life with tea parties and buffet luncheons for the old refugee crowd, for relatives and friends from London and from overseas who came to visit. These included the swelling number of my friends, who all felt welcome in the continental atmosphere of Rectory Terrace and savoured especially the potato salad she prepared for them, which reminded them of home. Her hospitality was inclusive and she became popular among my many friends. I learnt from her that everyone was equally welcome and everyone matters not for what they possess but what they are.

One winter's night, another drama unfolded. There was a great thumping on the back door next to the coal bunkers. It was Gabriel Stein, seeking shelter. He looked dishevelled and had a beard of many days' growth. Inside the sanctuary of our house he stammered out an account which seemed incredible. He was being physically assaulted and hunted by a local Jewish doctor of high standing in the community, because he had asked his daughter's hand in marriage. Moreover, the doctor had threatened to have the Home Office revoke his visa and throw him out of the country. He spent the night with us, and the next, and a very few months later his tormentor arranged the biggest wedding that had been seen in the post-war Jewish community. I don't know if it was the glaring hypocrisy of the charade or the effusive speeches or the excesses of the whole affair which made me drink and drink, until I was sick over my ballgown in the Ladies and was forced to go home to change. It was at this wedding that my brother met his nineteen-year-old bride.

My uncle had negotiated funds from the sale of the factory in Germany. My mother felt helpless in the proceedings, from which she would not emerge the winner. In the event, money was put in the bank for both families, but the political situation at the height of the Cold War was precarious. Across the border to the east in close proximity to Bamberg the future movement of the newly created satellite state of the German Democratic Republic was unpredictable and, at times, imminently threatening.

My mother therefore decided we should go on site, and as soon as term ended my mother, my sister and I flew to Germany.

11

Return to Germany 1951

Bamberg looked run-down but unscarred when we checked in at the hotel on the Schoenleinsplatz. Here, a decade ago, my world had been shattered and I had been thrust into a maelstrom of uncontrollable events. I wondered how a town's people could survive the transient horrors perpetuated against their fellow citizens – in which they had colluded – and how it managed now to show its face to us who had escaped.

Nothing seemed to have changed. My feet walked around the streets without instruction, guided by memories. The ghost of a small child walked in front of me, knowing the way. The air was soft with the whiff of summer, the dahlias were in full bloom, and high up on the cobbled Dom Plaza the air was perfumed with the lovely scent of roses from the gardens opposite. From all corners of the town and the surrounding hills the church bells sent their call to matins and vespers with the same urgent peal as before, and behind the gleaming window panes the white lace curtains twitched with curiosity as they did when the householders peered without objection or protest as the cattle trucks containing my grandmother and other human beasts rumbled past their houses on the way to slaughter.

In the packed beer houses, groups of pot-bellied men took deep draughts from their large tankards and wiped the froth from their lips with their sleeves with grunts of satisfaction, stuffing themselves with the sausages that sizzled on braziers, with veal and potato salad, schnitzels and sauerkraut. Enormous quantities of food were everywhere in abundance. In the Konditorei Kamm, opposite my grandmother's apartment, the windows were stacked with cakes and pastries bulging with mountains of whipped cream. The deli counter in each shop displayed every conceivable delicacy and at mealtimes people swarmed to the renowned Messerschmidt restaurant, to select a carp or a trout plucked from the surrounding rivers and lakes, swimming in the tanks waiting to be culled and eaten. The Marshall Plan had ensured that the Germans would want for nothing in their process of recovery. With our own experience of enduring austerity we gazed bleary-eyed at this incongruity and ate our share.

In Munich, where we had landed, my mother had collected the Deutschmarks owed to her from an agent, and took us on a shopping spree. Suddenly, awash with money to spend, we acquired the most ridiculous number of useless objects, persuading ourselves that we needed them and making up for the years of deprivation. The Dior-inspired cocktail dress I chose for its silhouette of tiny waist and billowing skirt was in black moire, off the shoulder. I also bought a red raincoat and a beret to launch myself in Paris where I was heading in the autumn for my year of intercalating. My sister, too, equipped herself for her new research job in the laboratories of Lyons & Co in London.

With her newly regained riches, my mother, who had not sat at the wheel of a car for more than a decade, bought herself a navy blue Opel in Bamberg and, once again, we crossed the bridge spanning the Regnitz to the Rathaus, where she demanded the renewal of her long-lapsed licence. This time, unlike the threatening employee of the Third Reich who had snatched a basketful of family jewellery from her arm, a cringing clerk in plus fours, desperate to avoid any discussion, fell over himself to issue her a permit to drive, no questions asked. Fortunately, our old manservant Sulzbacher, who had proved his bravery and survived at the siege of Stalingrad, sat in the passenger seat next to my newly empowered mother in her acquired toy. It made her very happy.

My mother adapted quickly to her old habitat, receiving visits in our hotel room, and accepting invitations to outings from acquaintances, neighbours, former staff and an accountant and solicitor who had been helpful in obtaining access to our money. How quickly they all accepted us fawningly into their midst! They pleaded their innocence, reminding us that they, too, had suffered and lost their men on the Russian front. They had no knowledge, most of them said, about the juggernaut that rumbled unstoppable to this defeat. All they knew was that God, who had sent them Hitler to protect them against the Bolsheviks and to make them rich, had failed them. There were glaring ironies, too. After her arrest, my grandmother's servant Kunigunde had been obliged to work in the kitchen of the Gestapo chief. Since the only food she had learnt to prepare in forty years' service in a Jewish household was chicken soup, potato latkes, *lokshen* pudding and matzo balls, this became standard food in the Gauleiters' household.

I wandered around the town of my childhood, its history stained with blood. Wherever I went, I held in my mind my grandmother's pain and degradation and the loneliness and hunger that engulfed her in her last years. I saw the debris still scattered over the site of our synagogue and a plaque on the wall in the entrance lobby of my brother's school, the gymnasium. On it were hand-painted tiles depicting twisted expressions of agony which had been assembled by the students, bearing the inscription 'In memory of the unbearable suffering inflicted on our fellow pupils'.

I began to feel ill, suffered a blackout and refused to leave my hotel room. My mother took me to Dr Mueller. He wore a long-belted white coat and spoke in low tones, conveying the compassion demanded by the occasion in English, because I refused to speak German. He said he could find nothing wrong but informed my mother in all earnestness that I was suffering from *Seelenkrankheit* – roughly translatable as melancholia. I supposed this diagnosis said more about him than about me, and by indicating his complete understanding of my condition and the reasons for it, he somehow wanted to identify himself with it and thereby exonerate himself from guilt. This impressed my mother and gave me some status because not long afterwards, we left the town with its horrible history, its terrible beauty and its simpering population trying to explain away their guilt. As for me, I vowed never to return again.

We settled at a vast resort hotel in Garmisch-Partenkirchen called Wigger's Kurheim, sprawled at the foot of a fir tree covered mountain. It had all the lingering features of a sanatorium; all its rooms had balconies facing the sun. It was clean and orderly and from my balcony at dusk I could see the twinkling lights of the cable cars gliding down from the peak of the snow-capped Zugspitze. In this perfect calm, surrounded by mountains, everything appeared different. The air was fresh and the town familiar and near enough to Bamberg for my mother to come and go. Its timbered houses, with their brightly painted facades and inns, were crammed with GIs on respite leave. There was every conceivable sports facility left over from the 1936 Winter Olympics. The ice skating rink (where, as a child, I had seen Sonja Henie practising and performing her ice dancing), the toboggan run and the ski jump must have been attractive to an army of occupation far from home. One could always recognize them by their long-limbed saunter, the loafers they wore, their crew-cut hair and their open, friendly smiles, sashaying around the alpine streets.

My sister and I enrolled at the riding stables of Gustav Lang, run by a lean dark-skinned former Russian cavalry officer called Ludz of dubious pedigree who had a sabre scar from a duel which stretched from chin to eyebrow and told Munchausen tales of gruelling and daring exploits in a turbulent past. He twirled a mean-looking whip constantly in his hand and used it liberally to scare us and startle the horses as we trotted and galloped around the sandy arena. I was assigned a huge chestnut stallion called Gauner and soon trotted out on this great beast on magical trips through the mountains.

Not far from our hotel, the villa of Richard Strauss was draped in black; he had died just before our arrival. My mother sang us arias from his operas and *Der Rosenkavalier*, which I had heard only on recordings, became a leitmotif for me. We teamed up with an English couple and toured the area. We visited Mittenwald, a little town squeezed in between mountains, and met the luthiers, who were eager to show us the instruments for which they had been famous ever since Mathias Klotz, pupil of Nicolò Amati, began to make violins there in the mid-seventeenth century. His bronze statue towers over the market square opposite the church. They took us to Hitler's mountain eyrie high above the village of Berchtesgaden. On Hitler's own terrace, from where he planned the destruction of Europe, we looked out over the wooded hills and fertile valleys of Bavaria. In the landlocked village below, people in the streets were mostly lame, disfigured and on crutches. This was due, our guide told us, to the incest and intermarriage rife in the enclosed and isolated mountain community.

The lakes and mountains of Bavaria were inexhaustible, and the summer sped by in a series of excursions. In a secluded valley we came across an entire village of wood carvers preparing to enact the Passion. Here in Oberammergau, in the single street with whitewashed houses and green shutters, the entire village was busy carving souvenirs. Most of the villagers had a role in the play, but he who played Christ was king. We met him in the huge theatre, preparing sets on stage in preparation for the play. He was very proud and had about him a sacred sort of aura.

To the sounds of an organ thundering out a Bach cantata, in a nearby forest clearing we opened the door of the Wies Kirche and stared in disbelief at the frothy pink and gold confection of camp rococo. But nothing could prepare us for the splendour of the frescoes and paintings and gilded furniture in the fairy-tale mock mediaeval castle of King Ludwig II of Bavaria, high up on a rock at Neuschwanstein. So *this* was the kinsman of the tenant in my grandfather's house in the Hainstrasse! Like my mother's mother, Louis adulated Marie Antoinette and, at Linderhof, another of his fantasy castles built like a miniature Versailles, he dined with her tête-à-tête, allowing no servant to interrupt the intimacy of his meals with her. For this purpose he had a hole constructed in the floor, through which food was hoisted up from the kitchens below. In a grotto adjoining the castle, he indulged his worship of Richard Wagner. For the composer of *Der Ring*, he built a theatre in the grotto where, in seats carved into the cave's wall, he and Wagner could sit together and watch Lohengrin, son of Parsifal, glide out of the watery wing on the small lake in a boat drawn by a swan (which was really her princely brother in disguise) to rescue Princess Elsa. In the event, Wagner never condescended to attend, and when, in the end, the niggardly Bavarians no longer tolerated their king squandering their tax money, they pronounced him mad and had him incarcerated in an asylum from which one day he walked out into Lake Starnberg and was never seen again.

When my sister left for London, I spent more and more time in the stables. Sitting in the stacks of hay, I listened in awe to the heroic exploits recounted by Ludz. Occasionally, some equestrian star or other arrived to jump over hurdles in the meadows in preparation for an international event. One, with the improbable name of Ingrid Ungewitter, befriended me and taught me, in a gentler fashion than Ludz, how to ride horses. I was surprised how sure-footedly Gauner clambered up mountains and was exhilarated when we reached the top, where the rule prevailed that the last rider to the summit had to pay for a round of schnapps.

One day, riding up a hill near one of the many railway lines that curl through the mountains, I heard the shrill whistle of the train as it emerged from a tunnel. Gauner reared up in fright and I was catapulted over the side and thrown down a steep slope. The horse had to be calmed and I was shaken but I knew the rule of the stable: you get up and ride your horse home if you have breath in your body. There was no schnapps at the inn that day, only broken bones and the end of my riding career.

The X-ray at the clinic showed two fractured metacarpals in my right hand and the plaster covered my arm from fingertips to elbow. At the stables, I became a one-armed visitor and captive audience and spent hours in the cave near the horses. But at the hotel, when my mother left for a business trip to Munich, I was alone. I suppose people in the Alps were used to skiing accidents in abundance, but on the sun-drenched summer mountains accidents were few, and my injury and dependence gave me celebrity status. At a dining table adjoining mine at the hotel, members of a film crew competed in cutting the meat on my plate. Among them, and most engaging, was Hollywood star Peter Lorre, a fellow refugee.

On my mother's return from her business trip, which had not been a success, a prosperous-looking little man who had been eyeing us up in the dining room introduced himself to her. He was short, rotund and round-faced with flabby pink cheeks, always dressed in a navy suit with a gold chain dangling from his waistcoat and was frequently visited by a liveried manservant. He presented himself as a Romanian financier, who had somehow profited from the post-war confusion. As he installed himself more frequently at our table, my mother poured out her concerns about her financial situation. He seemed to have all the answers, and, in advising her, showed great concern for my fracture and me. Little by little he impressed my mother with his wizardry in understanding the movement of funds, the transfer of foreign currency and how to rescue it all from the Russians, and he gained her trust. She was quite sure he could solve all our problems and confided in him increasingly, actually naming sums of money and where it was kept.

So grateful was she for his attention, that she begged me to be nice to Mr Guetter because he was so understanding and willing to help, and when he insisted that I accompany him and his chauffeur on an outing my mother urged me to accept.

I felt it rude to refuse, and so one bright morning after breakfast I found myself sitting next to this unpleasant little man behind the chauffeur in a large Mercedes. The conversation naturally began about my mother but soon he changed to talking about me and my upcoming year in Paris. Here, too, he could be helpful in easing my way financially. I listened with chilly courtesy and prayed for a speedy end to this farce.

At the top of the hill we stopped; I heard him say something to the driver, who disappeared down the slope, and I followed him from the car to a wooden bench overlooking the valley. We sat there together, I next to him, squeezing myself to the limit of the seat. After a while, he beckoned me to come and sit closer, and before I could remove it, his hand had pulled mine towards his protruding belly and into his lap, from where he had tugged a jelly-like little wiggly pink thing. All the while he looked straight in front and never interrupted his talk of how my mother needed his help to maximize her capital. Miraculously, the driver's head appeared over the parapet just as he released my hand from the clasp of his stubby little fingers and was fiddling under his jacket to button up. We returned home in silence.

I did not have the vocabulary to explain to my mother what happened on the mountain. It was only when she was about to sign away our small fortune to him in front of an attorney that I expressed my doubts about him. But then, a bombshell arrived and everything was put on hold.

A telegram came from my brother in Newcastle announcing his engagement to the nineteen-year-old girl he had met at the wedding we had all attended. My mother was distracted and inconsolable. She seemed obsessed with the folly of this, and sent an urgent message back to my brother to rethink: the girl was too young and about to start university, he had not the means to support a family and anyway he had known her too short a time. In her agitation, amongst the messages going to and fro, she informed him what she was about to do with Guetter, which sent my brother into a spin and onto a plane to put a halt to proceedings.

It was time to leave all this drama behind. In early September, with my hand in an elastic restraint, I boarded the Orient Express in Munich and escaped to my year in Paris.

12

Cité Universitaire, Paris 1951

An indigo sky without a whisp of a cloud greeted me in Paris, and I savoured the crisp scent of autumn. On the chestnut and sycamore trees shading the boulevards, the leaves were still shiny green and the streets were crowded with stylish activity.

Refreshed now that the torpor of August was over, the city had reclaimed itself from the tourists and was preparing for renewal. There was a fever, an urgency in the steps of the elegant men and women and the cafes were crowded with chattering bronzed creatures fresh from the beaches and mountains. On the quays of the river, the fuddled outcasts wrapped in newspapers were swilling the contents of bottles of red wine, in search of blissful oblivion in their diaspora on the cobblestones.

For me, Paris was no longer the unattainable mystic *domaine* of *Le Grand Meaulnes*; I now confronted the reality of the city, which was quite unlike the dream of it. Alone for the first time, face to face with myself, I tried to work out how I was going to make sense of my life. Separated from my family and the orderly existence of home, across the Channel from my adopted country, I had to rely on myself in this multinational, multicultural student population within whose midst I had landed and through whom I began to understand the world and myself.

Prowling the streets and the *quartiers* of Paris, my passion for the city was reignited and I experienced, in reality now, all my fantasies. My involvement with the city was complete, total, unexplained and un-analyzed and has remained with me always. I was dazzled by the sense of space from the Place de la Concorde; I watched the barges floating silently on the mirror-glazed water under the bridges of the

Seine and climbed to the white exotic other-world palace of the Sacre Coeur overlooking it all. Cultural events and the literary panorama, driven underground during the occupation, now appeared to be flourishing. Improbably, it had been only six years since the German Army left, six years since the city had witnessed executions and betrayals, deportations and hardships, and Jews were forced to display the yellow Star of David sewn onto their clothes, the cost of which they had to pay with their allocated coupons. Now, theatre, concerts, art shows and exhibitions were exuberantly announced on every visible surface, in the metro, on billboards, on noticeboards and on railings.

I shopped at the market of the rue Mouffetard and retraced my father's steps through the Luxembourg gardens; he too had been beguiled here by Anatole France's *Le Livre de Mon Ami*. I passed by Verlaine and Chopin on their pedestals in the avenues which transverse the gardens in a theatre of stone, and watched the children bouncing astride the revolving carousel's painted horses, competing to catch the little brass rings they had to prise from the outstretched hands of the old lady keeper. I felt at home as I had nowhere else before and I knew that here was where I wanted to be; a place that I would never want to leave.

In the Cité Universitaire, where the Ministry of Education had organized my lodgings, the student population was settling in for the academic year. They came, the brightest from Latin America, Africa, Asia and Europe, mainly holding scholarships, and lived along the length of the Boulevard Jourdan in the southern suburb in the residences built for them by their country in the style of their indigenous architecture. We ate our meals in the grandiose Maison Internationale, which dominated the landscaped campus. Here we slid our tin trays along the counters from where the meals were dished out and in a well-rehearsed ritual, the uninitiated were met with loud banging of cutlery on the trays of the seated diners if one was foolish enough to wear a head-covering. The *beefsteak* was really *horsesteak*, without much disguise of its stringy sweet taste, so I restricted myself to unadulterated greenery. Afterwards, my new medley of companions and I would emerge into the formal grounds, where the sound of every conceivable instrument floated out and filled the air from a dozen practice rooms on the first floor. For aspiring Olympians and athletes in general there was a gymnasium, and for the artists, sky-lit studios and a cinema where on Saturday evenings we noisily (and with wit) provided the soundtrack for the film on show.

The Collège Franco Britannique was a large red-brick building, one of nineteen student residences which had the pretension of a British country mansion. It was quietly self-contained and provided lodging for future cabinet ministers and stockbrokers and girls with no defined future at all. Set back from the main road in the midst of a hundred acres of tree-filled parkland and playing fields, it was very austere, as were most of its post-graduate residents. It had a distinct and sickly musty smell, due to a native fear of the *courant d'air*. Squarely positioned in the middle of the foyer was the lodge of the concierge, who enforced the house rules. Even when poring over his books through misty glasses, recording our comings and goings with arthritic fingers, his tangled white hair falling over his forehead, he made sure that the prohibition against the mingling of sexes in the bedrooms was strictly enforced, and so all social intercourse took place in the lounge at formal sherry parties for visiting academics from Oxbridge, or in the safety of the basement kitchen, where there were benches and tables and lockers for food storage.

There was a terrible stale smell in my shared bedroom, and it was only at weekends when Madeleine, my roommate, went to her home in the provinces that I could fling open the window and banish the foul air. To keep the parquet floor at a high gloss, a pragmatic housekeeping device obliged us to attach brushes to our shoes to polish the floor as we went; and so we constantly skated around, from bed to basin and from table to door, in a clownish sort of ballet.

Since my permission to reside at the college required a *carte de séjour*, and a *carte de séjour* required admission to the university, and admission to the university required a *carte de séjour* and my appointment as *assistante* at the Collège Octave Gréard required the lot, I spent my first week in Paris locked in circular argument with officialdom in a grim room with men in grey. Here, benches were stacked against the wall, and lost-looking immigrants sat semi-comatose, drooping despairingly, waiting for their number to be called and this stagnant bureaucratic process to somehow resolve itself. When I finally left, I had a pocketbook full of stamped, signed, sealed dockets which gave me the right to live, study and work in Paris.

Armed with all my documents, it was with a deep sense of destiny that I crossed the hallowed courtyard of the Sorbonne, which stretches from the Panthéon on the hill down to the Cluny alongside the worn stones of the rue St Jacques, for my first lecture by Jean Wahl. He was the doyen of existential philosophy, authentic and uncompromising, and had been responsible for introducing the German philosophers Husserl and Heidegger to France. In the vestibule, murals depicted the history of the university and showed the remarkable scientists Ambroise Paré (pioneering the tying of arteries), Cuvier (studying bones), Laennec (inventor of the stethoscope) and Arago (lecturing on astronomy). It was humbling to pass these on my way to the huge amphitheatre, to sit on the worn wooden benches which reached in steep semi-circular tiers to the ceiling. I looked down to the podium where Charcot, in his exploration of the human mind, had demonstrated to Freud how a hysterical patient reacted under hypnosis and, in doing so, had changed the course of the understanding of human consciousness and set the foundation of psychoanalysis. In this amphitheatre, too, Marie Curie had presented her discovery of radium in the use of medicine.

To my surprise, I discovered that the sternly orthodox character of the university, which in the thirteenth century governed Robert de Sorbon's theological college, remained restrictive in these sacred halls of learning. Then, it was a bastion against innovation and reform, with its repudiation of the Reformation, its persecution of the Huguenots and its encouragement of the burning of Joan of Arc at the stake; now, the elders of the institution were disputing with rigour the philosophical credentials of Jean-Paul Sartre, forcing him to give his lectures outside the aegis of the university. And although I had signed up at the Sorbonne to attend lectures in philosophy, it was to the Collège International de Philosophie in the Place St Germain that I went to hear Sartre.

It was standing room only in this imposing classic grey building opposite the mediaeval church of St Germain des Prés to hear the lucid argument of this small, stocky man with the round horn-rimmed spectacles, who, without looking at his intrigued audience, dissected his brilliant arguments with powerful reasoning. Afterwards, we would follow him to the mezzanine of the Café de Flore and try to get close to the round mahogany table where he sat, puffing on his briar pipe and drinking cup after cup of black coffee. This is where he worked, these were his headquarters; seated on the red-plush chairs and reflected in the gilt mirrors, where the smoke from his pipe mingled with that from our Gauloises, he answered with thoughtfulness any question that interested him. He was the existentialist in residence and cast a mode over a contentious, disenchanted generation in search of freedom. I understood that literature in Paris was conceived as a social function, and that since 1945 his publication, *Les Temps Modernes*, was the debating ground for the contestants – and that public lectures by Sartre were a media event.

At the Sorbonne, I occasionally attended for my entertainment the *Cours de Civilisation Française*. For the wide-eyed American girl students with time on their hands and money to spend, sent abroad to absorb culture and hopefully find romance, this was the new frontier. They were decorative in the amphitheatre, with their sincere desire to learn what measures the government was taking to repair the decline in the birth rate. One way, the prohibition of the sale of contraceptives, restricted all relationships, since the consequences of love-making carried a life sentence, or a back-room abortion, or being outcast from the family, or at best, a clandestine disappearance to Geneva where medical terminations of pregnancies were readily performed. There were of course other lectures on French history and literature, few of which I attended.

Realising that my philosophical grounding was insufficient to write a meaningful dissertation on existentialism (I had tried unsuccessfully to read Sartre's manifesto *L'Etre et le Néant*), I agreed with my professor that instead my thesis would be on the theme of 'Existentialism as Portrayed in the Plays of Sartre'. It was a pragmatic solution, given that every month one of his plays would premiere in one or other of the little theatres dotted around the city and that in the clipping file at the quaint Bibliothèque de l'Arsenal, every programme, review and discussion was available.

My teaching duties as *assistante* at the *collège* started at half past two in the afternoon, and when I was not leafing through clippings in the Bibliothèque de l'Arsenal, I spent the mornings exploring the city. Paris is small and its present is unapologetically informed by its past. It requires no guidebook, only the metro station bearing the name of the *quartier*. Its monuments and its associations picturesquely proclaim its literary, martial and sometimes bloody history. So I became familiar with the Paris of Molière and Rabelais, of Rodin and Balzac, of Proust and Baudelaire, of generals and martyrs from the names of the streets and the statues erected to them. On my way to the *collège*, if time remained, I sat in the nearby Parc Monceau, watching the armies of tiny children with their buckets and spades playing in the sandpits under the gaze of chattering uniformed nursemaids and the towering statue of de Maupassant, rolling their hoops and sending balloons into the sky. The small, elegant park just off the Boulevard Malesherbes is full of statuary and history, and, after eating my baguette, I would explore its shadowy copses and secret bowers and absorb its past, before entering the school and confronting my classes.

I managed to entertain a bunch of young girls in classes of twenty-five and was paid 19,916 francs each month for doing so. In addition, there was a subsidy for my rent, a cost-of-living allowance and a travel allowance. All together, my monthly disposable income, after deduction of social security contribution, came to the princely sum of 24,765 francs. And while I cannot say any of my pupils will boast that they were taught by me, I think I kept them amused, and hopefully entertained them in the English language, enough to give them a little hunger for the literature which inspired me. It also gave me the means of providing food for the hungry inhabitants of the Cité, stuffing my locker in the basement with basic food, and enough to buy snakeskin handbag for my mother and a present for my brother's wedding, which I attended in Newcastle in December.

On my return to Paris, I plunged myself into my dissertation. The pessimistic radicalism and the rebellion and insubordination voiced by his characters underpinned my existence also, though I did not have the confidence to express this. The total subjectivity which dominates his feelings through Orestes (*Les Mouches*), Estelle (*Huis Clos*) and Hugo (*Les Mains Sales*) empowers these characters until they ultimately achieve their absolute freedom. This freedom is passionate and disciplined and constantly under scrutiny, and the exploration of his characters in relation to their actions mirrored my own self-scrutiny. Life may be absurd, but, for the moment at least, I savoured every aspect of it.

Upending the perceived Aristotelian perception of helplessness in the face of predestination, the notion of responsibility and choice grasped the imagination of the Parisians. Literary activity was in the grip of existential debate and entwined with politics (Marxism, colonialism and religion). The discussion was breathtaking, and, enacted in the cafes of St Germain and Montparnasse, not without its battles. These spilt over and raged on the pages of the literary journals – especially Sartre's *Les Temps Moderne*. The whole of society seemed to be discussing writers, and the artists performing in the small atmospheric theatres dotted around the city – the Antoine in the north, the Vieux-Colombier and the Théâtre de l'Oeuvre – presenting the plays of Camus and Sartre, of Cocteau and Gabriel Marcel, Gide and Malraux.

When Sartre wrote a gloomy song for the talented elf-like Juliette Gréco ('Dans La rue des Blancs-Manteaux'), existentialism entered the nightclubs. In the Rose Rouge, dressed from head to toe in black, she sang her melancholy tales of sorrow in her smoky, conspiratorial voice and mesmerized her adoring audiences with her unremitting pessimism.

I quickly became acquainted with the Cité and its inhabitants. The teeming centre of activities was the American Foundation fronting the boulevard. It was open to all, held weekly balls, and housed a noticeboard advertising job placements and accommodation. Not surprisingly, it attracted touring Americans and all kinds of unsavoury people, including crooks and black marketeers. It was easy and uncomplicated to make friends; one was never lonely, and one contact led to a multitude of choices in friendship. From the Latin Americans I learnt to recognize (and imitate) every inflexion of Spanish from Cuba to Argentina. Everyone spoke French, but the French seemed to keep their distance. Next to our foundation was the Spanish house, a sombre forbidding structure, from which regularly emerged two young men, one bearded, one clean shaven, Jose Maria Garcia Llort and Juan Antonio Roda, their hands clasped behind their backs, as new to the scene as I was. They passed the Franco Britannique each day looking for miracles, and found me.

Partly because I could speak their language and partly because I could introduce them to other English girls, they came often to our establishment. They were both painters, on a tiny bursary from the Franco regime, on which they could barely sustain themselves without selling their drawings for a packet of Gauloises. So I began my career as a provider, offering them breakfasts of bread and cheese and bowls of *chocolat* in our basement. It was the beginning of my exalted admiration of genius and we made friends for life. It was a disastrous trend, one so transparent in its offering that I would fall easy prey to crooks and confidence tricksters. But in the meantime, at their shows in various galleries around town, they introduced me to Pablo Picasso who, eager to support his fellow Catalans, would scrutinize their work and offer his opinion.

Another of my breakfast regulars was a tall, handsome pianist named Peter from England. For the first time in my grown-up life I felt a tingling of attraction. He fulfilled all my notions of a romantic hero; full of sadness and disillusionment, he had determined never to touch a piano again since his teacher Dino Lipatti in Geneva had died from leukaemia. But after long soul searching and discussion, I persuaded him to book a practice room and stood next to the piano while slowly he began to play again. Peter never joined me on our evening outings. Our time together was spent agonizing over his dead hero and his intention to abandon his music. We had breakfast together each day but there was too much excitement spinning around in my head, and he became too intense and demanding. At the Valentine's Day ball, I was dressed in a red silk cloak with a multitude of embroidered black felt hearts, he offered to smuggle me into his bedroom, whereupon I withdrew myself and my breakfast facility from him.

Sex was for the brave in the city of free love and the brave girls quickly became known and in demand. I was not one of them, perhaps because of my mother's coded caution in my ears about sleeping with boys. For the moment, I enjoyed casual encounters and meetings of minds, and sheltered my lack of sexual confidence behind counselling the other girls. So I was anointed with the role of *la tante Lili*.

115

It was much later, after the end of term, that I fell hopelessly in love with Len. He was an alcoholic, blond-haired Canadian from Winnipeg with a thick growth of blond hair and a squint in his left eye. He sat next to me in lectures at the Sorbonne and I noticed he shook uncontrollably. He was passionate and knowledgeable about literature and was doing a doctorate on James Joyce. I attached myself to his crowd of friends at the Canadian House without making much impression on him. Until, one day, he noticed me.

I had moved to a little hotel round the corner from the Cité and used to haunt his favourite bar, the Chalet du Parc, where they all drank wine and played football. On one of those afternoons when I joined them, he said he would come to my hotel when they finished their game. I was waiting for him by the window of my room when I saw him coming up the narrow little side street lined by vine-clad terraces of doll's houses built for Napoleon's officers at the southern end of the park. Behind me, the wardrobe wobbled on the uneven floor, its door creaking open on its hinges. My typewriter was perched on the chest of drawers, which had a drawer missing. It was not the most romantic setting for a life event. I thought about what was to happen, the advice I had given to all my housemates at the Cité, but if this was how to get his attention, I would throw caution to the wind.

He knocked on my door and the bed beckoned in an unspoken summons. I put my head on the round bolster, used by the French in place of pillows, and he went about it in a hurried, if business-like way. As he made love to me, the cupboard door flung open, and his face started sweating. It struck me as very comical and a little painful, and when it was over and done with and we were lying side by side in silence, I felt I had been let into the secret everyone was talking about. From my ignorance of the language of passion, he realized it was my first time. He was horrified and felt betrayed, and from then on he avoided me like the plague. But I still spied on him and, after he left Paris, out of nostalgia I transferred my favours to his best friend, a sad Polish-born mathematician who was also mesmerized by him. He was grateful to me, even if he knew he was a substitute.

Meantime I had much opportunity to indulge my love for the

exotic. In the sky-lit studio at the top of the American Foundation Juanito Blanco de la Cruz held court amid his easels and his paintings, and fellow Hispanics indulged their homesickness with songs from their homeland and native drinks and had a rapt following of girls. The drawings on the easels were strangely ghostly, the result, I learnt, of a year's drawing technique honed in the city's morgue, forced on him by his teacher in Mexico City. Even after he had studied with Diego Riviera, whose daughter was one of our crowd, the paintings on the easels were masterly but dead. Sometimes, we all went to eat in the cheap restaurant in the neighbourhood. There, after our *steak frites*, one of the Latins would jump up, tap on his glass for silence and proceed to deliver a rousing oration to a make-believe 'bride'. I discovered that the Mexicans love learned discourse and legal disputes, and they certainly never missed an opportunity to entertain us.

There was a new fascination with the jazz played in the whitewashed basement *boîtes* and the *caves* where we students were lured for the price of a watered-down flute of white wine, to listen to a steady flow of Afro-American jazz musicians who, restricted in America, received an ecstatic reception in Paris. Their music was new to my ears and we listened through the night to Duke Ellington, Lester Young and Miles Davis. At dawn we would leave and roam through the deserted streets, where our footsteps echoed and the dustcarts began their dawn sweep-up of the night's refuse. Membership of Les Jeunesses Musicales de France entitled us to half-price entry and the best seats in the great concert halls of the Salle Gaveau and Pleyel, to performances by Heifetz and Gilels and to the Trocadéro, where I heard David Oistrakh perform four violin concertos in one go, his brow dripping with sweat. Edith Piaf sang at the huge venue of the Olympia; but even here she created an intimacy with her transcendent voice and her searing lyrics. Jouvet and Pierre Brasseur brought the classics of Racine, Molière and Corneille from the books I had studied to vibrant life at the Comédie-Française, and in the smaller theatres of Montparnasse Charles de Rochefort brought modern plays to the stage.

I became aware of my ill-fitting utility clothes, cobbled together from coupon remnants and curtains, and started to pay attention to my appearance. I discovered the fabric house Dreyfus, which sold fabric-ends from the collections of Schiaparelli, Chanel, Fath and Worth at the foot of the Sacre Coeur. I took the remnants I selected there to a seamstress at the Porte-d'Italie who draped them around me with deft fingers. And so began my Parisian wardrobe. I started collecting earrings, and learnt to make up my eyes with shadow and how to knot a scarf round my neck like French women to make it look like an important garment. The result was noted by the visiting friends and relatives from England for whom I found cheap hotels in my neighbourhood.

As I metamorphosed into a more beautiful being, more suited to my surroundings, I became more confident and walked tall into the luxurious restaurants to which I was introduced – the famous fish place Mediterranée in Pigalle by my Uncle Ernest and Maxim's by Bram van Santen after a performance of an Anouilh play starring Jean-Louis Barrault and Madeleine Renaud at the Théâtre des Champs-Elysées.

For the Easter holidays, summoned by my mother to a spa in Germany, I boarded the packed Orient Express at the Gare de Lyon. I had to sit on my suitcase in the corridor throughout the night all the way to Wiesbaden and consumed, with the help of two GIs, the entire bottle of Rémy Martin intended as her present.

My mother spent much of her time now in her old homeland; there she could enjoy some luxury, entertain her friends with the frozen capital not transferable to England and pay for her medical expenses. She distrusted all doctors, particularly English ones, and so returned for diagnoses and treatment to her old gynaecologist in Munich, who had seen her through three pregnancies. She seemed to adapt with ease to the circumstances and felt comfortable in her own language. She also seemed to tolerate the fawning, guilt-driven attention of the Germans. We agreed that in exchange for sitting through a performance of *Ein Walzertraum* at the Staatsoperette with her, she would spend a day with me at the casino and hope for the machines to spin out their loot.

Back in Paris, early summer had arrived. The skies were clear and cloudless and the warm air brought out subtle perfumes, natural and fabricated. At weekends a crowd of us now took our bicycles and headed for the nearest open road, into the countryside studded with chateaux built for royal mistresses and bastards. It was tame and civilized, so elegantly serene and untouchable. One dared not pick a leaf or a branch from a tree for fear of upsetting the delicate equilibrium of le Nôtre's landscaped symmetry. We delighted in picnicking on the manicured lawns and nothing could disturb our *partie de campagne*, not even the guardian frantically blowing his whistle and waving his arms in the air, yelling '*Defendu!*'. Only the swans in the lake were frightened by his wild gesticulation.

In Newcastle, meanwhile, there was great excitement when my sister brought Martin her husband-to-be, who worked in his father's factory making numbering machines, to introduce him to all our friends. The wedding was to take place in our home and for the second time that year my mother applied her talents to catering a wedding. There was some discussion about sparing me from attending, since they would be passing through Paris on the way to their Corsican honeymoon. But, armed with strawberries and Normandy butter and gladioli from the flower market near Notre Dame, I embarked on the boat train to Dover and made my way to Newcastle.

13

Graduation 1952

It was a new semester at King's. I typed my dissertation on a worn-out Baby Hermes typewriter, laboriously inserting the accents and circumflexes by hand in pencil, but I soon lost patience with this task, and handed it in as it was. I was not proud of my sloppy presentation, nor were my tutors. I found it difficult to concentrate in lectures and tutorials. I missed my Parisian friends, despite exchanging letters describing our feelings at the deepest level of our existence. I missed being understood in all the elations and depressions of life and I missed the exquisite freedom and vitality of the Parisian experience.

The final year honours course was demanding, the examinations exacting, and I much distracted. The wait for the results to be pinned up under the arch at King's was intolerable and a second class honours degree disappointing. I felt I had let down my mentors, especially my professor. My mother, returned from visiting her sister in Texas, was displeased with me and did not attend my graduation, nor was there any photograph to mark the occasion. Professor Girdlestone was a little disappointed, I knew, but he encouraged me to continue my graduate studies in mediaeval poetry and supported my application for a grant.

He contacted Professor Seguy in Toulouse – the heartland of the troubadours and their lyrics – and they decided that was the place for me to pursue my studies. In a letter tinged with irony, he wrote to tell me that he had handed my application to the county hall. 'You were predestined to study Old Provençal,' he declared; all I had to do was await the outcome.

This I was trying to do when my mother, who was about to depart

120

on her annual visit to Germany to spend her Deutschmarks, insisted the house must be closed up and I must leave. I found this unjust, since my brother and his wife were occupying the attic flat and I needed to await the reply from the ministry regarding my grant so that I could decide at which university to enrol. Being forced out of Rectory Terrace so suddenly meant that instead of taking a smooth path to an academic career, I was launched into a precarious future.

Whilst waiting for my grant to come through, I set off for Paris again. It was September and Paris was settling down to autumn. The leaves were curled and twisted on the avenues, and on the benches in the Luxembourg Gardens sat their perennial occupants. For the first months I sub-rented a corner room on the ground floor in the Fondation Deutsch de la Meurthe, a single storey vine-clad graduate dormitory set around a quadrangle which had no prying eyes of a concierge. Only a few of my friends had departed and the rest of us resumed our get-togethers and steamy discussions over red wine and spaghetti. The most interesting company were the Canadians, French and English; there was no hint of the enmity aroused in their separateness at home. They had a freshness, energy and enthusiasm about their discovery of Europe and the medley of our student population. Among the media students and writers was a mathematician and a future director of the IMF and Terry Gabora a virtuoso violinist. Nobody paid much attention to the appearance in the group of a large, fleshy man with greasy blond hair, a puffy baby face and an ambling gait. To anyone who cared to listen, he was the talented cousin of the actor David Heflin. He had come to Paris to study singing, and he soon persuaded me to support his musical ambition and write him weekly cheques for his 'singing lessons'.

One night after a party in the lodging of a ballet dancer, a suitcase stuffed with dollars disappeared from under his bed. It was the money the dancer had earned in a year of working the night shift in a factory to fulfil his ambition of coming to Paris to study with Serge Lifar. Suspicion fell of course on the concierge, which made the investigating gendarmes splutter with rage. When they finally suspected Heflin, no evidence could be brought against him, but it was I who was most frequently interrogated at the gendarmerie, singled out as a promoter of his singing career, which in their eyes made me *'la petite maîtresse'*.

It was only the following year, that I learnt that a colossal fraud had been perpetrated by him; he had placed a series of advertisements announcing cheap Christmas flights to Canada, which were eagerly taken up by Canadian students. When they arrived at the airport for their journey home, however, there were no such flights and no Heflin. It had been so easy for this total sociopath to infiltrate our easy and inclusive gang.

My Catalan painter friend Roda had returned from designing tapestries for the French painter and textile artist Jean Lurçat. One day, he asked me to accompany him to the campus infirmary, where a Colombian labour leader, crippled from birth, was recovering from a series of operations to make him walk. It sounded like a fairy-tale ending to a life of despair.

Born in the desolate industrial plains of Colombia, where his father barely managed to earn a living for his eleven children in the mines of Bogota, Arnoldo Palacios was struck by a disease at the age of two which destroyed the nerves in his legs and left them hanging lifeless from his body. Helplessly watching as his siblings played in the sandy streets, he painfully learnt to manipulate the crude sticks they had fashioned for him, which dug deep into his armpits. With these, fiercely determined, he could make his way to school, where he learnt to read, write and discover the world. At night, his brothers would carry him across the fields and lay him down under the stars, where he would dream his dreams. Through his efforts and persistence, he achieved remarkable success, growing up to represent the labour movement. Some months before, travelling on the metro on his crutches, Arnoldo was approached by a strange man who challenged him to let go of his crutches and stand up unsupported. Arnoldo had laughed in his face, but accepted the calling card of France's most renowned orthopaedic surgeon. He told Arnoldo he could help him to walk and would operate on him without charge. Despite the initial doubts which led him to this quasi-miracle, it gave him hope and the unfaltering expectation that he would make a full entry into the life of which he had always dreamed.

Lying in his hospital bed, propped up on mighty arms, Arnoldo greeted me with the polite warmth with which one welcomes the friend of a friend. His eyes, wide with wonder, glowed and expanded out of his dark face, his deep and emphatic voice giving a value to his words which impressed each one on my mind. He listened intently to the news Roda brought him, and his laughter came deep and melodious from inside his body, ill-defined under the sheets. There was a feeling of ease and intimacy in their conversation which made their words seem unnecessary, a mere concession to the human convention of talking. He spoke thoughtfully and with conviction and his slow delivery had a prophetic quality. Although he addressed himself to Roda, he included me in his complete delight in this contact with the world from which he was separated but to which he had been given reason to believe he would be reconnected and to which he directed a gigantic effort of his energy and his thoughts. He asked me my name again and pronounced it slowly, as if to savour its sound and commit it for all time to memory.

I visited him regularly, and he came to rely on my companionship more than on the flowers and fruit I brought him. Sitting at the foot of his bed in the hospital, I listened to his intense commitment to humanity, his wide understanding of literature and his belief in our responsibility to a world where, as individuals, we must make ourselves heard. I confided in him my anguish about life and literature, never realizing that after months of sequestration, my visits and the intensity of our conversation had led him to high expectations of our relationship.

In the early autumn he was discharged to a friend's sixth-floor apartment on the Quai d'Orsay. He had progressed to an armchair and was no longer inaccessible across the safe divide of the hospital bed. He had the same triumphal laughter, though, and I saw for the first time how dwarf-like in stature he was. It was then that I realized the expectations I had aroused, and the delicacy and tenderness of his feelings for me were almost unbearably intense; he was going to make a pact with the devil, he said, to come and visit me if I did not return. To my shame, I took flight. My visits grew fewer, his letters – so beautifully penned and poetic – grew more ardently wounded and deeply disappointed, as Sundays came and went without my visit. In one of his letters that autumn, he expressed his deep disappointment by writing only a line of a poem by Neruda: '*Nosotros los de entonces, ya no somos los mismos*' – 'We who were, are no longer the same'. I despised myself for having entered into a bond which I was too inadequate and too small to honour.

I began my research into the troubadours. Letters from my university and from the British Consul, along with my photographs and fingerprints, finally gained me access to the shrine which contained the mediaeval manuscripts and actual handwritten lyrics of the troubadours, which thrilled me. I had been seduced by these young musicians who roamed around the countryside from castle to castle, singing the verses they composed and enchanting the ladies. Their courtly lives were recorded in the langue d'oc, an other-worldly language between the Latin of Caesar and the Old French of the north. They composed ballads and pastourelles and evensongs and elegies. But mainly they sang songs adoring the ladies of the court they addressed. The most dashing of their princely tribe was Guillaume de Poitiers who, after returning from the Crusades, devoted himself to the art with wit. He is recorded as being seductive and completely irresistible to the women to whom he addressed his poetry.

The Bibliothèque Nationale was in the rue de Richelieu attached to the colonnaded Palais Royal. It was a place of privilege, housing the archive of the recorded history of the French republic and the royal houses which predated it. It was staffed by war veterans, *les anciens de la guerre*. They limped and shuffled around in grey belted overalls with berets to match, and displayed a terrible enjoyment in making life difficult for researchers. It took most of the morning to obtain the folders requested for the day's study, and they had to be returned by the same process each evening. But it was a small ransom to pay for the privilege of touching and scrutinizing the hand-written texts of nearly a thousand years ago.

Since my grant had not yet come through, I was forced to take on a job as a tour guide. It was a toll too far, and it happened only once. As I stood next to the driver yelling out the names of my cherished landmark discoveries to a coachload of beer-filled Bavarians, it struck me that it was impossible to share the Paris to which I alone had the key, the Paris that has to be lived in and experienced in all its highs and its lows, thrills and depressions, and that I would rather starve than spend another day in this ridiculous occupation.

By early September, I still had no news of my grant and my money had run out. I scoured the job columns in the *New York Herald Tribune*; before I could respond to the five replies to my applications inviting me to interview, I saw a notice on the board in the American House in the Cité. An American couple living in Neuilly were looking for a babysitter for their four-year-old son, Nicky. In exchange for two evenings of my time they were offering free accommodation at the top of their apartment building and some pocket money. I was interviewed and moved immediately into the maid's room under the roof, one of which was allocated to every bourgeois apartment from the time of Mansart. From a previous incumbent, I inherited a small oil-fuelled stove on a stand and a large packet of Betty Crocker's Cookie Mix, on which I lived for two weeks, making pancakes and nearly suffocating from the smoke. On my evenings on duty, in their apartment, I found their fridge was stuffed with American supplies from their commissary, and hungrily shared Nicky's supper.

The Mallets were my first encounter with the beguiling open charm of the New World, completely uncontaminated by European fossilized class-consciousness. Mr Mallet worked as a Mutual Security Agency Special Representative in Europe for the State Department which administered the Marshall Plan. When he learnt that I was fluent in four languages, and needed to support myself through graduate studies, he arranged for me to apply for a translator's job in his Agency.

The examination took place in the gilded splendour of the Le Meurice hotel, the former HQ of the German occupying high command. It overlooked the Place de la Concorde and the Tuileries gardens. The examiner, Mlle Pascal, was a diminutive dynamo of a woman, with snow-white hair and a bossy personality. She gave me four official documents, and with the help of dictionaries, I managed to translate accounts of trades unions negotiations, monetary transactions and litigation into English. A few days later, I learnt that I had passed with flying colours. I was going to have to forsake Guillaume de Poitiers and his romantic pursuits for as long as was necessary to support myself.

My grant came through three weeks into the job. Due to some administrative confusion, county hall had informed Professor Girdlestone instead of me. In a letter apologizing for the mix-up which had led to the delay, he wrote: 'Well I think you have done well to keep your present position and to decline their tardy offer. Your enthusiasm for Old Provençal was undoubted, but I wonder whether it would have resisted the grind which accompanies all investigation?' and he congratulated me on having obtained 'such an excellent position'.

There now began a life of ease and prosperity, and, for the first time, the infinite possibilities which a large weekly cheque provided. I moved back to the Deutsch de la Meurthe, unwilling to sever my ties with student life and my friends, and reported to the office in the rue de la Trémoille. It was another of the prime venues requisitioned by the US government to supervise the reconstruction of Europe on their own terms. We were five in the office, the only male being a relaxed Italian called Bob who, his feet parked on his desk, provided the gossip, the politics and romantic intrigues in the organization. Mlle Pascal allocated our daily documents for translation and threatened us with impossible deadlines.

The Champs-Elysées was five minutes from my office, and I felt a part of the animated, glamorous end-of-day crowd that promenaded on the wide pavements and drank in the bars and restaurants. At lunchtime, I chose oranges and bananas, flowers and cheese from the women crying out their wares at the Alma market, while taxi drivers hurled abuse even more shrilly at the pedestrians who were transgressing on their right of way. Or maybe they just shrieked for the hell of it.

With my American friends I went to a concert in the academy of an old crank, Raymond Duncan. The pianist that night was Victor Gil, who claimed to be in direct communication with Chopin, whose grave in Père Lachaise cemetery he visits for guidance in the interpretation of his music. He was big and fat and old, with a remarkably young face. Strips of white hair reached over his shiny bald head and drifted half way down his back. He wore no shoes and bits of dirty lace adorned his cuffs and waistcoat. He played as in a trance, throwing his hands about and lovingly gazing at a young male admirer in the first row, who seemed to be writhing with emotion as he hung on to the strains of music. After the performance, Gil put on his diamond bracelet, renewed his lipstick and disappeared with the young man to wild applause.

Listening to his music was an exquisite experience, a transportation into a past era. Perhaps Chopin really *was* communicating from the next world. I too paid homage to Chopin in Père Lachaise. It was while wandering around the literary history of the world, following the little paths where Abelard and Eloise lie near Molière and La Fontaine, Balzac, Victor Hugo, Sarah Bernhardt and even Oscar Wilde and Gertrude Stein, that my attention was drawn to a recent tombstone. It was carved in shimmering white marble, a violin straddling the grave. I remembered a recent plane crash in which twenty-two-year-old French violinist Ginette Neveu had died, clutching her Stradivarius. A nun was kneeling by her grave in prayer, tears streaming down her face. Along the wall, bullet holes marked the executions of the Resistants of the Commune, lined up there barefoot and shot.

Now it was late November; autumn had turned to winter. Though Paris had taken hold of me, the intimacy which I had formed with the city was fatiguing, so, my finances enabling, I decided to spend some weekends travelling, like the best of Parisians.

My first outing was to Amsterdam and the van Santen household, to where we had fled from Germany when I was a child. Their youngest son, Joost, became my guide. As he accompanied me through the city, the attraction between us left us both without words and we wandered as in a trance over the bridges and by the canals. We ended the afternoon in the cinema and the evening in deep conversation; afterwards, we corresponded, and the poetry he wrote for me expressed a depth of feeling which was, for the moment at least, reciprocated by me. A gifted artist, hidden and almost converted by Cistercian monks during the occupation, he was locked in a battle with his father which he was bound to lose: Bram, a pragmatist, insisted he first study engineering before pursuing the art he so desired. I left in a daze, unbelieving that such electricity could pass between strangers.

Spending Christmas at home, I met the first baby in the family. My brother's baby daughter, Naomi, lived in the attic of our house. My mother's connection with the family business, which had been created with so much sacrifice and in the face of so many obstacles, was failing, and she had no option but to surrender her shares, their value now pitifully small, to her brother-in-law. Severing her ties with a past in which she had played so dynamic a role left her feeling betrayed.

In April, I invited her to Paris, her first visit to the city. She stayed at the Hotel du Parc Montsouris, where she put up with having no bathroom, and held court in the evenings with my friends, who seemed to adore her. After work, she waited for me to take tea at the marquise de Sévignés across the Champs-Elysées, and in the evenings we went to the opera and the Comédie-Française or ate with friends in the little restaurants near the Cité. David Heflin, not yet exposed as a thief and a fraud, was to be her escort on the metro, supplied by me with first class fare to avoid mother being squashed in the crush and protected from the stale pungent smell of unwashed bodies spiked with cheap cologne and a hint of garlic. My mother was too polite to tell me this never happened. But she did mention that she had lost the diamond from her solitaire ring.

In early summer, the McCarthy witch hunt in the US spilled over into my US Agency's activities. Two thugs sent to Paris from Washington investigated our translation department and as a result, job cuts hung over us all. They searched out communists everywhere and justified their extravagant stay by instigating redundancies, mine among them.

I returned to the troubadours with small appetite, due in part to my bewildering frustration with the daily routine of retrieving my archival sources in the library. I experienced also the depression that can descend upon one with the emotion and agitation of Paris life, which results in what Parisians call being *fatigué*. One day, walking wearily down the Avenue de l'Opéra on my way home, I saw a poster outside the Israeli travel bureau. It showed an expanse of golden sand stretching into the horizon under an opaline sky, and smiling faces of girls and boys in shorts. I decided then and there on a career in pioneering; in Israel I could do something really useful, and I would see my hero Gaby Stein and his wife again in Jerusalem. My friend Ilana Lourie, whose parents had been founder members of the State of Israel, guided me through the visa hurdles and directed me to an English-speaking kibbutz, where I would enter a new life.

14

Israel 1953–1954

Midnight in the limbo of no-man's-land, Italy, en route to Genoa to catch a boat to Israel. As the train snorted to a halt, the carriage door opened, letting in a rush of dank autumn air. A man in uniform, hand raised to his peaked cap, demanded passports and visas. A lot of animated chatter in the corridor, then more door slamming. The train briefly pulled up in the station before restarting its journey through the night. All I could see of Italy before I dozed off was my blurred refection in the window as the train flew through the ghostly landscape and into the unknown.

When I woke up, one of the three friendly young Englishmen sharing the compartment informed me that we were nearing Florence. They must have noticed that I was flushed and shivering with fever, and suggested a *pensione* where an Irish landlady was fond of taking in English students. It was in the Piazza della Santissima Annunziata, though I was too ill to appreciate the colonnaded beauty of the square behind the Duomo when the taxi deposited me there. The lady who opened the door asked no questions; she simply led me to a cool room where I passed out.

In bed, burning with fever, I heard the unfamiliar sounds of Florence filtering through the window in the still afternoon air. Red roses danced on the black wallpaper before my eyes as I listened to the tramway on its way from San Marco to the piazza. The sultry late summer air was very different from the sharp cold autumn air of Paris, where a legion of friends had come to see me off at the Gare de Lyon. They had tried to dissuade me from going until the very moment I boarded the train. Marianne Gellner even accompanied me on my journey as far as the border.

One evening as I was recovering, Signora Morandi, the landlady of the pensione, appeared at my bedside on her way to Benediction in order to perform her ritual stabbing. She used a very large needle, more adapted to the hind quarters of a cow, to inject my bottom with antibiotic, but it probably saved my life. She was a large lady who, gesturing wildly with her hands, told me I had been very ill with pneumonia when she had called a doctor who prescribed the penicillin. She told me her story of how in Ireland, the oldest of seven children, she had been driven by a craving for adventure and the desire to escape to take a post as governess to a young gentlewoman in the house of a Florentine nobleman. Her reward had been this magnificent palazzo. She spoke with pride of Florence and the civic spirit which created the communal art and the harmonious structures. She also confided in a conspiratorial voice her conviction that 'as clear as the shamrock is green, it was the Jews, the communists and the Masons' who were at the bottom of all market competition and its resulting evils. I listened in silence and never admitted that I belonged to this guilty axis of evil!

When some strength returned to my limbs, I climbed up into the Tuscan hills above Fiesole which hide in their folds so many Roman memories, with their theatres and baths and sumptuous villas and the ancient Etruscan gardens of the Franciscan monastery. It had the imprint of the landscape of my childhood. It was there that I took my leave of the old world, with which I could no longer identify and which had preoccupied me too much. I made a pact with myself not to live on memories, but from now on to create my own.

I spent my last four days in Florence exploring the dazzling beauty of Renaissance art. The convent of San Marco was round the corner from the *pensione*. Here the walls of the monks' cells were decorated with the simplicity and the grandeur of the holy images of Fra Angelico. At the end of one corridor, I came upon a painting of the Virgin, interrupted in her payers, leaning forward to receive the news from an angel that she was destined for something important. Inside, in a palette of soft colours, were depicted the life and death, the mockery, the entombment and the resurrection of Christ. There were the angels and onlookers, their garments draped around their bodies in cascading folds of exquisite half-tone colours of lilac and mauve, of aquamarine, orange, azure and yellow on gold, their faces astute, knowing, curious, involved in the spectacle they were witnessing and gossiping about. And outside, astride a tall bronze mount, the hooked-nose face of Savonarola, steeped in the bloody history of the city and tortured to death for his politics. In the Pitti Palace I saw the smiling Madonna and the chubby babies in her arms and, in the round tondos, the fey androgynous creatures of Botticelli. How different from the foreshortened, childlike Gothic figures of Northern Europe. I gazed in a trance at the gold-trimmed amethyst folds and draperies of Ghirlandaio; but it was in the Accademia that I longed to touch the statue of Michelangelo, to feel the knotted muscles breathing inside the marble bodies, the life and movement contained in stone and bursting out of the flesh-like form in which it was sculpted.

It all seemed like the decor, the props of a dream of long ago. I walked through the streets and said a last goodbye to the Old World. I prepared myself to go pioneering in an even older one, wondering and apprehensive of what was to come next.

On 1 October I boarded a rusty, crusty relic of a boat in Naples. Standing at the prow of the ship, the sea air rushing through my brain, I regained my optimism. A blond, freckle-faced crew member told me that only five years ago this boat had heaved under the weight of illegal immigrants attempting to break the blockade to Palestine. On this boat, like on the *Exodus* and any other barely seaworthy vessel that could be commissioned, the remnants of tortured and traumatized European Jews had been shunted back and forth across the Mediterranean. The lucky ones were interned in the barbed wire enclosures that still stood by the port of Larnaca, waiting for the end of the British mandate and for outrage to explode in the international community before they were finally allowed to land in a Jewish homeland. The unlucky ones were returned to camps in Germany, from where they had recently been snatched.

At dusk after five days at sea, we entered the port of Haifa. Mount Carmel rose steeply from beyond the harbour shimmering with a zillion flickering lights. 'Each light that you see on the mountain,' an Israeli passenger whispered in my ear 'represents a life rescued!'

Immigration officers boarded the ship and set up trestle tables in the lounge. They were all young, blond and very good-looking. When it was my turn to produce my documents the young man in khaki shorts sitting opposite me at the table exclaimed 'Loebl? But that's my name too!' There followed the most extraordinary conversation in which he decided that, since I was undoubtedly a family member, he must bring me home to his mother. I persuaded him that I was a Loebl with a mission, but promised to visit.

I checked my suitcase in the port's left-luggage office and asked directions for the kibbutz in Galilee to which my friend Ilana Lourie had directed me. The bus station was just outside the port and a bus was due to leave for kibbutz Sasa in half an hour. In the queue, white-robed Arabs, with rakishly tilted black cords coiled around the kefiyas on their heads, were talking, gesticulating wildly and crunching sunflower seeds. They extricated the kernels from between their teeth with a loud sucking noise and spat out the shells in front of them, so that they landed in a fine film on the back of my neck. I noticed that a young woman in a tailored jacket and trousers with turn-ups had arrived next to me in the queue; she too was headed for Sasa. Her claw-like fingernails were painted scarlet and with her crimson-painted mouth and mascara-tinted eyelashes, this was not the picture of a fellow pioneer I had in my mind. She told me she was hoping that the kibbutz would mend her broken heart and give her a new purpose in life.

Soon, Teddy the driver mounted into the cabin. He was a large red-haired, bearded young man in light khaki shorts, who ran the service daily from the kibbutz to Haifa. We started out in the rickety bus along the green coastline, past the Crusader town of Acre with its pink-stoned prison. Beside the road, Arabs squatted cross-legged on their haunches next to piles of water melons, swatting insects away while puffing on their hubble-bubble pipes. They seemed to be in a daze and unconcerned whether or not they sold the fruit. We stopped to let off passengers at the seaside resort of Nahariya – nicknamed the German colony because of its settlers – and climbed through changing scenery past mounds of barren hills, soft, wavy and immobile, purple-tinted in the fading light. The smoky whiff of horse dung mixed with charcoal drifted through the windows from the Arab villages inhabited by Druzes.

As darkness descended, the road began to climb abruptly and we arrived on the hilltop at Sasa. Girls with babies in their arms, their young faces creased and leathery from exposure to the sun, welcomed the passengers spilling out of the bus. No one appeared to be curious about us two odd young women who had landed among them, and simply ignored my well-groomed companion and me. More than invisible, we were unwelcome. I learnt soon enough that they felt hostile to visitors who came and went, prying, unsettling and unproductive and, during their short stay, often disruptive. Finally a girl in khaki shorts called Yaffa came over and talked to us; assuming we had come together, she showed us to a wooden hut with two iron bedsteads and straw mattresses, indicated the dining hut and the toilets down the hill and disappeared to join her family.

I woke up at dawn and stepped out onto the stone-strewn path. The valleys of Galilee stretched out before me as far as my eyes could see, villages dotted among the softly curling hills rising out of the mist in a violet glow. To the east there were glimpses of the mirror waters of the Kinneret and to the west, terraces of olive trees descended to the Mediterranean Sea. Inhaling the air, fragrant with the early morning dew, I absorbed this scenery and felt elated. This was land unchanged since David grazed his flocks and the Maccabees reigned over their tribes. I was going to be happy, and it would be right for me to belong here.

Yaffa welcomed us in the dining hut, where long wooden tables were set with bowls of fig jam, olives, white cheese and huge chunks of brown bread. The community had eaten earlier and gone to the fields, to the cowshed for the milking and the hen house to gather the eggs for market. I must have convinced Yaffa of my commitment (indeed, our friendship was to continue long into the future), because she showed me round the community, persuading some of the members that I wasn't one of the unwanted drop-outs that drop in. My travelling companion, however, left the next day on the morning run.

Before the end of the week, my name was regularly on the roster pinned on the wall in the dining hut, and I worked hard to prove myself. My first assignment was in the dehydrating plant, designed and set up by one of the men to process onions and figs in a basic, ingeniously designed smoke house. It was perched on a mound overlooking the hen house and the landscape beyond, and employed women and recovering patients not equipped for heavier tasks. There, we peeled and sliced the onions delivered to us in large quantities each day from the district cooperative, then we spread them on wooden slats to dry inside the hut before packing them ready for market. In the spring, figs replaced onions for drying. It was a low-cost production which brought in valuable income all the year round. I learnt a lot of gossip there, but wanted more challenging work.

There were boot repairers and carpenters and metal workers and Shlomo's mechanical works shop, which provided a lucrative service for broken-down vehicles from all over the neighbourhood. The women were occupied with the children, with laundering and repairing clothes, and anticipating the approach of winter bringing mud, they urgently needed help in the fields. Soon I was detailed to a group of men in charge of the orchards, and on my shoulders humped 6-kilogram bags of phosphate and lime deep into the wadi where the red earth, starved over the centuries by wind and rain, and decimated by the Turkish occupants, was being reclaimed and prepared ready for planting vines and fruit trees.

The work was back-breaking. We started at dawn and after a breakfast of black bread, white cheese, red peppers and olives, worked nine tough hours in the fields with only a twenty-minute break, when cool water in Arab clay jugs were brought on site by Shoshanna, a founder member of the community and engaged working with the children. The air was delicious and the company stimulating. The man in charge was Israel's renowned poet Elazar Granot, and when the rhythm of labouring permitted, we had good conversation. At night, after a meal of vegetables, white cheese and bread, I returned, exhausted, to my bed under a vigilant moon suspended in the sky and all the starry magic constellations which I had never dreamed existed and which I learnt to recognize. With aching limbs and face burning from the wind and the sun, I would turn up the volume of my radio so that the *Pastoral Symphony* would drown out the blood-curdling howls of invisible jackals surrounding my hut. Eventually, exhaustion triumphed over terror and the silvery trill of cicadas soothed me as I succumbed to twelve hours of restorative sleep.

I was kitted out with work clothes and oilskins from the communal store and on *erev Shabbat* (Friday evening) together with all the members, I received my allocation of grainy cigarettes, writing paper, candy and cookies. My private hoard was a bottle of Israeli brandy which I had bought in Haifa when I picked up my suitcase, and shared with anyone who appreciated it.

In charge of all activities, according to their training and ability, were the veteran founder-members from North America and Canada who, after a stint in the US army, had joined the crews of the *Exodus* and other blockade-running ships carrying Jews to Palestine. Unsavaged by the Holocaust, they had come together and prepared for their common aim over a decade: to pursue their aspirations and realize their ideal for a persecution-free homeland for the Jews. With this shared ideal, they brought to this way of life their own culture and a socialist democratic ethic. I lacked the background of their dogma but I felt I owed it to their dedication to match it with my commitment.

This wind-swept mountain-top assigned to the group after the War of Independence was a hastily abandoned Arab village, sustained exclusively by the lucrative traffic of hashish. The deserted and destroyed houses made of stone and clay clung to the slope of the hill and seemed to merge with its contours. Only the skeleton of the opulent mosque on the summit, silhouetted against the sky, remained witness to their wealth. The remainder of their crop of hashish and tobacco had been destroyed in a gigantic bonfire, and wooden block huts now housed the kibbutzniks.

The social organization was complex, a microcosm of any community anywhere. I noticed to what extent they had stopped being *Jews* and were now *Hebrews*. There was a hierarchy of responsibilities, though not of privilege; the least able, probably neglected by society, occupied a place of importance in total economic equality. Money was allocated only where needed and barter was excluded. The commune was the shared responsibility of each individual in the role assigned to him or her and democratically ruled by committee. This met on Friday evenings, was conducted in Hebrew, and dealt stringently with economic progress, successes and failures and child rearing. Only signed-up members were admitted and had a voice. The infants born in Sasa took priority, followed in importance by the herd of cows. The children's house, in which they were communally cared for, was beautifully appointed, with tiled stoves in the kitchen and a bathroom and indoor toilet, while their parents roughed it in improvised wooden huts. Only on Saturdays did they spend the whole day with their parents. Their separation from their young parents was a continual source of dispute and reassessment and remained chronically unresolved.

The herd of cattle was the pride of the *meshek* (community), in the charge of Yakov, an ex-marine from Chicago who had taken on the role of cowboy with gusto. He was contagiously high-spirited, and became my drinking companion. He rode out of the stable shed each morning on his Arab steed like a mediaeval knight before any of us blinked into the sunrise, leading his grunting beasts to graze on the plain below.

With winter came the rain, and with the rain the endless *botz* (mud). The nights were icy and the floor of my little house was squelchy with soggy mud; but the kerosene stove which heated it kept me reasonably warm. It was here, after a day's work, when all the fathers had gone to fetch their little ones from the children's house, that I was surprised to receive, washed and shaven, each in turn by prior agreement between themselves, evening visits from the left-over bachelors in the kibbutz who couldn't believe their luck or forgo their chances with this windfall creature that had landed in their midst. But the person I quite fancied was someone else's husband, so the bride they sought was not available.

Instead, I spent some time on the wheel in the pottery in one of the abandoned houses which had been set up by a visiting ceramist from England. The raw material was the clay I dug out of the earth outside and I was triumphant when my pots kept their form as they spun round on the wheel and were worthy of firing in the kiln.

One of the intact Arab houses was a designated music room with a magnificent Steinway grand piano contributed by one of the parents. Inside, I discovered all sorts of music recorded on vinyl discs, presents from enthusiastic American supporters and famous musicians who came to assist at the kibbutz. Sometimes in the evening, Yak the cowherd would invite me to join him in lighting up a few grains of the hashish he had clandestinely saved from the conflagration. I didn't like the smell, and it did less for my mood than the Gauloises I used to smoke in Paris, but it was exciting to taste the forbidden. It ended when we were denounced by one of the young radicals from the movement. We were then hauled in front of the Friday evening committee and severely reprimanded, with a rigorous reminder of the ethos of the society, which rejected the use of drugs.

Early in my stay, Archie, the leader in the community, a Canadian mathematician from McGill University, taught me how to handle a Sten gun. The Uzi was a primitive object even to my simple mind. After two lessons and some target practice, they entrusted me with guarding the sleeping community from the threat of fedayeen terrorists crossing the perimeter fence from Jordan. It was called *schmirar* (watch duty). On my first night, I was partnered by Amos; together we were to circle the terrain and raise the alarm if any intruders from across the border crept into the kibbutz to steal poultry, cattle or murder the inhabitants. We were also to be on the lookout for raiding parties who cut down young trees and uprooted the slender saplings.

One night, soon after the moon had risen, I saw a fleeting silhouette, no more than a trembling shadow, crossing the barbed wire fence and disappearing behind the henhouse. I looked round for Amos; he had vanished into one of the stone houses, no doubt to keep a romantic tryst. Hoping the shadow was my imagination and not wanting to grass on my partner, I foolishly took the risk not to raise the alarm, and when the sun rose in the morning, the door of the henhouse was miraculously fastened and secure.

I continued to volunteer for night duty because it freed me in the daytime to go with the trucks to the Hule lakes where the men went to tend to their fish ponds. The road followed the northern border with Lebanon, through endless stretches of barren land. Every now and then, in the midst of the emptiness, the sound of Bach and Beethoven filled the desolate landscape. It announced the presence of another of the string of kibbutzim dotted over the land in a defensive ring, another group of educated idealists who gave up the comforts of home to create a future safe for Jews, bringing with them their love of music and the culture in which they grew up.

We reached the flatlands reclaimed from malaria-infested swamps – now green with vegetation – and the vast areas of the Hule lakes, where the men waded thigh deep into water teeming with carp to gather in the nets, test the state of the shoals and the quality of the environment.

One *erev Shabbat,* when everybody had had their hair cut, was cleaned up and wearing their best clothes, the barber needed a lift home, and I went along with Peter in the jeep to his village, Bar'am, in the north. We left Sasa by the high road through the wild and barren hill-scape of Galilee, speeding along on the spindly road which winds through scattered hills. The earth was dry and the scrubby, undulating hills were studded with clumps of olive trees. In the background, the mountains were velvety black, overlooked by the snowy peak of Mount Hermon.

We arrived in the village when the sun had completed its course and was changing to a bright red glow. The scattered houses, stone cubes with single openings for windows and spherical domes of baked clay on the roofs, showed no light, no smoke. We parked the jeep and, invited by the barber into his house, entered a large neat room where the peaceful and friendly family were sitting. They served us with tiny cups of sweet coffee, the ever-present front line of hospitality, accompanied by piles of pitta bread stuffed with olives and *leben* (a sort of yogurt). They giggled at the clumsy way I handled it all.

Later, we made our way amid the straggly cows and heaps of dung to the top of the village to buy liquor. The moon seemed to be leaning heavily now on the cushion of the sky, which was pure indigo and swarmed with stars. The sound of barking dogs and restive cattle filled the stagnant air. Groups of young men stood about and stared. In the doorways, women were rocking babies in their arms. Inside, the rooms were lit up now with smoky lamps and we could see the men sitting, just sitting, puffing on their pipes. I thought how friendly they were and how resentful they must feel.

Winter descended on Galilee with a blast; it was cold and the rain lashed the ground and turned it into a slithering sea of mud. I became focussed on keeping warm and dry on my straw mattress, and aimed to go as little as possible to the *bet kisset,* located over the brow of the hill, far removed for sanitary reasons. When dysentery gripped me and my intestines were exploding in my weakened body, it was all I could manage to get to the toilets crawling on all fours.

When Shula the cook fell ill, they asked me to replace her in the kitchen. The catchword was Paris, and much was expected of me, and I used all my skill to meet their expectation. The dining hut was the hub of the commune, where people stopped to talk and discuss plans, and I enjoyed my new-found social life there. I picked armfuls of the wild flowers that grew in a profusion of colours between the cracks in the rocks at the foot of Mount Jermac, and filled jam jars for the tables with cyclamen and poppies, orchids and narcissus and mottled grass blades. That was the easy part of my job. Turning the handles of the huge cooking vats, adapting family-size quantities to feed 120 people and plucking the feathers from dead chickens on the kitchen stoop was much more difficult, and when I had to put my hand inside the slaughtered beasts to extract the giblets for the Friday night soup I did it with my eyes closed and a great sense of revulsion.

Some Friday evenings, when everyone was relaxing from the toils of the week, Avram would start blowing his mouth organ; someone would set the tables against the wall and in the centre, a ring of dancers locked arms and the hora would erupt. To mounting excitement, more people would break the chain to join in the ring of whirling, stamping dancers, swaying to the sound of the music and the ecstasy of the frenzied rhythm, until the wooden hut heaved.

I learnt only the kitchen vocabulary of Hebrew; it seemed pointless to persevere without a commitment to a future in Israel. But I was fascinated by the beauty of the language, which had stopped evolving (unlike Provençal and Old French) two thousand years ago, and which had to create a vocabulary and improvise an idiom for this age and which in its intonation and verbal mimicry had such warmth and humanity.

Taking on the role of cook presented a challenge: malnutrition was a problem, appetites jaded from the endlessly repetitive carrots, beets, onions, oranges and lemons which were dumped daily in hessian sacks on the doorstep by the cooperative. There was no variety, no luxuries, no comfort food; occasionally there were eggs and on Friday evenings, chicken. So one day I ventured out on a limb and, drawing on the glut of available onions, garlic and stale bread and some stock cubes, I prepared a Sasa-version of French onion soup. It was devoured with enthusiasm and voted a great success, more, I suspected, for its novelty than its gourmet quality. My reputation soared, people paid attention to me and counted on further imaginative innovation to their diet (like my mother's little jam-filled pastry envelopes), and there I stayed, until one morning I lost the tip of my index finger in the hole of the machine designed for chopping carrots.

I was spirited away to the infirmary for inspection by the American lady doctor with much secrecy, so that no one should be put off their food knowing it contained my fingertip. It was eventually retrieved and surreptitiously disposed of. Archie, summoned to support my trembling arm while it was being dressed, slid down on the concrete floor in a faint on seeing the nerve ends pulsating on my severed finger. His place was taken by Abba, who nearly did the same. In the end, they bundled me into the jeep and drove me to a clinic in nearby Safed.

The ancient little town was perched on the face of a green mountain overlooking the Kinneret, or Sea of Galilee, and had a turbulent history of conquests, earthquakes and destruction. The most recent massacre by Arabs in 1929 had wiped out the population. But 400 years ago, it was the cradle of Hebrew mysticism and poetry, where, after the exodus from Spain, I was told, the rabbis of the Kabbalah had danced in its narrow winding streets. Now, in a well-equipped medical unit located in an Arab house, my truncated finger was expertly bandaged. Afterwards, we visited a local artists' colony, where a friend of the kibbutz, an American woman painter, made tea for us. They said of her that she had brought female homosexuality to Israel.

One episode made me glad that I was no longer fit for purpose as chef. Standing by the sinks one afternoon I saw a strange procession, headed by Archie, and followed in a straggling single file by Arabs trailing a bullock. They were making their way to the caves used for storing supplies and slaughtering livestock. I sensed from the tension and bewilderment among the kitchen staff, that it was best not to ask questions. But when soon afterwards our men came in with huge bleeding hunks of meat, which they placed in the freezers, and the Arabs miserably shuffled their way downhill, I discovered that the bullock, their only bullock and the source of their livelihood, had been butchered.

I was told it was a regrettable lesson; an existentially pragmatic outrage in which the end had to justify the means, because, despite repeated warnings, the villagers had continued to water their bullock in the well which supplied the kibbutz, and their own village, polluting the water and risking the health of all. Since the well-being of the community (and of course of their village) was at stake, draconian methods, the only language the Arabs were perceived to understand, had to be used. The decision was regretfully taken; water supply is life; cholera and malaria are death. That evening, the discussion raged over the meal and continued into the meeting of the elders. But the deed had been done and the dissenters were in the minority. Anyway, it was too late. The debate moved on to future projects.

There was a spell of fine weather and sensational sunsets and dawns but then the rain started again, and with my finger in a large bandage, a placement was found for me to assist pregnant Rifka from Mexico in the laundry at the top of the hill. We worked to the hum of the washing machines churning over the toil-soiled shirts, exchanging the latest gossip and finding satisfaction in the fresh smell of newly ironed clothes. We hung up hundreds of nappies on the line, sewed patches on frayed elbows, looked down and watched everyone busy in their tasks, the girls playing with the children, the boys doing the heavy work. Winter seemed to be the time for working on the kibbutz. Houses where married couples could be installed were being built using the stones from the demolished Arab dwellings, and trees were being planted in the valley below. The Arabs, the only hired employees tolerated by the socialist movement specifically for this task, were harvesting the olives. They hurtled themselves at the trees with long rakes and blood-curdling shrieks and tugged the ripe olives from among the shuddering leaves. At night, I went along on the trucks that took them back to their home in the neighbouring village of Jish.

While my finger was still healing, I met with another accident. I had heard people speak in near mystical terms of an oak tree standing below in the middle of a mine-strewn no-man's-land on the Lebanese border near the rock caves which riddled the side of the cliff-face. European vegetation was said to be growing in profusion at its base. No one knew how it had arrived there nor for how long it had cast its shade over this hostile border. It was a bad risk but, for me, irresistible. I would have to negotiate a precipitous climb past the honeycomb of ancestral burial chambers hewn out of the rocks. Jewish or Byzantine, their bones had long ago been plundered and were replaced now with stacks of guns and ammunition, a massive defence arsenal constantly replenished by the government and furtively maintained by senior members in the event of attack. The caves were seriously out of bounds, referred to only in whispers among the initiated.

One evening, I exchanged my muddy boots for hardy Jesus sandals and clambered down the rocky path. There, in the forbidden area, like a mirage, the oak tree appeared in the dusky light. Its trunk was covered in moss, its ancient branches bent over clusters of tulips, snowdrops and lilies of the valley, daffodils and crocuses, an enchanted oasis of unseasonal European vegetation.

Thrilled, I was heading towards it, running through the tall grass when I tripped over a metal object and heard a muffled bang. I felt a searing pain in my right leg and believed some dreadful punishment had been visited upon me. I turned away from the tree and scrambled back up the path. My knees kept giving way and my legs wobbled. The warm trickle of blood from the soft flesh in my calf was turning into a flood. I bent down and tied the kefya from my head around the wound as tightly as I could. When I reached the top, I hoped no one would see me. Worse than the gaping gash on my leg, was the fear that my escapade and its consequences could not now be concealed by the blood-drenched cloth.

I was evasive when they questioned me about where it had happened; but they guessed I had stepped on some sort of partially exploded mortar shell or unexploded mine and hauled me to the infirmary muttering about my lucky escape. By that time, it was too late to stitch the four-inch long cut; the doctor warned me this would prolong the healing process, and the pain lasted a long time to remind me of my wicked folly.

I could sense the underlying anger of the senior members of the community, though they never challenged me. Not only had I disobeyed an unspoken rule by intruding on their secrets, but I had caused problems with my injury, as a result of which I was useless in the workforce and had become a liability with my accidents. Their compromise solution was to send me travelling to discover the Holy

Land. I was to return only when my finger and my leg had healed, making me a useful member of the community once again. And so I was dispatched on a sightseeing tour of the country, beginning with a lift from Motty, who was taking the truck to Jerusalem for a conference.

Our early morning departure took us down the roads from Galilee; where they converged, we entered the breathtakingly beautiful valley of Jezreel and on to the coastal plain. It was studded with kibbutzim and the trees in the dense young orchards were a fresh green, zealously planted and watered by clever irrigation and the heavy winter rains. I thought about the remnants of my people, who had survived the most brutal treatment conceived in the human brain, tortured and humiliated beyond any imagining, who had begun again to recreate this fertile land with their toil and ingenuity, in the hope of living again and raising their children without fear.

In Tel Aviv we stopped for a juice and a falafel at a roadside kiosk before continuing our journey south. The road to Jerusalem was narrow and twisting. As we approached the Judean hills the tortuous ascent to Jerusalem became slow and steep. Clusters of Arab villages peered out from the dense woodland overlooking the winding road. From these positions in the hills around Jerusalem after partition in April 1948, Arab artillery had attacked and wrecked the convoys taking vital supplies to the city under siege, in an attempt to break the spirit of the newly created state. Burnt-out armoured cars lined the narrow pass, rusted corpses of vehicles that never made it to Jerusalem. They were a monument to the men and women who battled through the ambush to breach the blockade and rescue its citizens from dehydration and starvation and, ultimately, defeat.

The landscape changed now to the rocky hills of Judea. We reached the top of the hill and there was Jerusalem spread out at our feet, a huddle of ancient stone basking in the luminous evening light, drenched in stillness and steeped in a sense of eternity.

This, then, was the city fought over from the beginning of time. Its streets had run with blood in the fight for the fulfilment of a dream to possess it. Here, King David had desired Bathsheba, King Solomon had built a temple in which Isaiah and Jeremiah had proclaimed their prophesies, and the Maccabees had cleansed the city from desecration and ruled over it. Greeks and Romans, Byzantines and Babylonians inhabited and dominated its people. The Crusaders destroyed it, and yet the Jews, despite the infighting among their tribes, despite massacre, exile or humiliation, had preserved it as our religious centre and drifted for centuries through the world, always yearning to return.

Landlocked in the middle of the wilderness, it looked so small, so compact. After two thousand years, our history resumed here. At last, our people were no longer despised, murdered, spat upon or destroyed, the objects of tyrants and the scapegoats of history. And the boys and girls of Sasa and their comrades had helped to secure it for us so that we could lead normal lives and die normal deaths. It was a place in which to feel at home, and as we drove down into Jerusalem, a deeply felt attachment came over me and has remained ever since.

I went to stay with the Steins and saw my old friend and hero Gabriel going to bed with a hot water bottle. Their warmth was embracing, their circle of friends inclusive. We lit the candles on Friday night and celebrated the Sabbath with the ageing parents he had rescued from the Holocaust. Gaby took me to his laboratory where I met his fellow researchers in physical chemistry. They had adapted to the divided city.

The holy places of my ancestors were tantalizingly barred. Since capturing the Jewish Quarter of the Old City, the Trans-Jordanian League had remained entrenched in the crennelled towers of the Citadel of David, their red-checked head cloths and cocked rifles peering out from behind like characters in a menacing puppet theatre. Great rolls of barbed wire piled on top of each other in huge pyramids divided the city in half. At every point where I tried to penetrate the demarcation line, I encountered minefields, firing positions and concrete walls that prevented my access to the Old City with its narrow alleys, the Church of the Holy Sepulchre and the landscapes of Jesus. The Western Wall, sacred remnant of the temple and holiest of places, for Jews was a dream away from the descendants of Solomon who wanted to plant their prayers in the gaps between the stones.

There was no place in the City of David where I could walk, and on the Temple Mount where the golden roof of the Dome of the Rock beckoned, only the Arabs had access to the stone where Abraham was spared from sacrificing his son Isaac and from where Mohammed had risen to heaven. Mount Scopus, the academic centre of learning, was completely encircled, an inaccessible enclave in the heart of the city. In the daytime, I wandered through the accessible quarters which constitute the mosaic of the city, the Russian and the German, the French and the American; they all staked a claim to its eternal history. At night, the city hummed with the ghosts of past lives and the sky teemed with stars so it was never completely dark. Sometime through the still dawn air, one could hear the chant of a muezzin from the top of a minaret across the divide. In the day it had a smell all of its own, of chalk dust and crumbling rock and unforgettable.

I boarded the Egged bus in the Jaffa Road to make good my promise and complete my tour south to the Negev desert without much enthusiasm, because my leg ached. The driver invited me to sit next to him and talked me through the journey, which started through the shingled gravelly hillocks of a wasteland, bare but for the scrubby tufts of vegetation. In this sparsely populated desert, Bedouin encampments appeared like some weird vegetation between ridges and furrows of the black volcanic hillocks. Almost invisible, they blended with the desert, except when the breeze lifted up the flimsy covering of their mobile homes which they dismantled and moved to wherever an oasis or some greenery could be tracked. Scrawny camels and goats surrounded the tents, which were decorated with black goatskin and woven carpets. Occasionally, a date palm or two pointed their spear-like ribs, silhouetted against the sky. Only the sound of the jewels which adorned the flowing robes of the veiled women jangling as they exchanged their shrill chatter broke the stillness. They cast no glance in the direction of our bus, which intruded upon the age-old sanctity of their habitat.

It was market day in Beersheba, where we were to spend the night, and all the inhabitants from the wilderness had converged there. Barrels of locusts, aromatic plants and dates, baskets of semi-precious cornelian, agate and onyx were arranged on the stalls in the mud lanes, and Bedouin tribesmen, standing beside their camels, their faces like carved mahogany under their dark robes, were bargaining with their customers.

I declined the bus driver's invitation to spend the night in his home, and searched out the only hotel of the town for commercial travellers, where I rented a bed in a dormitory. Under the sovereignty of Turkish high command the little garrison town had prospered, but it seemed that all hotels must have been destroyed in the defeat of the Ottoman Empire. And so I slept soundly with seven pioneering men and no partition or modesty – saving curtains – between our beds.

Next morning, after bending over the deep and perilously exposed Well of Jacob, I continued my journey to Eilat. The Negev desert changed now into gigantic phantasmagorical sculptures, hewn from heaps of limestone into forms of endless variety. It was a panorama of nightmare shapes, craggy heights and weirdly carved sandstone cliffs, with contorted rocks rising out of arid gorges and deep stream beds. And in the early morning light, it felt dramatically silent and undisturbed, both menacing and mesmerizing.

For many hours I absorbed the desert, but I welcomed with relief our arrival at the Gulf of Aqaba when we reached Eilat. I swam in the turquoise waters of the Red Sea and stepped on the gleaming shells and fragments of coral which littered the sand. The only sign of habitation was a little brown wooden fisherman's hut, where I changed my clothes and ate the food we had bought at the market in Beersheba. The bus driver did what he came to do in the tiny colony of inhabitants, and beckoned me for the return journey.

Back in Sasa, the months passed. Chanukkah came and was celebrated with much excitement. Work clothes and rosters were discarded for smart wear and there was leisure, wine and grown-ups and children were swept away in heady dancing. Spring exploded in the Galil and the bandage came off my leg. Blossoms appeared on the peach trees we had planted in the fall, the apple orchard promised a plentiful harvest and the hills were covered with wild flowers. With it came the stifling khamsin wind, carrying the heat and particles of sand from the desert. It blew up, choked the pores and whirred and hummed and made everyone irritable and uncomfortable.

There was increasing pressure from my mother for me to return home. Alarmed by my letters filled with happiness, she was fearful I would want to stay on in Israel. She reminded me of my promise never to leave her when my father died, and expected me to accompany her to Texas on her annual visit to her sister.

The prospect of departing from Sasa represented a threat and kept me awake at night. I could not remember when I had last been so contented and felt so at home, being accepted for what I was, appreciated for my contribution and looking forward to the future in which every year would be a better one. I loved to prepare the earth before planting it and valuing water above gold. I loved the absence of pretentiousness and formality and the peace that echoed from hill to hill. If I belonged anywhere, it was here.

And yet I realized that, despite my longing to be one of the manual toilers who debated political theory and discussed Dostoyevsky while they turned over the land and pruned the fruit trees, here too I would be an outsider in their midst, because I did not share their collective history. My mother's demand for my return home became more and more insistent; she told my cousin Werner she would throw herself into the Tyne if I remained. But while I resisted this pressure, I knew that ultimately my restlessness would take me away. I think Yaffa knew it, too. She also understood that I could not abandon my family and that my mother would never uproot herself again. An added consideration was a murmur in my heart and arthritis in my limbs – diagnosed by a doctor in Jerusalem to whom Gaby had taken me on one of my trips there – which needed attention and which might cause problems to my friends here.

And so I reluctantly booked a passage home. At my farewell party they presented me with a chronicle of drawings by Yaffa of my stay and a photo album of all my friends, who demanded my promise to return. I drank and drank sweet Carmel wine until it was time to get on the morning bus to Haifa. I said goodbye to the friends who came to the boat to send me off. I was leaving the Galil and the people with whom I loved to be, the much trodden paths and the stones and the hills and the *botz*, and I wished that I was going back with them. Instead, I walked as though in a dream and boarded the *Messapia* and sailed to Venice at sunset.

15

Galveston 1953–1954

My mother's excitement at my return to the nest from Israel had been short-lived. While I was awaiting my American visa and preparing to accompany her on her annual visit to Galveston, Texas, she seemed quite happy for me to disappear. I also needed to earn money and decided to head back to Paris. Here I felt the same exhilaration as ever, although there was a different atmosphere among the student population. Most of the close-knit society of friends I had left behind had returned home. So I broke my bond with the Cité Universitaire and migrated to the Latin Quarter, where I took residence in an attic room in the Hotel Soufflot, round the corner from the Panthéon.

It was not difficult to find a job. Paris was about to launch its haute couture season and I signed up with a press agency in the Avenue Duquesne, where the enterprising Madame Golda Antignac realized my usefulness with her US clients and instantly employed me. My assignment initially was to interpret for a Texan professor of fashion journalism and shepherd her around the collections. Appreciative and generous, she eagerly accompanied me to the shows and was quite infected by my enthusiasm and familiarity with everything Parisian. Soon, I graduated to reporting the shows for the *Philadelphia Inquirer*, and my copy went unedited into the women's pages.

I sat on little gilded chairs reserved for me in the salons in and around the Avenue Montaigne, redolent with perfume and buzzing with the high octane atmosphere created by clusters of buyers, designers, celebrities and wealthy clients. I witnessed the unveiling of Dior's H-line, the violent magenta colours daringly introduced into her collection by Schiaparelli, and attended the shows of Patou, Fath and Worth and Balenciaga, and applauded the lavish embellishments which adorned

148

their sumptuous clothes. I developed a new way of seeing things, a passion for clothes and a feel for fabrics. I fantasy-wrote about the fledgling high-fashion Renaissance in France, its feast of luminous fabrics, styles and colours inspired that season by the paintings of Velazquez and Vermeer that hung in the Louvre. I think my cultural references and a little Paris-acquired art erudition introduced into the vocabulary of my text must have met with approval and my job continued to the end of the season. I stayed to see the Christmas decoration in the boulevards, the sparkling and magical window displays in the Galleries Lafayette and the rue St Honoré, then returned home to prepare for America.

In mid-winter, my mother and I boarded the Ropner line cargo boat *Daleby* bound for the Gulf of Mexico. It was a foul evening in the Glasgow docks. The air was raw and filled with the acrid stench of urine. We groped our way through a pall of thick fog and climbed the makeshift gangway. The sea looked menacing and I felt sick the moment I set foot on board. My mother was in a bad mood and ignored me, still seething from the desperate rows with my brother that had taken place over recent days. The shrill exchanges as he demanded an injection of cash into his expanding instrument-manufacturing business rebounded throughout our house, where he and his young family still occupied the attic flat. With all the shouting and recrimination, he seemed insensitive to my mother's need, after years of financial precariousness, to enjoy at last the security which the newly received reparation money from Germany afforded her. For me, the stark realization that I was a long way out of university and had no job, no career and an unfinished post-graduate degree in an unfashionable subject hit me in the face. It was an inauspicious start to pioneering the New World.

A fierce storm broke out over the Atlantic as we left port, rocking the small 7,000-ton boat. It heaved and pitched in the waves from side to side and from prow to stern. Any unattached objects flew across the cabin which I shared with my mother and I was violently sick. Feeling near to death, I took to my bunk. Day and night there seemed to be no respite from the relentless pounding of the ocean and no relief from my retching. The nausea, exacerbated by the food smells drifting up from the galley, saturated my body and penetrated my sleep, and I believed there would never be an end to it. I wanted to die.

On the morning of the fifth day I woke up with a sublime feeling of calm and well-being. Gone was the rocking; the boat seemed to glide over a mirror-like ocean. I heard the engines humming steadily and ventured on deck to watch an escort of porpoises playfully weaving and diving around the prow. From the second mate, between watches, I learnt the law of the sea. I vaguely registered that it was he who had come to visit me in the cabin during my seasickness with offers of help. He was tall, smart and crisp in his starched white uniform, and had a faraway look in his sea-blue eyes. His thick hair was the colour of corn, and being with him was more enticing than the company of the bridge-playing couples wandering around the decks. For the remainder of the journey, I spent most of my time in his cabin, when he was not working. My mother, meanwhile, concerned about my disappearances, entertained the other passengers, enquiring on her rounds of the boat if they had seen her daughter. If by chance any of those dear people had seen me vanish into a crew member's quarters, they conspired to keep it a secret, and merely marked my reappearance in the salon at mealtimes with a nudge.

At dawn on the ninth day, excitement stirred in the ship. We had reached the mouth of the Mississippi and were only one hundred miles from port. A descending fog brought the ship to a standstill; when it lifted, one could tell it had class, this wide expanse of water which presented itself calm and glistening in the early morning sun. On either side we could see willow-fringed banks emerging out of the swampy shore, and, as we approached New Orleans, we waved to the women in their wooden huts on stilts at the water's edge, who were hanging up their washing. They were chattering with each other across their shabby abodes in high-pitched patois, and laughing at us across the water.

In New Orleans, my mother and I went on shore to continue our journey to Galveston on land. I was desolate to leave the *Daleby* and my second mate behind, and felt cheated not to meander with them around the Gulf ports. We exchanged addresses and agreed I would meet the boat on its return journey from the Rio Grande.

My Aunt Antonie met us at the quayside moved to tears – so

much had happened since she last saw me. We had landed in the middle of the high jinx of Mardi Gras. The teeming streets were draped with garlands of exotic blooms. On the balconies of the pink and white stucco houses, with their iron lace-work balconies, gaudily dressed people in all shades were chanting and singing to the rhythm of the bands parading below. TV cameras were filming the floats in the parade and movie stars jostled through the crowds. The strange Creole mixture of languages was steeped in the town's history as a French and Spanish enclave before it was acquired by America from Napoleon with the infamous Louisiana Purchase, and one could sense that adventurers, revolutionaries and buccaneers had all left their own brand on the town.

We were emerging from a patio restaurant on Bourbon Street where, in the middle of lunch, Gordon McRae, a singing star from the cast of the film *Oklahoma*, had serenaded my mother. Suddenly, sashaying down the street at the head of his band, Louis Armstrong came flinging his trumpet from side to side belting out the tune 'When The Saints Come Marching In'. The crowned King of Jazz had returned to ignite the streets and dominate the town where he was born, and where he had been abandoned in a home for waifs by his prostitute mother. Now, his gritty croaky voice exploded from deep down, his lips spread round his gleaming teeth and the laughter lit up his face, as he let out a sound, intimate yet urgent. And when the high notes burst from his shiny horn they were tinged with melancholy, eerily hinting at the origins of the blues. I was transfixed. This was jazz, but not as I had heard it before, not even in the *caves* of the left bank.

In Galveston, we were received like royalty. My Aunt Antonie's and Uncle Fritz's small house with the wooden porch on 11th Street was stacked with welcome presents for us from friends, with that unstinting generosity systemic in American life. They had been adopted by the cluster of Jewish families as their token refugees, and had been showered with care and concern. My aunt earned money as a seamstress, taking up hems and repairing dresses, and reciprocated in the best way she could afford and in the manner of her European upbringing. When customers came to pick up their alterations, there was always something baking in the oven, and they did not need much persuasion to stay on for coffee and cakes, served on beautiful porcelain. My uncle had been found a job by Carl Brehm, a successful former fellow hop merchant, in the brewery of Mr Autry, a dashing Mexican who loved to gamble. My uncle rose early, grumbling, to attend the brewery laboratory, feeling anxious and ineffective in his hurt pride at taking such a lowly job.

There is little to Galveston, an island-city cradled in an inlet of the sea, to betray its turbulent history as part of Mexico, a pirate's nest of looters and robbers and finally, the reluctant 100th state of the Union. At the turn of the century it enjoyed great prosperity due to the pirates (Lafitte), the buccaneers and the Bodanskis, Novikis, the Annigsteins and the Tinteroffs, whose parents came with packs on their backs from the European backwaters and ghettos of Poland to make their wealth from the natural resources, the cheap labour and from the land that belonged to anyone who claimed it. They were late in surrendering their independence from the Union and defiantly continued to live by their own rules, proudly dismissing laws they did not like by simply disobeying or repealing them.

The inhabitants were friendly, expansive and prosperous, their wealth implicit, not talked about. Everything was on tap, like a ubiquitous *Schlaraffenland* (land of milk and honey). For everyone, that is, except for black people, who were poor and sat at the back of the buses behind a movable 'Whites Only' sign. I avoided arrest but incurred cautions each time I rode in the black section of the bus because I was pretending to be a non-English speaking foreigner, not comprehending, and therefore not responsible, for their rules.

As I experienced the Galveston way of life, it became a mystery to me how Aunt Antonie, a sweet, gentle, childless lady of great dignity and devotion to her husband, who had needed an escort to cross the town square in Bamberg, had managed to exist side by side with gamblers and millionaires in this gaudily lawless barbaric tail-end of the American continent, into which she had been parachuted by her rescuers.

Announcing our arrival, the local *Tribune* wrote: 'Galveston this week has an extremely attractive new resident' adding that I had come straight from Paris. It was enough to open the floodgates for the

152

male population, for whom Paris spelled erotic adventure, and they were hungry for its promise of liberty, fraternity and free love on their doorstep. There was no end to the callers, young and old, who presented themselves at the house on 11th Street with high hopes and barely concealed intentions.

The invitations came fast and unending; we were invited to barbecues and clambakes, lunch parties and cocktails by families eager to offer their hospitality and display their opulent homes. I was astonished to see the nostalgia for their ancestry, and a bizarre personal taste represented in the most eclectic of styles, mimicking every phase of European architecture and fanciful design from mediaeval cloister to baroque castle; there was a house in the shape of an ocean liner, and one like a toadstool. It was pure Disneyland.

On that first weekend, we were driven by Carl Brehm to his ranch in West Texas and for a day I was a cowgirl, dressed in my blue jeans and embroidered leather boots purchased at J.C. Penneys department store. Jake, the chief cowboy, saddled up a horse for me and side by side we galloped unencumbered on the wide open endless space of the prairie. The speed and freedom of our ride was exhilarating. After a few hours, we came upon the herd of grazing longhorns, clustered around a water hole. There must have been a thousand of them, long, lean and large, restlessly lumbering, munching on the parched tufts of grass, as far as the eye could see. They all had the branding mark of the Brehm ranch on their brown hides. The cowhands were friendly and touched their broad-brimmed hats in greeting. They wore pointy-toed shoes with high heels which kept them from slipping through the stirrups and were preparing to round up the cows and nudge them along to new grazing grounds. I watched them corralling the animals that strayed with awesome skill and accuracy: they twirled the rope shoulder high then swung the noose to snake, spot-on, round their necks, tugging them back to the fold at the end of the rope. Their vocabulary was economical, their vowels curved in a lingering drawl. The beasts contentedly nuzzled up to me as I sat high in my saddle and I made contact with their warm bodies. As we rode home into the setting sun, I wondered whether they knew that they would all end up as giant steaks on the tables of insatiably hungry Texans.

Back at the ranch, as we stabled the horses in the corral, there was a commotion in the yard; a huge black snake was slithering through the hibiscus bush and climbing up the low-built ranch house. Mr Brehm tossed a gun into my hands and hovered over me with instructions to shoot. I had never killed anything before, but I knew what was expected of me in this fierce and violent Texas environment.

I had sent my documents to Rice Institute in Houston, one of the most highly thought-of and heavily endowed academic institutions in the South, with the intention of rescuing my thesis and the hope of getting a grant. On the way to my appointment, I had a chance to look round Houston, where the discovery of oil accounted for the display of dazzling prosperity in its glass-fronted skyscrapers, its extravagant homes and glossy shops. I walked through the gilded paradise of the Neiman Marcus department store and could not believe my eyes.

At Rice, the dean received me with warmth, and invited me to audit a final-year BA philosophy class where, to my astonishment, the professor put over his subject to his students at the level at which we had been taught for Matric. This, I was told, is to give them maximum time for the *real* curricular activities, such as ball games and contests for Most Popular Boy, Beauty Queen and Most Dated Girl. In the course of the lecture he asked the class the meaning of the word 'hedonist'. No one was able to supply the answer, and this lack of verbal awareness recurred throughout the classes I attended. But although I could not see my life in their midst, I was taken with these crew-cut athletic boys and pretty pony-tailed long-limbed girls, who preferred to display their skills on the playing fields and skating rink than in the lecture hall, and I envied them. Riding back through the sprawling wealth of Houston, across the causeway next to the giant oil derricks and storage tanks that lined the route like mediaeval knights in glistening armour, I decided once again to give up on my studies, to make my stay in Texas as short as possible, and resume my studies in New York. But first, I would have to earn my way out of here, because I was penniless.

There was a vacancy in the cotton gin of Harris L. Kempner, one of the three powerful families who dominated the economies and ruled the society of Galveston. I was hired to test the tensile strength of cotton, teasing apart the little white cotton buds with their pink centres, and splicing the fibres to stretch them into the machine. For this I received health insurance and was paid generously enough to move out from my aunt's house into a flat and save up for my getaway money.

The warehouse was located near the docks. The open bales were stacked, awaiting sorting, to be hoisted eventually onto the ships when they arrived in port. My glass-enclosed laboratory was located right at the end of the warehouse and my boss, an Irishman called Jim, was in charge and very gallant; he had never had a female on his team before. From his office next to my lab, he commanded the workforce of blacks and the longshoremen who moved the bales around. He was kind, tolerant and good-humoured. A bottle of Jack Daniel's was lodged at the base of his desk, ready for a swig or two, and I became accustomed to the smell of whiskey on his breath when he leaned over my apparatus. There was always a smile on his ruddy face. He walked with a lopsided gait and a springy step, hoisting himself from one leg to the other with his hips as he made his way through the stacked cotton bales. I was reminded of my grandfather's warehouse, except the smell of the hessian sacking overpowered the dry, sickly smell of the cotton. The season was slack and there was not much to do; games of poker, to which I was invited, happened spontaneously and warded off boredom. As the only woman, I was very pampered by the ten men, who bit their tongues rather than swear in my presence. Sometimes the air-conditioning in the sample room crashed; then the heat rose to 96°F, and with the high humidity it was draining and exhausting, tempers flared and the slightest effort was strenuous.

I threw myself into social life but with an underlying ever-present sense of despair. I never really knew what I was doing trapped here without resources, aside from pleasing my aunt who missed her family, and I was filled with a sense of futility. Sometimes it felt as though I was walking on a tightrope over the pitfalls presented by this violent edgy existence, to which my uncle and aunt were blissfully impervious and from which I learnt to extricate myself, as when I had to escape being physically overpowered by Mr Brehm on one of those friendly outings into deep sand on the beach, when his Studebaker got stuck in the sand and I had to wriggle out from under his bulky, sweaty entrapment. Letters arrived from my friends wondering what I was doing on this island off the coast of America. My professor wrote to tell me – with his consummate irony – that '*ma fille a epousé un marchand de gaine*' – 'my daughter has married a manufacturer of lingerie' and I thought of my friend Anne, so in love with Dimitri, a young Greek naval architect student in our crowd, who had deserted her for a union with ships, and she had succumbed instead to the bourgeois requirements of her station. I hoped she would be happy nevertheless.

The young men from good families were at my beck and call and sometimes I went out with one or the other. Our date always started out with long rides on the beach, and ended more often than not getting stuck in the sand. The Bodanskys and Novicis, and the Tinteroffs – mostly associated with research in the prestigious and highly endowed teaching hospital – all encouraged their young men to entertain me. One of these was quite willing to drive me to the *Daleby* on my final, fraught assignation with my second mate. A crate of beer, donated by my Uncle Fritz, was our password on board the boat as she docked in Houston that night, and I parted forever with him on the waterfront amid the smell of diesel as the hoists cranked the huge crates on board. My companion looked on, puzzled, but knew it was with him I was coming home.

Although Texas was a dry state, most people (apart from the Jewish inhabitants) were drunk most of the time. They obtained their alcohol from private clubhouses, where you had to ring a bell to gain admittance. Everyone had bars in their living room, stacked to the rafter with every conceivable bootlegged drink. The unrelieved heat and still, overcast air made one rush to accept glasses clinking with ice and filled with stimulant for relief. Carl Brehm, whose bar dominated his living room, and was in action from early morning, had taught me how to drink, and very soon I could keep up with the best of them and was proud of my new skill. My Uncle Fritz was no slouch with his beer himself and laughed at my Texas-acquired talent.

At night, when the ocean breeze brushed across my face with the promise of refreshment, I walked to the beach. But there was little relief from the clammy heat. The air was heavy with the cloying scent of the oleander with its poisonous sap and the bougainvilleas which lined my route. Nor was it possible to bathe in sea in the daytime; the murky water of the romantic-sounding Gulf of Mexico was full of deadly predators, and the waves seethed with an inner ferocity. It was easy to fall prey to the large crystal balls that floated peacefully on the surface, concealing their lethal poison-filled tentacles under the water. Huge sand-coloured jellyfish littered the shore and stingarees hid in the shallows. Few people were enticed into the sea; they merely enjoyed the beach with its hamburger stands and jukeboxes, and many had pools in their homes.

My mother departed for home and I decided it was time to move out. I shared a rented flat with a forty-year-old nurse who worked at John Sealy Hospital, staggered home blind drunk every night and slept with a .32 gun under her pillow. Not before warning me, though, that if the wife of her lover appeared with a pistol expecting to find them together, I was to hang on to the phone ready to call the cops. The betrayed woman's late-night visits became a habit and were increasingly frenetic. I don't know why she persevered, because the lover was always gone before she arrived to scream her threats and ultimatums. I grew tired of throwing a chair at her – as instructed by the nurse – and weary of the ever-present threat of a shoot-out. 'Lili,' the nurse would drawl as she stretched out on her bed and waved her beer can through the air, 'It's all shit for the birds.' After a few weeks, I decided to spend the rest of my time in Galveston with my aunt and uncle.

At last I had saved four hundred dollars and was able to prepare the getaway which I had earned. The last hectic days in Galveston left an indelible mark on me. I reassessed my sense of drama, which had exaggerated the excesses of good and bad. Sonia Findlay, a family friend who had often visited us in Newcastle, packed my bags; she invited me on a Caribbean winter cruise on the *Stella Polaris*; the Brehms gave me lingerie from Neiman's, the boys in the sample room chose earrings, the Tinteroffs, eau de cologne.

On Saturday, 3 September, my uncle and aunt and half the population of Galveston waved me goodbye on the *Texas Chief* and as I crossed the causeway onto the mainland. I reckoned I had survived

Texas; I had neither perished from the heat nor become an oil millionaire. I collapsed in the luxuriously cool lounge and set out on the longest train journey of my life.

16

New York 1955

As the train rocked through the long night, I took stock of my life. Physically, a two-week diet of grapefruit and hard-boiled eggs before leaving town had restored my inflated whiskey and steak-fuelled body weight to normal. In my wallet I possessed a prized Green Card entitling me to work, four hundred hard-earned dollars and a few addresses in New York. Apart from that – no plan.

There was certainly no going back. Since a perfectly smooth path to an academic career had been scuppered, I could not see my way, as my mother was pressuring me to do, to returning to university involving Professor Girdlestone once more to enable me to do so. Nor could I ever think of putting myself again into a situation where I was financially dependent on my mother's handouts. I had learnt to build up a resistance against unwelcome influences and claimed the privilege of rejecting people I didn't like and who irritated me, and, once in a rare while, finding someone who talked my language. For all the things I had become, I felt I had left my family behind. I did not know if I was prepared to seek their understanding of my uncompromising way of looking at things, defend myself against their challenges or be terribly hurt at not receiving it. I knew from experience that one gesture or one word from my sister could disrupt me. I discovered, to my surprise, that the existential way of thinking which had seen me through my despair following my father's death empowered me to make my own choice of whether or not to endorse the set rules which society offered. This gave me the prerogative of my own morality, which needed no explanation and set me apart, in situations and in my relationships with people who did not share my values.

I left the train in Chicago on the second morning of the journey for a brief stopover and a restorative sleep with friends from Bamberg. The scenery from their apartment was dazzling; I had never seen anything like the soaring spires, the mirror images of the glass-fronted skyscrapers sparkling in the sunlight reflected on the waters of Lake Michigan.

In New York, I spent a few days with my cousin Erica in Queens, but found suburban living stifling. I needed to find a centre, and gravitated without much imagination or spirit of adventure to the environment I knew best: International House, the post-graduate students' residence on Riverside Drive. Here, removed from the stark gridiron verticality of midtown, the campus of Columbia University was set in a quietly residential part of uptown Manhattan with access to all educational institutions.

My residency depended on enrolment in a graduate programme of studies. At the beginning of the academic year, I presented myself at the registrar's office to enrol in a course on the Provençal language, on which I chose to underpin my thesis on the troubadours. I was told that to complete their requirements for a post-graduate degree, I was short of an astronomical number of points. The trouble was, Rice had irretrievably lost my papers; without copies of my degree I could not enrol for my course. I wrote to the registrar at King's, who wrote back saying he would deal with it. But I would not hear from him for a long time.

Nevertheless, they allowed me to start my classes in Provençal; probably because interest in the subject was limited – we were very few students on the course. I was able to extend my stay at International House because I had befriended the receptionist, Anne Carlisle, who not only included me in her circle of friends, but appealed to the directors, who bent the rules of residency. I felt at home here; although the atmosphere was different from Paris, there was the same easy, fluid encounter and lively conversation with serious young people, many active in music, theatre arts and design. Inevitably, there were also the roving outcasts of society who hang around universities – a few geniuses, and drifters who prey on a trusting student population. I had paid my dues to this activity and stayed clear of any approaches. For now, anyway.

Spending leisure hours in the lounges, and on a bench outside

Grant's Tomb, I regained a sense of camaraderie and a feeling of belonging. Unmistakeably, an undertow of disquiet and disillusion seeped through our discussions. The McCarthy trials had percolated through all creative and liberal-thinking Americans, and there was a feeling of helplessness about the present and of pessimism about the future. I heard from Bill Epstein, a Canadian in the UN whom I befriended, that a member of staff had thrown himself from the rooftop of the UN, a victim of the witch-hunt. His was not the only suicide. For this and historic reasons, they all seemed to cherish the hope of following Henry Miller and Ernest Hemingway, F. Scott Fitzgerald and Gertrude Stein to Paris, to write the Great American Novel in the Luxemburg Gardens. They discussed their existential anxiety and disgust and probed me for my first-hand experience of Jean-Paul Sartre; they were deeply engaged in evaluating his philosophy in terms of their everyday life. Meanwhile, many supplemented their grants as short-order cooks at Prexis.

Two weeks into term I moved out and rented a room round the corner from nearby Juilliard, the performing arts school. It was next to the overhead L-train which roared by my window and through my head at ten-minute intervals, day and night. My next habitat was even more disastrous. It was on E 116th Street, jammed between the slums of upper Manhattan and the elite residences of university personnel. Two Dutch Puritan sisters let the flat, took an instant dislike to my libertarianism and made life uncomfortable for me and my visitors. They were mean and called me to account with their expressed complaints, challenging my every move in the flat. I decided to resort to my Parisian habit of living in hotels.

I discovered just the right, run-down establishment on 114th Street, south of the Columbia campus. It bore the aspirational name of Arizona Hotel and was set up in self-contained units of separate corridors with four bedrooms, home to old people dumped there by their relatives, and students' overflow from the halls of residence opposite. I did not mind the shared toilet, the chipped kitchen sink, nor tripping over the cracked lino on the communal bathroom floor. The rent was reasonable and I could come and go unmolested. I was blissfully content.

My neighbour on the corridor was a Sephardic eighteen-year-old

music major with huge hands and an even bigger personality; he had
prodigious talent and supported his parents playing the piano in bars
at night. Performing with seasoned and sophisticated jazz players
probably explained his precocity, exposing him to a life experience
beyond his young years. Once a week on Fridays his mother arrived
with Tupperware boxes containing exotic highly spiced ethnic Turkish
food she had prepared for him. He guarded these like the crown
jewels and very occasionally let me have a taste.

His name was Raymond Cohen and he briefed me on the importance
of the concierge who, Cerberus-like, guarded the entrance of the
Arizona and manned the telephone connection to each unit, which
gave him control of our social life. Abe knew everyone and their
business, used it mischievously when expedient, and acted as a sort
of mole for Mr Reissberg, the landlord and his boss. His creased
russet-coloured face was framed by a mop of wiry grey hair and he
lacked upper teeth behind his cheeky, all-knowing smile. His malice
could result in the eviction of anyone threatening to lower the tone
of the establishment with unsuitable behaviour; it was wise to humour
him and feed him his diet of gossip with harmless titbits.

Ray was jazz crazy; he could not get enough of it and sometimes,
after a gig we went together to Birdland, where the entrance was free
after four o'clock in the morning. Jazz addicts would sit, bleary-eyed
and mesmerized, ingesting the hypnotic sounds from the small stage.
By this time of night, the musicians seemed to be deeply introverted,
probably drug-sustained, playing as though for themselves, impervious
to the audience, improvising in that almost mystic musical logic of
the jam session. It was at Birdland that winter, in the dimly lit smoke-
clouded club room, that I heard Dizzy Gillespie, Duke Ellington and
Thelonious Monk, John Coltrane, Art Farmer and Miles Davis. The
applause of the thinned-out audience of aficionados was desultory
and a sort of bewitched state hung over us all. Just before dawn, we
would make our way home. In the attenuating dark of the downtown
streets at the end of the night, our footfalls echoed in the silence.
Ray explained to me that New York was the only place where the
black musicians who made the sounds we had experienced were
allowed to enter by the front door.

I had presumed to have left segregation behind in Texas. At

International House, a flamboyant black actor drifted in and out of our circle. He received attention with his sibilant campness and provocative charm, which, instead of concealing his still outlawed homosexuality, exaggerated it. His acting and directorial skills were finally acknowledged and he went to fulfil his dreams in Hollywood. I had experience of the great divide when I met up with my friends from Paris. One of them, an artist called Tim Bowden, bitterly accused me of racism when I rejected his intimacies on my visits to his studio in the Bronx.

One day, in the campus cafeteria, I met John Barrett. It was a casual meeting, a coming-together of two Brits, amid the clatter of cutlery and plates. Little did I know it was to have a profound effect on my life. He was tall, slender and soft-spoken and gave the impression of not wanting to be there at all. His blond hair fell over his forehead and his eyes were a misty blue. He seemed to disown the grey flannels and corduroy jacket that covered his body, his tie swinging loose from his shirt collar. I strained to hear him across the table where we placed our trays. He was on a teaching fellowship from Jesus College, Cambridge, lived in John Jay students' residence and was disparaging about Columbia. He did not enjoy the food and did not really like America. Together we walked to the Dutch sisters' flat where I was living at the time and I promised to cook him a proper English meal.

At first we met sparingly; I had many friends at International House who, together with my companion of the corridor, were quite possessive of my time. Although I was aware of my habitual recklessness in throwing myself deep into relationships, I could not help being drawn to this sensitive, gentle somewhat remote person who had attached himself to me and kept calling for me when I moved to the Arizona Hotel, and I had absolutely no premonition of what was to come.

Winter had set in with biting cold. Winds blasted through the gaps between the skyscrapers and lashed our faces like a knife blade. We went for long walks in the freezing temperatures, sat in Central Park watching the skaters on the lake, went to the Rockefeller Centre to see the giant Christmas tree and to the fake mediaeval building of The Cloisters. In the evenings after work, we would go downtown to Times Square, with its shabby buildings animated by hyperactive flashing electric signs, its cacophony of noise, and its continual ticker tape announcing worldwide and local news. We both loved ice hockey matches in Madison Square Gardens. The fierce-looking players in their spacemen outfits moved fast and hit each other hard and harmlessly in their protective armour, and the music blared through the unyielding ice-cold interior.

I realized in our time together how restrained he was and how attentive to me and my concerns. Yet, even while trying to be ordinary he was guarded, always economical with his words, suppressing some demons inside his head. I was aware of his great compassion and his depth of understanding, and when a bewildered look crossed his face, belying his precise and careful gestures, I could see he was troubled and disconnected but I adapted to doing what pleased him. I knew he liked being with me and I respected his English reserve and blithely tried to carry him with me in my energy and my enthusiasm.

We went to parties at the flat of John's mentor, Herbert Robbins, a professor at Columbia. John told me he was brilliant, a widely published pioneer in mathematical statistics who clearly valued him and entertained a large circle of people who mattered in letters and science. He was single after a failed marriage, and the ladies we met at his flat had no doubt been vetted for the perfect woman the professor admitted to be searching for. He was suffering from some sort of ill health, which probably explained why he received his guests sitting on the toilet, door open, at the end of the corridor. This was only one of the eccentricities of this brilliantly articulate man with a great sense of humour. His status in the world of applied maths (he had obtained his PhD from Harvard at twenty-three) seemed to entitle him to set his own rules of conduct, and his parties, on the many occasions we attended, were animated and sometimes hilarious. I felt at times he knew and hinted at the complications surrounding my involvement with his talented student.

The rooms at John Jay were strictly out of bounds to females and a curfew was generally enforced. In the beginning, our evenings together terminated with him rushing back to meet the deadline. Later, if Abe could be distracted and Raymond avoided, he spent the night in my room. Even in our intimate times together, John was chaste, engaged always in a struggle to cope with his physical desire and some deeply unconscious guilt which seemed to prevent his pleasure. I found this bewildering, but still felt attracted to him.

I had been earning money babysitting for the Epsteins, and writing advertising copy for the delightful Mrs Hull from Paris who, I suspect, invented work for me in order to be able to stuff some dollars into my handbag at the end of an evening. She lived downtown in Murray Hill, in a frothy all-pink boudoir sort of a place, and plied me with Bourbon whiskey all through her drawn-out preparations for our evening meal together.

The Provençal course occupied only one afternoon a week and was boring, so I found myself a job in an insurance company. My brief at AFIA (American Foreign Insurance Association) was to translate policies, contracts and claims from worldwide clients. They were in French, German, Italian and Spanish, written in minuscule print and were incomprehensible to me and I suspect to everyone except lawyers. But I enjoyed my daily trip to the cavernous heart of Wall Street on the IRT downtown, squeezed body to body against the working population of New York, who had a very clean smell of deodorant and Old Spice aftershave. The offices were like teeming prison cells, with typewriters instead of bars and routine instead of jailers. The staff in the vast open-plan offices – a mix of Italian, Irish and Puerto Rican second generation immigrants – were welcoming. I was one of only two translators. The other was Camilla, a twinkling Puerto Rican, who soon perceived my restlessness at my office desk and chronicled my progression throughout the day, with walks to the water fountain, telephone calls and private letter writing. Receiving a weekly cheque compensated for the routine.

Among the many invitations from fellow workers, in which John was included, was one from my Italian colleague to his farm in the Catskill Mountains. I think it was the only time I really saw John happy and able almost to express his feelings. He thought it wonderful and 'full of the things that make life worth living'.

One evening in spring, John came as usual to my room at the Arizona. He appeared more in retreat than usual and beads of sweat trickled down his pale face. I assumed he had a feverish cold and remembered my father's infallible medicine of hot red wine. He was gladly sipping the warmed up plonk I brought him, when he remembered he had not eaten all day and asked me for some food to line his stomach. I went to find the remains of a loaf in the kitchen and offered it to him. After one bite his body suddenly became rigid. He began to tremble and he looked at me in torment. I realised the significance: this was the Eucharist, the blood and flesh of Christ, and in the desperate process of resolving all his conflicts he was undergoing his epiphany. He jumped up, leaving me stunned and frightened.

I did not hear from him for many days. Nor did I attempt to leave messages, half fearful of intruding and half not knowing how to help him. Somehow, I felt that I was part of the problem. I did not realise to what extent he had imperceptibly contaminated me with his darkening mood and taken me with him into a deepening depression which neither of us seemed able to confront. So when, one afternoon in late spring, I returned to the office from lunch to find a note on my desk that John had called, I had a premonition of disaster. I could not reach him at his residence, but before the afternoon was out I had another call. This time it was he; I was to come to the psychiatric floor of the hospital where he had been admitted. At least he was safe.

I rushed there on the subway. The receptionist at St Luke's at the edge of the campus directed me to the secure ward on the top floor. I rang the doorbell and waited while they fetched him. He shuffled into the hallway with a sheepish grin on his face. His hair was tousled, he was dressed in an unbelted green dressing gown and made a big effort to communicate, bewildered at what had happened. He had no recollection of what brought him here and begged me to go to his room at John Jay and bring him his recording of Mozart's *Don Giovanni.*

I waited till the coast was clear and found the door of his room unlocked. The room was in an almighty disarray. On a chair, cut in half with its sawdust stuffing spilling out over the floor, was a small toy alligator, an imitation of those found in the swamps in Florida, which he had bought on one on our nocturnal outings in Times Square. I tossed it in the bin, swept up the repulsive contents of the room with my hands and found his records, debating with myself if it was good for him to listen to the hell-raising tale of guilt and retribution, with its spine-chilling D-minor overture, which accompanied Don Giovanni's descent into hell. But I respected his wish; the terror he felt listening to the music clearly obscured his own.

I never discovered what event had caused this catastrophe. There was a hint that the police were involved. I visited him whenever I was permitted and soon, with the benefit of a heavy drug regime, he became calm and rational. Before he was released there were many formalities to arrange, including his passage back home. I accompanied him to the boat. We promised each other to meet again soon in Cambridge and I took a photograph of him standing on deck, his back half turned to me, hesitant and forlorn. It was my last glimpse of him.

I went to see the only person with whom John had really connected in the hope of making sense of it all. Herb Robbins had anticipated my visit. 'Well, Lili,' he said to me when I arrived, 'Now that society has taken care of John, what are you going to do with your life?' It was a cruel blow, intended to shock me into the reality that John was more sick than even he had suspected and I more gullible than I had allowed myself to believe. That it had been a love affair that never was, an impossible attachment without ordinary outcome, was not an unusual end to my entanglements.

My friends at AFIA surrounded me with comfort and treats and in my leisure time I returned to the fold of International House. Anne Carlisle had moved into an apartment on Riverside Drive and invited me to evenings with her new boyfriend, a musician called Leonard Cohen. Over spaghetti and red wine, he played his guitar, sang the songs he had composed and told us about his stay on the Greek island of Hydra, where he led a blissful hippy existence. He was gearing up to return to his family in Montreal, who, he said, did not feel he could make a living as a musician and were urging him to start a 'proper career'. It was warm and soothing, and gave me time to avoid the pain of my experience.

Life in New York after the disastrous adventure with John was not negotiable and I did not feel I could stay on. My studies had fizzled out when I was only one of two students in the class which now took place in the professor's house in the Bronx. When I heard my old friend Gabriel Stein was in New York, I rushed to him. It was soothing to tell him about the events of the past months, but my hope that he could help me in my raw and troubled state was an illusion; the comfort he extended to me was hazardous, maybe because it reawakened the unquenchable crush I had on him and he just barely rejected my advances. Nor was I able to accept the Jerusalem lifeline he threw me. I was simply too weary to start again and decided to head for home. Bill Epstein advised me to try becoming a translator/interpreter at the UN and I decided to delay my departure and sit the exam. Depending on the result I would square things with my conscience and my mother. Throughout the summer, I continued in my job. Faced with leaving New York behind, I was reluctant to renounce its freewheeling sense of possibilities, the freedom which definitely existed over and above what was admissible in England and a type of frankness in people, a rejection of pettiness and an unstinting generosity. In Cambridge, John was back in hospital receiving shock treatment for advanced schizophrenia. His letter to me from the Male Admissions Ward at Fulbourn Hospital in Cambridge was a cry for help which he knew was unavailable; his precise exquisite hand-writing was muzzy and irregular. He seemed to be expecting my return and explained the visiting hours to me in detail.

Without much enthusiasm, I presented myself along with a large number of candidates to take the interpreter/translators exam in the UN building. It was difficult but manageable and the results would be forwarded to me in England.

The next day, 22 September, seen off by many friends bearing gifts, armed with many addresses of Herb's network of friends in London, one dollar from my aunt with which to rent a deck chair and various telegrams, I set sail on the SS *France* for home.

17

Bloomsbury 1956–1957

I had mentally rehearsed my homecoming and reunion with my mother who, in my letters home, had become my confidante, more intimately beloved and admired in my imagination than could realistically be sustained. I wanted desperately to be accepted in my new persona, and was eager to share the new me with her, my brother and my sister. But the euphoria which dominated my arrival at home, the promises and plans, was short-lived. Nothing at home had changed and I knew I was placing myself in a precarious situation. As a family, we were excessively involved with each other emotionally, due probably to our shared traumatic experiences. As for being back in England, I came up against everything which had made me feel ill at ease here and the reason why I had left in the first place. In building on a subjective relationship with my mother, I had shared my New York life with her, expressing my wavering feelings and unsteady frame of mind; the effusive care and concern which steamed off our correspondence would be hard to incorporate into the reality of living face to face. In the first excitement of homecoming, I desperately wanted everyone to acknowledge the new me. But after twenty-four hours everything was as it always had been.

Two things *had* changed in Rectory Terrace in the past eighteen months: my mother had acquired a lodger and bought a car. The former, an ex-commercial pilot, was living in the attic flat newly vacated by my brother and his family. Philip Wood had a game leg which he trailed around ostentatiously and with braggadocio, the cut-glass accent of the upper classes and the pedigree of the son of a father knighted after the Boxer rebellion. I half resented his invasion of the family home with his blustery bonhomie, but despite the fact that he was so lusciously camp, or perhaps because of it, my mother was delighted with him. He offered on-tap companionship, served her little aristocratic snacks with exotic cocktails at teatime and paid her much respect. She was therefore not well pleased when he included me in his extravagant attentions and insisted on improving my driving skills in wild outings up and down the country's motorways in his red convertible MG.

As for the car, my mother proudly showed me a greyish Mini Cooper with mahogany panels. With the quite illegal extension of her 1935 Bamberg driving permit, she obtained an international licence, without practice or road experience. But the enjoyment of the freedom and independence it gave her silenced all protest, and left us in permanent jitters as she tried to negotiate her way out of the garage and into the back lane. The many scars on her little vehicle, notwithstanding the limitations of petrol rationing, showed us how much she used it and she bullied my brother into letting her drive into her nineties. Needless to say, I was not allowed near it.

In the beginning I enjoyed coming down to breakfast, to a table set the night before by my mother, with tablecloths appliquéd and embroidered with cherries, Rosenthal china and homemade raspberry jam made with the fruit hand-picked by her.

My brother had obtained a Ministry of Defence contract, which had ensured the survival and prosperity of his business. There was talk of the family becoming shareholders in a further extension. But I felt this was precarious; I did not have the adequate capital, and it might cause problems between shareholders, and furthermore I felt I had absolutely no claim to anything that might have accrued to my mother. I just hoped she had acquired over and above her needs for the next decades and that she should live as comfortably and as well as her frugal nature would allow her.

I had acquired an interest in money by osmosis while translating financial documents at AFIA (my firm had just paid out $15,000,000 dollars in liabilities connected with the pirated ship *Andrea Doria*), and had keenly followed the drop in the pound resulting from the Suez crisis to ensure the best possible exchange for my small savings, which, had I worked another six months, would have ensured a degree of security. I also knew that what my mother really expected of me was to be happily married and settled, preferably in nearby Jesmond, with an addition to the grandchildren she already had and was active enough to enjoy.

I satisfied my craving for mediaeval buildings by visiting Norman churches, Georgian squares and any old buildings. It was always damp and chilly, but a profound aesthetic relief after New York. None of the outings to Scotland and to Paris, which had been mentioned as an enticement to come home, materialized.

After a few weeks of living comfortably, I became restless and felt compelled to confront my future. It was certainly not going to be in Newcastle. Nor could it be in Israel, where I had never stopped yearning to be. My mother was actually traumatized by the thought and it was a pain I could not inflict upon her. In response to my letters of application to every editor on Fleet Street, I received only two positive replies inviting me to interview. One was from Reuters news agency, the other was from *Woman's Own*, a weekly publication read avidly in the women's union at King's College for its tips on beauty, diet, its agony aunt and gossip columns and its serialized love stories.

I opted for Reuters. Philip Wood drove me to London and deposited me in a boarding house near the British Museum which he had selected for me. For the first time since the Blitz, I found myself in London, on Fleet Street, in a wonderful Lutyens building. In the vast, open-plan newsroom, I had to man the clattering ticker tapes, and re-write the financial information from around the globe, which was spewed out in an incessant mind-crunching cacophony of sound, assigning each story to the relevant publication. At lunchtime, I participated in the ritual visit to the bar of the Cheshire Cheese, where all the big names of Fleet Street congregated.

I did not stay long. A phone call to *Woman's Own*, my second choice, revived my application and I organized an interview with Jimmy Drawbell, the managing editor and head of the Newnes & Pearson empire. The interview was brief; he picked a random copy of the magazine from a pile next to his desk, and invited me to do a critique of every feature in the issue. He warned me to resist praise – the sales figures of 6 million were proof enough of the high quality of his publication. My assignment was to find out what was wrong with it and report back in three days' time.

I retreated to my attic room in Bloomsbury, rang my sister-in-law Anne, an English graduate and an avid reader of the magazine, for ideas, and on 27 May, soon after submitting my text, I received a letter inviting me to join the organization at the majestic salary of 15 guineas a week.

The office was in the tower of a building overlooking Covent Garden at the end of Maiden Lane. With my increase in salary, I could live comfortably at the Madigans' boarding house and have money left over to save. The editorial area was under the skylight in the tower and I worked with half a dozen experienced subs around a very large table. I had to pick up swiftly the language of editing, the symbols, the grammar, punctuation and house style. I had to learn what a 'widow' was (the short last line of a paragraph that appears at the top of a page), how many words to a line and how many copy inches to a page. One of our lighter tasks was to invent letters to Mary Grant the agony aunt, because the originals were too indecent to publish.

The chief subeditor was a big young man with intimidating black spectacles and a brusque manner. For some reason, he took me under his wing and patiently taught me everything, indulging me in my errors and really never letting go of me. Even after he left, headhunted by a competing publication, he plied me with letters and tentative invitations, full of self-deprecating humour, tempting me with his love of Beethoven and nature, laying out all the possibilities of the relationship with me he so desired. As a leaving present, we had embroidered a handkerchief with all our initials. I did not realize how deeply he wanted to involve himself with me ('When you walked in, I saw you were the only woman, and you were a woman alone') and regretted the hurt I must have caused him by failing utterly to reciprocate his feelings or take up his humour-cloaked entreaties.

At the B&B, the regular clientele were commercial travellers. But in the attic, my neighbours on the drab landing were an Afro-American medical student from Indianapolis in transit to university at Ibadan in Nigeria, and Jeanette Durand, an 'au pair'. She was a young Russian girl who served us our breakfast and we became the nucleus of a gang of friends who spent all of our leisure hours together.

We went sightseeing in London, visited the Tower of London and the museums, and walked for miles and miles. In the evenings we went clubbing at the Kismet Club in Soho and the Tahiti near Leicester Square. For the price of a drink one could meet up with friends, listen to records by Elvis Presley, whose 'Heartbreak Hotel' had just burst onto the scene, and dance to rock and roll. On Charlotte Street, not far from our lodgings, a coffee house had opened, the first in London. Its attraction for the crowds of people sitting there was a brand new Gaggia machine, which hissed and gurgled and spewed out a dark brown elixir topped with white froth, just like in Paris. It became a favourite meeting place after work. Its very novelty created a sort of social melting pot, where foreigners and locals met and talked, quite unlike anywhere else. The owner, whom we befriended, acted as confidante and message-taker and, occasionally, go-between.

We were joined in our group and in our outings by the de Barovier sisters from Jamaica. The daughters of the prime minister, they lived in a boarding house on Gower Street. When the Madigans increased their rent, there was an exodus to Dyne House, to join them. Once a one-family house, it was converted to its present function by dividing the rooms into small living spaces with clapboard walls, which, lacking all sound-proofing, created a sort of anonymous intimacy. The person on the other side of my thin wall was a young Tamil accountancy student from Ceylon who introduced himself and eventually spent more time at my side of the room than on his.

His name was Indra Kanagasabai, one of the persecuted minority on his island. He lived on enormous subsidies from his father's tea plantation, and had the robust ego of a very spoilt young man with high spirits who had great flights of fancy and a vision of the future filled with Lagonda cars financed by a thriving business of his own. But in the light-hearted few months we spent time together, we grew more attached than either of us had reckoned, and I came nearer to marrying him than any other man before.

I had not completely recovered from my first and protracted encounter with mental illness and my fragile self-belief had been severely dented. Slowly, I began to feel more comfortable, and immersed myself deeply in the small tight-knit crowd of people from all over the world passing through, who meant things to each other, developed a strong attachment and longed for a continuity in the relationships that held us. But it merely confirmed my status as an outsider and my situation seemed stagnant. I had never felt at home in London and there was nothing and no one to keep me here. I therefore worked up my courage; I would go back to New York. It had to be better than this. My US visa was nearly running out and I had to make a decision. On one of my weekends in Newcastle, my mother felt uneasy at my lack of commitment and my rootlessness, and was quite willing for me to go back to America – in fact, she encouraged me to do so.

It was with a feeling of weariness riddled with doubt that I booked my passage at the beginning of winter, my escape strategy fraught with uncertainty and depression. On 29 November 1957 I left behind on the platform a sad little community in whose midst my absence would leave a big hole, but hopefully no hearts were broken. As the ship left the shore, abandoning the shelter of home, I had the feeling I would never return.

Part Three

Newsweek

18

Newsweek 1958

I returned to the Arizona Hotel, to the teeming upper reaches of Broadway and the life of its exiles that cascade into the streets at day's end, and was embraced by my former corridor mates. The scenario was unchanged: Mr Reisberg the landlord had raised the rent, Justine the cleaner still frittered about polishing the ashtrays in the hallway with a rag, and Abe provided the soundtrack with his contrapuntal snore. I had not many choices; the chief one was to survive financially, make sense of what came before and create some continuity in my errant life.

My job options were upgraded now by my Fleet Street pedigree, and while applying everywhere, I took the first job offered me. It was at *McCall's Needlework & Crafts*, preparing their spring-summer edition. The offices straddled Park Avenue over Grand Central Station. The editor was Nanina Comstock, a large-boned earthy lady in sandals and homespuns, who was rumoured to excel at divining water sources by dowsing with a cleft stick, and who was on a mission through her magazine to persuade Americans to 'do it yourself'.

For a time I was kept vaguely amused, checking knitting patterns, describing rug-making, tile craft, mosaics, weaving and needlepoint, and how to make bead curtains. It reminded me of the war years, when we had to make absolutely everything including footwear, with coiled rope soles to replace shoes. I performed all these functions, did everything that was expected of me, lunched with the girls, contributed to collections and signed cute cards for anyone who was ill in bed or getting married.

After a few months, though, I had had enough and when a job came up at *Charm* magazine, I transferred myself to Madison Avenue, the buzzing centre of the publishing and fashion world.

My boss in the promotions department was a manic lady from the Shattuck dynasty who owned Shrafft's, a popular chain of eateries in the US. She was explosively energetic and very self-important, with her buttoned-up little figure, hair stretched tightly back from her forehead and her face encrusted with make-up. She stalked around on very high heels with pointed-out toes, issuing commands on the trot and expecting action everywhere, and immediately. Despite my fancy title (assistant to the director of the Promotions department) on the masthead, I watched everyone from the outer fringes of the staff, as they plotted and schemed for the plum assignments around Europe, Hawaii and Haiti while I, meantime, had to find sparkling vocabulary to entice the reading public with the merchandise they brought back, and run errands for my boss, collecting her clothes from the dry-cleaner.

New York seemed to have outgrown its torpor and now, in the waning fifties, was beginning to rock. Yet the little community around Columbia was strangely indifferent to the upheaval in Hungary, the Suez crisis, and the descent from the Sierra Madre of Fidel Castro; most dismaying of all, was that the student body appeared unmoved by the discovery of a faculty member's body, fished out from the bottom of the Hudson River with his feet cast in concrete by Battista's thugs. How we would have marched in protest in Britain!

My room at the Arizona overlooked a dilapidated courtyard; it had an air of decay which no one should have had to breathe in, and the chair covers were decorated with flowers which nature never intended. Raymond was in his final year now, friendly and funny and resilient and helpful in keeping me aloof from any new calamitous involvements. His friendship was endearingly secure and we continued to confide in each other. As for my other friends from International House, Anne Carlisle was living out the embers of her love affair with Leonard Cohen in Canada, and Bob Verberkmoes, an aspiring theatre director, was trying to come to terms with his homosexuality after a disastrous affair with a young idol, agonizingly chronicled in his letters to me in London, and was pursuing his career with a play in a fringe theatre.

I began to see more of an Israeli pianist called Nathan Mishory, who was preparing for his debut recital at Carnegie Hall. Intuitive and supportive, he had been a silent bystander who kept his distance while the drama with John Barrett was playing itself out and had awaited eagerly my return to New York. My life now revolved mainly round concerts and ballet rehearsals, in the company of the charismatic Balanchine, among others. Through his connection as *répétiteur* for Martha Graham and Anna Sokolow, I grew to understand a little of interpretative dancing.

As we became close, Nathan understood more than anyone the restlessness in me, my self-doubt and the longing for something that did not exist. He also sensed my reluctance to allow myself to be drawn into a love affair that was real and meaningful; he suspected that while my compromise with the demands of life were cheerfully enacted, in the end they had no meaning and little content for me, merely disguising a deep negativity which made me run for refuge and hide. I perceived every attempt by others to get close to me as temporary, as 'being and gone', as one rejected boyfriend reproached me. Nathan tried his best to persuade me that our sense of futility resided in the world outside and not inside ourselves. In our time together, I found him to be the finest human being I had loved and rejected. His talent transcended his experience of music and gave him a deep insight into poetry and literature, despair and renewal.

I was very nervous when he walked on stage for his concert at Carnegie Hall, but it was clear from the beginning of his programme that his performance was going to be accomplished and stylish. He delighted the audience with a beautifully shaped, disciplined Bach English Suite, following it with a Schubert sonata (Opus 20), which sounded clear and sweet. The Beethoven he played (Opus 10) was unknown to me, chosen without doubt for its depth of feeling and profound poetry. But he challenged the audience most with the evolved musical language of modern composers he loved: pieces by Béla Bartók, Paul Ben-Haim, Stefan Wolpe and the atonal Arnold Schoenberg showed off his pianist skills with elegance and a touch of mischievousness. His performance was applauded and enthusiastically reviewed and it marked the end of his studies in New York.

One evening before his departure to Israel he took me along to a party to meet his patroness, Charlotte Bergman. She lived in a penthouse which laterally spanned two apartment houses on Riverside

Drive and was filled with one of the most extraordinary collections of modern art I had ever seen in a private home. On the pale cream-coloured walls were absurdly beautiful paintings by Picasso and Matisse, Braque, Rouault, Dufy and Kandinsky. On little side tables sat sculptures by Henry Moore, Epstein and Maillol. The dedications inscribed on portraits of herself as a young woman revealed her friendship with the artists, and I learnt later that her husband, a man of wealth, had supported and encouraged these artists in the early days of their struggle in Europe. The room was teeming with diplomats, governors, politicians and other VIPs who came to the party to be entertained by Nathan and his brother and other young Israeli musicians studying at Julliard. Over cocktails, I found myself in a group with a short, tanned, balding man, with an aura of spicy aftershave, and a Belgian accent. He was the foreign editor of *Newsweek* and after a few glasses of champagne he invited me to come and work at the magazine.

Nathan gave me a parting gift of little wooden carving, an earth-bound bird, a Brancusi, and set out for home, via a once in a lifetime tour of European cities. From each city that he experienced on his travels, from London, Paris, Geneva, Amsterdam, Rome and Florence, he chronicled for me in his letters, so full of longing, his magical and perceptive discovery of the mediaeval and baroque. Each time, I wrestled with my feelings, weary and disillusioned with myself. My mother stopped over from Galveston on her way home, and braved a stay at the Arizona. Her appreciation of Nathan was marred only by the fear that I would marry him and live my life in Israel.

One early summer afternoon, coming out of Prexis doughnut shop, I was crossing Broadway in the unbearable heat when I noticed a man dressed in a black suit of woollen cloth making his way up and down by the gates of the university. His hands, tightly clasped behind his back, could not straighten out the stoop in his body. We came face to face; I saw the close-cropped black beard and the deep black eyes of my old artist friend, Jose Maria Garcia Llort. In disbelief, we embraced. Much had happened in the past six years since the Cité. He had married Martha Crockett and was awaiting her emergence from her Columbia summer school course. Sadness clouded his face and darkened his look and in a voice husky with emotion he told me that he was in mourning for his father, whose death in Barcelona had been announced to him only yesterday, too late for him to reach him. He felt the deepest remorse about not being by his bedside at the end. The best way he could assuage his grief and show respect to his father, who raised him and whom he quoted to me as saying 'We have to suffer for what has yet to happen', was to sweat it out in this sombre attire of mourning. He and Martha had come for the summer from Louisiana, where she was teaching art at Louisiana College and where, in the pine woods teeming with songbirds and lush vegetation, he grew to appreciate America and feel less alien as he painted the colonial houses, the exotic animals, and the landscape and trappings of the colonial history of the South.

My reunion with this dignified compassionate friend and his wife was profoundly meaningful. Jose Maria carried the sadness of the world on his shoulders. Joined by our friends Armando and his painter wife Ellen, who were living in Greenwich Village, we found solace during the hot evenings in their all-green painted flat on Riverside Drive, where, by clever contrivance of two open windows, a flow of air brought relief to the oppressiveness, and where masterly meals and evocative wines were served by the Llorts, and we retraced the past, discussing the meaning of life and the struggle to maintain ourselves while compromising in a phoney and destructive world with values in which none of us believed and to which none of us entirely belonged.

It was a renewal of historic friendships. The plot of our lives had moved on from the uncertainty when we parted. My friends had sealed their destiny, while I plodded on in the reflected peaceful resolution of their unions. We vowed when the Llorts returned to Louisiana never to lose contact again. When they left, Jose Maria gave me a painting of the face of a woman, whose eyes were so sad, her look so troubled, that sometimes at night when I looked at her from my bed I felt compelled to get up and turn the picture to the wall. Jose Maria said that when he dies, the painting will utter a horrific cry and then I would know he had gone. This did not happen for another fifty years.

At my interview at *Newsweek* on 42nd Street and Broadway, Olga Barbi, a little Italian-American lady, explained the career structure. I would do my apprenticeship on the mail desk, progress to the clipping desk, and, if my spirit was unbroken, I would graduate to be a researcher, on trial for six weeks, ending up as editorial assistant. It was almost a caricature of gender selection: girls were recruited from Smith, Brown's and Barnard, foot soldiers and flunkies whose task was to serve up educated information on a plate to the writers. Only socially was the company of females desirable. At the New Weston bar across the road after work, the men unwound before taking their trains to Westchester and their domesticity. Then we changed into social creatures, drinking companions who, when excess of Martinis took their toll, heaved the writers into taxis to send them homeward bound to the outer suburbs to their awaiting wives.

I ran around Manhattan, clutching a street guide, delivering and fetching brown envelopes for the mail desk; at the end of the day, I was exhausted. I became well acquainted with the city and the organizations which ran it. In the office, my habitat was in a corner of a sprawling smoke-filled newsroom. I had an overview of writers who sat hunched over their typewriters; the editors were encased in glass-fronted offices. The wire room was central, its machines clattering non-stop with instant reports from correspondents and news agencies around the globe. I had never been so in touch with world politics.

Not long into my apprenticeship there was a change of foreign editor. Arnaud de Borchgrave was replaced by an English editor headhunted from *Time* magazine, and the atmosphere changed. From the first, Eldon Griffiths filled the chair with an air of unchallengeable authority; he was tall, had red hair, a thrusting chin and a highly disciplined mind. Soon after his arrival, feeling that he could draw on my Fleet Street training and my European languages, he asked for me to be instantly promoted to the foreign news department, and so I was spared the tedious task of tearing up newspapers all day long. He nevertheless set me a test, an engrossing assignment: it was to produce an exhaustive report on Outer Mongolia. I immersed myself with relish into the frozen regions on the outpost of the Soviet Empire, and discovered yurts and yaks and Ulan Bator, and Lake Baikal and the Trans-Siberian Railway which crossed through it. My boss seemed to approve the result, although I don't think he ever used it.

My premature promotion did not please the head researcher, and when I befriended the writers, it became a cause for extending the pre-requisite six weeks trial period. By the time I was confirmed in my job, *Newsweek* had moved to Madison Avenue, a proper building in midtown Manhattan. I had my very own cubicle and my newly acquired status, and in the morning walked excitedly into the high marble-clad lobby along with the morning crowd, immaculately turned-out men and women, pressing the little red triangles for the lift and waiting for the polished brass doors to open slowly.

I began to inform myself with every New York and regional newspaper landing on my desk in the morning, and to extract in my mind which were the important and not-so-important events locally and worldwide. Tuesdays started the week, with an editorial conference in Eldon's office, to which the girls were not invited. The week geared up in pace and reached its peak on Friday night, when all copy had to be checked, updated and processed, often through the night, before being sent to the printers in Dayton on Saturday for appearance on the news stands on Tuesday.

I was asked to write a brief on Albert Camus when, in early January, travelling back from a six-week holiday in the family home in the Vaucluse, he crashed his Facel Vega against a tree and died instantly. I felt privileged, and wrote a very informed five-page appreciation, quoting seminal lines from his writings and detailing his huge influence on the literary world, which had so informed my own academic and philosophical development. I included, among other significant quotes, the final passionate outburst of Meursault, mechanical man in *L'Etranger*, when, on the eve of his execution for murder, he realizes that after all he wants to live: 'Every man alive is privileged... All alike would be condemned to die one day; his (the privileged one) turn too would come like the others.' It was immensely tragic that at 47, Nobel laureate and with a young family, his turn had come. Very little of my text was to find its way into the magazine, but this was communal journalism after all, and I had no complaints.

My job as researcher developed into a news gathering exercise when the (French speaking) African continent was rushed into independence, and sent their representatives to take up membership of the United Nations, and I was sent to interview them. They were all young graduates from the universities of Paris, trained in the French parliament, who returned home from their years of enlightenment abroad, highly sophisticated and politically ambitious, and were glad to connect with me through the French language. I was invited to their celebrations and could count on the valuable briefings with which they entrusted me. I discovered that the UN bar was a source of endless political positioning and gossip which supplemented information from *Newsweek* bureaus, and from where I gleaned and submitted a smattering of information, trends and developing events.

I found being a researcher boring, and I was not very good at it. I misfiled the envelopes containing the clippings in the library and mixed up their content, to the despair of the librarian. In fact, I was much better sitting cross-legged on the desks of the writers discussing politics. But somehow I managed to provide the required information verbally or in writing and check their copy before going to press. I could not have foreseen, in those early months, the professional excitement that lay ahead which was to take over my life, nor that I was about to be plunged into a tragicomedy of global significance.

19

Congo 1960

That summer, extraordinary events occurred on the international stage and propelled me into a role unprecedented in ordinary Madison Avenue reporting: the Belgian Congo suddenly became independent and a prize pawn in the Cold War.

One Sunday morning in late July, I received an urgent call from my editor to go to the Barclay Hotel on 48th and Lexington to interview Patrice Lumumba, the prime minister of the Congo, who had arrived without prior warning to argue his case before the United Nations.

Until a few months ago, the Belgian Congo had barely existed on the political map of the world. It was just another colony, huge and unknown. Patrice Lumumba, who had gained prominence in the trade union movement, headed a government of only sixteen college graduates, who had no experience or example to follow in running a country. Now, only days after historic momentum had forced King Leopold to proclaim independence in Leopoldville and the Congo had acceded to membership of the UN, inter-tribal riots erupted, the army mutinied against their Belgian officers and Katanga, the wealthiest of its provinces, seceded and set off a dangerous contest between the Soviets and the West. The chaos which ensued took over the agenda at the UN, in Washington and Moscow and was never resolved, despite the best military and political brains, and endless heated all-night Security Council meetings. At stake was control of the sprawling former colony in the heart of Africa and its cornucopia of natural resources coveted by all.

New York was not prepared for this group of Africans who had abruptly descended in their midst and the hurried improvisation gave me a head start in reporting. For the desk clerk at the Barclay Hotel, who had never heard of Lumumba, he was just another black man from Africa, and he had no hesitation in informing me of Lumumba's room number on the fourteenth floor. There was only a cleaner in room 1451, but downstairs in the dimly lit bar, three tables had been put together for what turned out to be the entire youthful government of the newly independent Congo.

They were trying to order food and had difficulty in making themselves understood. Young and immaculately turned out in shirtsleeves, they looked a little bewildered on the pony-skin bar chairs, like a Sunday school treat ending up at the vicarage for tea. A portly, more mature man in a brown suit and bow tie introduced himself as Joseph Okito, vice president of the senate. He was thrilled to find someone who spoke his language. In reply to my request to meet his prime minister, he told me he was at the UN with Secretary General Dag Hammarskjöld, but I would be able to find him at the hotel at six o'clock. As I pressed them for information about Lumumba, it was clear he was adulated by this group of travelling companions, who referred to him affectionately as 'Pat'. But I learnt also that he was a hard taskmaster – sometimes calling them in the middle of the night to dictate a telegram – that he had tremendous drive, made snap decisions and had the passionate desire to build and lead a united Congo.

Reluctantly, and in the line of duty, I agreed to have a drink with Antoine Kiwewa, a secretary of state to an undefined ministry, despite his insistence that it took place in his room. Sitting in his stockinged feet on the unmade bed, he ordered whiskey from room service and for the duration of an hour, his nostrils quivering, his steely grey eyes glinting, he gave me a complete and impassioned overview of the drama unfolding in the Congo, describing the totalitarian administration of the Belgians, the non-existent education, except by missionaries, and the erupting tribal conflict. Independence had been sprung upon them, without preparation or an executive and with only sixteen graduates to run the country.

His impeccable French had the measure and rhetoric of the language of the seventeenth century, with a touch of precociousness and many imperfect subjunctives. Other members of the delegation came and went. Flirtatious suggestions and sexual innuendo crept into the conversation ('Perhaps Mademoiselle can provide some divertissement for tired politicians?'), but I thought I had done my job for my magazine and made my getaway.

Instead of going home, I found myself at the IRT station at Lexington Avenue, boarding the subway to Harlem, persuaded by Vice President Okito and a white-haired man in the uniform of a naval commander of the Liberty ship, the *Booker T*. The commander took the vice president round the local shops, shaking hands in all directions, and to a nightclub where Count Basie was billed. The Count had just left, which did not concern Okito, because he had never heard of him. At Small's Paradise, Harlem's oldest establishment, Pop Small proposed a special dinner for Lumumba, which Okito had to decline, but he was overjoyed that everyone in the street was African.

We had arrived at the intersection of 125th Street and 7th Avenue. A meeting of the Negro Improvement Association was in progress, but the commander decided it was time for him to put Okito on display. 'How about a word from the vice president of the Congo?' he asked the little crowd. He had worked his magic. There was a stunned silence, then a great outburst of clapping and shouting. Okito straightened his shoulders and shuffled through the wedge that was being cleared for him. I hung back, but knew what I so dreaded was inevitable: I was to translate. In the still summer night, the air was charged with electricity. I was ringed by expectant faces raised towards me, dark eyes shining, gold teeth gleaming. I felt I had no business there, that I was intruding on the most intimate union of a black people on a little piece of their own territory in exile.

I was being pushed by the crowd. The Chinese orator, whom we had usurped from his perch, introduced Okito as 'Our brother from the Congo'. A cluster of people had gathered round a ladder that had been found propped up against the wall. They pressed forward for his autograph. Instead, he climbed clumsily up the rickety ladder rung by rung, and waved to me to climb up behind him. Pressing his legs against the steps, which wobbled dangerously, he planted his hands on the top rail, threw his head backwards and raised his eyes to heaven. In the silence which rippled through the spellbound crowd, not a sigh or car horn or police whistle could be heard, as he began: '*Frères et soeurs...*'. 'Brothers and sisters,' I translated to the expectant faces. Okito had been transformed from a bumbling, stumbling overweight man into a political leader. The crowd was completely stunned. More and more people gathered on the outskirts of the crowd around us, spilling into the street at the intersection. With his right hand waving to me to translate, he continued: 'I bring you greetings from my country, which is also your country.' A burst of clapping. 'Monsieur Lumumba and I have come to ask the UN for assistance in making our country free from the oppressor.' Cheers. 'Africa is the country of your origins, though you were brought up far away from it and in ignorance of it!' More cheers. Okito went on to speak of the immense wealth of the Congo and the future plans for his country and for the entire continent of Africa, and I translated faithfully, sentence by sentence.

At my elbow, they were nudging me, saying 'They can't hear you!', and from the back of the crowd came cries of 'Louder, louder!' Suddenly, I felt myself changing in the same way that Okito had changed. I simply existed as the mouthpiece for an oracle; the voice that came out of my throat as I perched on that ladder was not mine at all. When he outlined Lumumba's plan for rescuing their brothers in South Africa, the cheering of the crowd became a wild frenzy. Okito raised his voice to say 'Let everyone shout, "*Vive le Congo!*"', which needed no translation. I had the feeling I was not in America, but in the heart of Okito's Africa. There was not a single policeman in sight, but behind the stepladder, a blue car was parked; peering through the window, Patrice Lumumba, the saviour of Africa himself, was watching the whole event.

With the promise of an interview the next day, I appeared again in the lobby of the Barclay Hotel, which seemed to have become my home away from the office. I saw the doorman smirking as I passed by, and the bellboys greeted me with an insolent knowing look. Bernard Salumu, Lumumba's twenty-four-year-old private secretary, was surrounded by a number of crew-cut important-looking American business men, waiting their turn to be admitted into Lumumba's presence. A man called Detwiler was deep in conversation with Bernard, speaking pidgin French and gesticulating wildly. It occurred to me how grotesque it was that this bright, petulant child should determine who should get to see his prime minister. I reeled when hearing why this man must be given priority; before leaving the Congo, Lumumba had signed over investment in Congo's entire mineral resources to this known conman, and I urgently prompted him to advise his prime minister to instantly annul all business dealings with him, which thankfully he did.

The days passed in socializing with the delegates, and it was only when Lumumba was leaving for Washington that I came face to face with him at last. He was waiting in front of the newspaper stand in the lobby, next to a small stack of suitcases. He was already grasping my hand firmly with both of his when Bernard moved over to introduce me. His goatee was neatly trimmed and his brilliant eyes locked directly into mine, relaxed and smiling. He was wearing a dark suit and a light grey pullover and kept tugging at his bow tie. Very gently, he put me at my ease. He had heard, he told me, that I was a writer and that I was British. Did I like living in New York and where had I learnt my fluency in French? *He* was interviewing *me*. His French was incisive and well-modulated. The conversation continued in generalities, the questions that I had prepared no longer relevant. Events in the Congo had moved on swiftly and he was not about to brief me on any reassurances he might have been given by the State Department and the Canadian president. In his hand, he clasped a statue, a present for President Eisenhower, whom he was about to visit. It was a tubular lampshade carved out of alabaster and decorated with grotesque nude figures, already wired up to be plugged in. Outside, the Cadillac was waiting to drive him to the airport. Lumumba shook me warmly by the hand and seemed disappointed that I declined his invitation to continue our conversation on the way. With Bernard by his side, he disappeared into the waiting saloon car.

I had become considerably involved with Lumumba's entourage, and was able to report all the information surrounding his schedule in the US, and his disappointment at failing to obtain the agenda which had hastened him here. Sometimes his entourage needed to be rescued from the hangers-on who preyed on their inexperience and naivety, although when it suited him, Bernard Salumu seemed perfectly capable of dealing with the army of people who wanted to get at the prime minister. Their appetite for sex seemed to inform their presence in the West, and I was in the front line. To deflect their focus from me, I introduced them to colleagues from the office, (all young and pretty) and even one of the writers who spoke French. They were too strange to be really friends, and yet too fascinating to be mere acquaintances, and after they had left I passed the Barclay Hotel on my way to work with the feeling that something was missing.

The Harlem episode had vaulted me into a disconcerting notoriety. To my consternation and everyone else's excitement, Walter Winchell of the *New York Daily Mirror*, more accustomed to salacious celebrity revelations, hinted darkly about Patrice Lumumba bedding a staff member of *Newsweek*.

In the office two days later, the telephone on my desk rang and the operator announced a call from Washington. It was Bernard Salumu calling from Blair House. He said he and Patrice had given much thought to the matter and asked me if I 'was disposed to make a journey'. I thought he was inviting me to Washington and promptly declined. 'No,' he said, 'A longer journey.' Bernard rarely said anything in a direct manner, it was always in Chinese whispers and it tired me. 'I mean to my country,' he clarified. I gasped. What in the world, I wondered, had I got myself into and how would I extricate myself without hurting or offending anyone? He was offering me the job of minister of information in Lumumba's government in Leopoldville. The situation was ridiculous, but he had an answer to every one of my objections. I said I already had a job. He said it didn't matter. I said French wasn't my native language. He offered to teach me. I said I had no experience in government work. He said I didn't need any. He said I had won a place in the hearts of the Congolese leaders. I said governments weren't run in people's hearts. He begged me to think it over, so I promised I would. In the open-plan newsroom in the office, everyone had listened to the conversation in disbelief and there were hoots of laughter. When the implications of the call had sunk in, Bob Massie and some other colleagues thought it a marvellous idea and a great opportunity.

I turned Bernard's offer down on their return from their trip to Washington and Ottawa and invited him to dinner that night at a lovely, cool five-room apartment on Sutton Place, which had been lent to me for the summer by Bill and Edna Epstein, who were away on a US mission.

It was fascinating to hear Bernard's background. One of fifteen siblings in the province of Stanleyville, he had been vaulted from being a postal worker into his current prominent position, having shared imprisonment with Lumumba, with whom he had forged a bond of steel. Everything had looked up since the revolution. About politics, he was generally vague; but the portrait he sketched of his country was a road map for disaster. He considered himself to be a non-communist anti-Russian Marxist, and was obsessed with the idea of revolution as an 'international war to the death', referring to it as '*La Lutte*' – 'The Struggle'. In the meantime, he lived in great style in his villa in Leopoldville.

I had invited my friend Denise to join us, and when she arrived he came into the kitchen to whisper in my ear that we must invite Pat over, because he misses this sort of company so. I said we weren't that type of girls. At that moment, thankfully, Gordon Heiner, a writer from the office and my friend, joined us and was received with some truculence. Sprawled deep into an armchair, Bernard became arrogant and argumentative.

After dinner we went to Small's Paradise in Harlem, where the manager put us next to the band. Bernard didn't like the cool jazz, he wanted African music. He also deliberately annoyed the waiters by talking French to them. Denise said she wanted to dance, but he said he didn't know how. Actually, our friend did not like Harlem. Next evening, instead of attending a party at Ghanain headquarters in the suburb, we all went to Denise's flat on 12th Street, where he made himself at home. He inspected her collection of stuffed animals, beat restlessly on an African drum, and made me realize that beneath all the bravado, there was a very homesick man, a little bewildered by his great mission and anxious to get back to his villa and his houseboys in Leopoldville. On a final stroll round Greenwich Village, he liked the atmosphere, the mixture of all colours and nationalities, the guitar players and the chess players, and kept wishing his hero were here. He told us that this was impossible because the agents of the Belgians were all around waiting to assassinate him. With his announcement that on his return home he would lecture on the American way of life, he left us to go to the Ghanaian party.

My last glimpse of Bernard was as he stood waving on the side of the street, waiting for a taxi that would never materialize. No yellow cab driver would pick up a solitary black man at that hour.

It was the last I ever saw of him. He promised to return for the UN General Assembly, but by September, President Kasavubu had ousted Lumumba, Lumumba had in his turn removed Kasavubu and the army had stepped in to enforce a political truce. In actual fact, the UN was now governing the Congo. Bernard had been sent back to Stanleyville 'to gain maturity' where he set up a brutal Marxist state. And by February of next year, Lumumba was dead.

20

15th Session of the UN 1960

As the situation in the Congo disintegrated into Civil War in the autumn of that year I witnessed and reported the struggle for power which dominated the agenda in heated emergency debates at the UN. In Leopoldville, the *coup d'état* by army head Mobutu, ostensibly to settle the leadership contest between the combatants Kasavubu and Lumumba, created total confusion. Moise Tshombe, seen as the puppet of the reviled Belgians, had taken the state of Katanga, where the Union Minière du Haut Katanga supplied endless riches, out of the equation, and had no intention of coming back into the fold. The promised supply of doctors, nurses, teachers and technicians had not materialized, nor had the threat of secession by Kasai, yet another mineral-rich province, been averted. In the UN, accusations and recriminations along regional power-political lines were hurled across the floors of the General Assembly and the Security Council by the most vitriolic orators in pungent rhetoric. And as the debate deteriorated into weary adjectives and over-hackneyed phrases, I sat listening to the heated vocabulary of abuse being aimed at the protagonists: 'lackey', 'pawn' and 'stooge of colonialists and imperialists' were regularly thrown around. There was little relief from the rhetoric on the rostrum, and it seemed to me, sitting in the gallery, that the audience seemed to welcome the slightest sign of mere oratory or any compelling thought.

Although Congo had been formally admitted to the United Nations, the dispute raged as to which faction should take the allocated seat in the third row of the chamber.

Chief contender for the role was the thirty-two-year-old Foreign Minister Justin Bomboko, representing the splinter government of

President Kasavubu against a rival left-wing Kanza. He told me of a legend among his Mongo people, that when God created the earth he forgot the sun. A fly nestled under the wing of the eagle to give him good council. After many trials and adventures, the eagle, still with the fly tucked under his wing, came back to earth with the sun; when, finally, Bomboko obtained the coveted place for his country and returned to the Congo with his President Kasavubu, it was indeed with a bit of the sun which radiated from him.

Meanwhile, surely no foreign minister in the history of twentieth-century politics had been burdened by a trickier assignment. Medium in build, light coloured and lithe, Bomboko walked with an elegant, rather mischievous jauntiness and an air of bewildered detachment. The 6,000 miles which kept the events of the Congo far away from deliberation presented him with a big problem and exposed him from moment to moment; he had to be at the ready for any surprise, that could either topple his position, or set him up as leader of his government. In his heavy pig-skin gold-engraved briefcase he carried a message from his president which had still been unread in open forum. I admired the way he somehow maintained the greatest statesman-like composure, the tact of a unique diplomat in the seething centre of warring factions and would-be friends. He was also a remarkable source of information for me, with a cynical view of the myth of African solidarity which exposed that Ghana and Guinea were not averse to prolonging the chaos in a prospering 14-million strong nation.

Once again, I was drawn into the Congolese upheaval. I became his informal interpreter and provided him with information about events to which he had no access; he in return kept me informed of in-depth factors, motivations and personalities at the centre of the dispute. One of the sixteen who had managed a higher education under Belgian rule, he was a graduate in primitive sociology, history and ethnology from the Université Libre de Brussels and was well-versed in philosophy and French classics. Throughout these harassing days he was patient and thoughtful and a good companion. At a penthouse restaurant where I had reserved a table for us, we were refused entry when the staff came face to face with my companion. Bomboko spared my fury and embarrassment by suggesting that no one would bother us if we dined in my flat where we could order in food. As a precaution, and to his dismay, I asked my brother, visiting at the time from Newcastle, to join us and we feasted on Chinese takeaway. Bomboko's present of a miniature rain forest meticulously replicated by a local florist was the only gift I kept of the many that arrived at my door.

With my adrenaline running high, I rushed out each morning at dawn to buy the *New York Times* from the stands on First Avenue, to catch up on the latest news in the saga of Leopoldville, Stanleyville and Katanga, and sat late at night and weekends through highly charged meetings in the Security Council, feeling quite affronted by the rude, confrontational dialogue between educated and well-bred men.

From the press gallery, I listened day and sometimes all night to the big powers struggling for domination of the newly independent giant in the heart of Africa. Within the framework of democratic procedure and parliamentary probity, the greed and acquisitiveness was undisguised. The pretext was ever the shady mission of restoring world order. Overseeing the proceedings, only their heads and shoulders visible behind the green marble dais, were the three wise men who looked like impassive judges arrayed up there, under the sloping organ-piping walls which merge into the dome with its imposing strength of a Gothic cathedral. In the centre sat Secretary General Dag Hammarskjöld, a mild-mannered genius with iron resolve who between sessions was flying back and forth from Africa unsuccessfully attempting to mediate and reconcile the warring parties. The year in which he was to be the target of a great UN-wrecking campaign by the Soviets had already been launched by their chief deputy, Zorin, with his shrill accusations of betrayal, partiality and neo-colonialism. The secretary general absorbed it all with extraordinary even-mindedness and the fortitude of an international civil servant.

It was three days earlier, in a chance encounter on Madison Avenue, that Justin Bomboko had stammered out the news of Lumumba's murder. He was deeply distressed and agitated and seemed at a loss at what needed to be done and begged me to help him. I was shattered, as much by the brutal death of a freedom fighter whom I had met and for whom I had great respect, as for the fact that a

195

minister of a great country in the heart of Africa knew of no procedure or precedent in such an event and was left stranded, having to seek advice from a newspaper reporter on how to act. I could only offer to consult the wires for news from Leopoldville and advised him to cable the coup leader for instructions. He and his inexperienced young colleagues had no mission base or administrative staff and were operating out of a hotel room. Was there a protocol, I wondered, in the event of the betrayal and murder by his own people of a revered leader, who not many months ago had proudly led his government through independence and onto the world stage?

Even in the shocked delegates' lounge, the information was scanty. Lumumba had been arrested on the orders of Mobutu, the incumbent leader, and with the connivance of the Belgians, sent into Katanga where he would be ambushed by his arch enemy, Moise Tshombe; it was a death sentence. It had been common knowledge that there was a murky CIA plot, endorsed by its head Allen Dulles, to eliminate Lumumba by lacing his toothpaste with poison. But before they could commit this ridiculous outrage, Lumumba's compatriots and the single-minded Belgians had done the deed for them. From his bloodied appearance it was clear that he had already been tortured in the prison in Leopoldville, and must have been aware of his fate, for he had penned this message to his wife: 'I prefer to die with my head unbowed, my faith unshaken by my profound trust in the destiny of my country.'

On 17 January, at dead of night, in a summary execution, an officer in the Belgian army fired the bullet that killed him. They buried him in an unmarked grave and later destroyed his body in sulphuric acid. His proud belief was misplaced. Civil war, poverty and destruction ensued under the military rule of the self-glorifying Mobutu, and the problem of the Congo has yet to be resolved to this day.

There had been little free time in those heady crisis days. When summer came, it was a relief from the scorching heat to go on weekend outings to Jones Beach and East Hampton. I had finally left the Arizona in the spring, and together with my friend Jeanette from my Bloomsbury days moved into a flat-share with Dimitri Nabokov, the son of *Lolita* author Vladimir. It was an end-of-lease arrangement on E 56th Street; Dimitri had already made a name for himself as an opera singer at the Scala and would be moving soon to Milan. He was tall and good-looking and entertaining company. Father and mother Nabokov dropped by to visit. Ironically, I thought, my sweet, waiflike little Russian friend was not unlike Lolita, the twelve-year-old nymphet heroine travelling around America with an elderly European intellectual in the novel which had so stirred the literary world. For all his notoriety, Vladimir was a mild-mannered, heavily accented, ironic, unassuming man, deeply caring about his son on his visits. An unfortunate car accident on a double date with Dimitri had left me with a broken nose and a whiplash injury to my cervical spine for which, against my wishes, Dimitri and his friend claimed compensation. After many months, innumerable X-rays and meetings with lawyers I was eventually awarded $1,000, most of which was invoiced by the lawyer.

It had become imperative now to live on my own, and properly, what with my burgeoning social life connected with the UN. On 16 September, one day before the beginning of the General Assembly, for the first time in my hotel-dwelling past, I had signed a three-year lease on an apartment on E 58th Street. It was the front half of a ground floor in a town house not far from the East River and within walking distance of both the office and the UN. I furnished it with a sofa bed and some armchairs bought from the Red Cross depot. It was basic, but sufficient for my immediate needs.

Soon after I moved in, I was in bed one midnight when I was awoken by a loud banging on my front door. Unnerved the previous evening by a face poking through my window mouthing lewd words, I took cover under the duvet. The knocking grew more frantic and a voice begged me to open the door. I looked through the peephole; outside stood a man, stark naked under an open raincoat and clutching a Siamese cat under his arm. What could this man be doing without clothes at midnight outside my door? He explained, shivering, that he was my neighbour on the ground floor, that as he had put out the trash for collection Augustus the cat had run out after him and that the door had slammed shut. His wife was in Chicago visiting her parents. I opened the door, draped my raincoat over him and there we sat, until the superintendent unlocked his apartment the next morning. According to the law of unintended consequences, we became friends and remained so, even when he and his wife – and Augustus – moved to a larger apartment.

By mid-September, the streets were buzzing with the arrival of presidents and prime ministers from Europe, Asia, Africa and Latin America, who were to take up residence in Manhattan with their entourages. The city had not seen anything like it in its history. The international flurry had begun when Soviet leader Nikita Khrushchev declared his intention to head his delegation to the 15th Session of the annual UN General Assembly. It was a signal for the leader of every self-respecting country not to be left out. Macmillan, de Gaulle, Nehru and Nasser, Haile Selassie and Tito were just some of the luminaries descending on Manhattan. Soon, their presence in the city was felt by traffic-halting sirens screaming ahead of the galaxy of political stars. An army of security officers and the NYPD choreographed the passage of limousines, which whizzed back and forth and up and down on the city's arteries. On the UN Plaza, new additions to the flagpoles strained against the breeze whipped up from the East River.

The 15th Session opened on one of those balmy end-of-summer days. Suddenly, the air was cool after the suffocating heat and the city could breathe again under a clear cloudless azure sky. I decided that Paris, Jerusalem, London and Rome are made for eternal spring; fall belongs to New York alone. At the entrance of the UN, chauffeurs leaped out and opened car doors to delegates in orange kente cloths, peacock blue boubous, loose kurta pyjamas, saris, dhotis and desert robes, which were briefly reflected in the glass of the revolving door before disappearing on the rolling escalator up to the carpeted landings of the assembly floor. The French West Africans appeared gloriously attired in hand-woven cotton kentes draped over one shoulder, over starched white under-robes in embroidered brocades and satins, strolling on the soft carpets in pointed white moccasins. From the Gulf states, the men wore the clothes of their desert habitat. They were mostly tall and superb and clearly delighted to meet their fellow delegates on this world stage. New Yorkers muttered about the paralysis of their mobility, caused by streets barred for the comings and goings of fleets of delegates' limos, and yet were enthralled by these exotic foreigners in fancy dress. Senior news correspondents came from the Washington bureau and the White House to boost coverage, accompany the president, and assess the Soviet position.

In the words of the assembly's president, Frederick Boland, the stage was set for what turned out to be 'the greatest and most momentous diplomatic gathering in history'. I listened transfixed in the press gallery as the wolves tore into the flesh of the half-defunct Congo, to which the West was desperately trying to hang on, in order to prevent the fifteen newly-independent African states from falling under the shadow of the hammer and sickle, while Khrushchev was trying to harvest the pickings. The stakes were high, the agenda far-reaching; the UN's role was debated in a spirit of bitter division in which the seeds of criticism were planted and exploited with tireless reiteration by the Soviets and their satellites.

I quickly assimilated into the system which drove the whole UN operation. The debates on disarmament, national integrity and the dismantling of the colonial empires had little impact on the ground. Resolutions were passed but rarely adhered to. In the daytime sessions, the speeches ran their course and were rarely more than window dressing, but the *real* business was transacted and kept on the boil outside the chamber. The wheels of international affairs were more likely to be set in motion at informal gatherings.

Key speeches followed well-rehearsed policy lines. Eisenhower pleaded non-interference in Africa and long-term development aid. Khrushchev's theme on disarmament without inspection and the destruction of nuclear stockpiles was met unequivocally by Harold Macmillan. But the real Soviet blockbuster was the demand to dismantle the UN by replacing the Secretary General with a troika. Khrushchev quite bluntly demanded that Hammarskjöld do the right thing and resign.

Worn down by the vitriol of the Soviets and their satellites, I believe Hammarskjöld had prepared a speech to do just that, when I noticed that he suddenly left the dais. I followed him down the corridor and rushed to the bank of elevators, signalling to my photographer to follow me. There he stood, in a defining moment of the world organization, bent over the text in his hand. Before he disappeared into the lift, we shot an image of him which circulated around world publications, telling the whole story. Shortly after, he returned to his seat with his alternate speech and, in the most dignified and unforgettable manner, announced why he would continue in his task. 'It is a question not of a man but of an institution,' he said. 'I would rather see that office break on strict adherence to the principle of independence in partiality and objectivity than drift on the basis of compromise.' And in response to Khrushchev's 'We do not trust *Mr* Hammarskjöld' (neglecting protocol by omitting his rank) 'and if he himself does not muster up enough courage, we shall draw the necessary conclusion', the secretary general replied, very quietly and with finality, 'It is very easy to resign. It is not so easy to stay on. It is very easy to bow to the wish of a big part. It is another matter to resist. If it is the wish of those nations who have seen the organization their best protection in the present world, we shall do so again.' The loud applause when he finished drowned out the petulant Khrushchev, pounding his fist on his desk like a frustrated villain in a fairy tale.

But Khrushchev did not let up, accusing, maligning, at times cajoling and peevish. The heads of state and government kept a composed stand-off at his vaudeville performances, because of the immeasurable power and importance of the man. Later in the session, when a Filipino delegate challenged the attack on Western Imperialism by saying that the Soviets had swallowed the whole of Eastern Europe, I watched in disbelief, and the assembly gasped, when Krushchev removed his shoe from his foot and banged it on the table in front of him. To this day, his display had been disavowed in Russia; for them it did not happen.

I acquired an expertise at recognizing stories for my magazine and my boss Eldon trusted me as long as I provided pungent information and an occasional march ahead of the competition. I developed a stamina for lunchtime drinking at the delegates' bar, where discussion with relaxed and free-talking delegates provided not only background information but quite a few scoops. I had their confidence and their trust, which I never betrayed, and succeeded in getting more in-depth stories for the news articles in the magazine. It was a place of easy access; often I found myself in the company of Alistair Cooke and Jonathan Miller, who were absorbing the atmosphere for their own accounts of the activities. I typed up my reports, checked the articles in which my pieces were incorporated, and quite savoured the excitement on which I thrived. Official briefings to the press in the basement by an American employee of the UN merely commented on the business upstairs and revealed little. For the news stories, I rushed across town, trying to find access to world leaders in their quarters.

Not all visitors to New York were treated with respect, and there were unpleasant occurrences. I learnt from a bitter Marshall Tito that members of his entourage were kicked, insulted and attacked and the police were slow in coming to their aid. The African diplomatic corps were smarting under many hate letters and refusals of service in restaurants. A minor car accident in Harlem's tinkling nerve centre, when a Mercury car rammed a taxi, became a major diplomatic incident. The car was driven by Guinea's UN chief deputy delegate, a fact that he failed to convey to the cabbie who asked for his licence. A scuffle ensued in which the incensed ambassador lunged at the cabbie and the police were called. Since nobody could understand what the other was saying, the ambassador was allegedly beaten with heavy objects and unceremoniously taken to the police station. The misunderstanding and underlying racism was much exploited, and fuelled the movement for moving the UN to a location where strangers, particularly Africans, would be more considerately treated.

Fidel Castro's treatment caused particular upheaval. Not very welcome in the US since the revolution, he had gained legitimate access to New York via the back door of the UN. Since the cash-strapped Cubans, including their diplomats, were confined to Manhattan and only the Hotel Sherbourne downtown would accommodate them, Castro had no choice but to bring live chickens to his room, where he cooked them on an oil stove and fed them to his delegation. The New York press had a field day, and the Cubans were evicted. In a huge publicity display, the president of the assembly intervened, and alternative accommodation was found for them at the Hotel Theresa, which Castro provocatively called 'a humble hotel, a negro hotel in Harlem', and whose owners had no choice but to welcome the Cuban delegation. The press declared that the Cuban delegation was living in a brothel, and it was here that I interviewed Castro and Che Guevara as he was entertaining the staff of the Hotel Theresa, while Eisenhower was entertaining the rest of Latin America at the Waldorf Astoria, a juxtaposition not left unremarked by Castro.

Castro's moment on the world stage, delivered in the General

Assembly in Spanish and heard through earphones in translation, lasted for four and a half hours and was frequently interrupted by the partisan applause of countries with whom his uninhibited vitriol against imperialism resonated. In the clever oratory, delivered in an aggrieved, husky voice, he displayed a studied mixture of humility and aggression. He gave an overview of his country as a victim of geographical history and described the role the US played before the revolution and afterwards. A demagogue to the hilt, he swayed the majority of the audience of nations, and made the captive audience of Western-aligned countries squirm in discomfort. When he finally emerged smiling to applause, his khakis immaculate, he was unruffled and at ease as he returned to the Hotel Theresa, where I came face to face with him in a delightful encounter.

The other half of the comedy double act took place that night under a balcony in Park Avenue: Khrushchev was giving a press conference at his Park Lane residence, and we all scuttled uptown. It was dark, and he was standing on the illuminated balcony like some latter-day Romeo, obliging us with capricious answers to the questions we flung at him in Russian, fully aware that those fists he so comically flung around contained the power to set the world on fire.

On most mornings, engraved cards with crests arrived at the office inviting me to various parties, and I became accustomed to the lavish hospitality, whether on the Starlight Roof of the Waldorf, or in the ballroom at the Plaza. Nibbling exquisite national foods and canapés, holding a champagne glass which was never empty, it was an opportunity to grasp events through relaxed protocols and informal chat and to move around the representatives of their country, appraise the importance of their rank and their views, and by assessing their phraseology and intonation get a sense sometimes of what was brewing. History certainly was not made at cocktail parties, but many a deal was.

But I much preferred the private invitations to African High Life parties, spontaneously arranged in their residences. Under their tuition, I quickly learnt to dance a mixture of rumba and merengue, with lots of freedom of movement in between, to the drum-beat of the Latin American music. And so did young diplomats from all over the globe, for whom this became the prime entertainment after gruelling sessions in the UN.

202

Perhaps because he could not be seen talking to a Jew by members of the Arab League at the UN, Omar Adeel was my closet informant, and made up for their strict inhibitions in the warmth and intimacy of his apartment. He headed the Sudan delegation and was at the beck and call day and night of his personal friend Dag Hammarskjöld. Sometimes late at night after a harrowing session the UN, he would ring me and, dangling the tantalizing prospect of fresh inside information, invite me to his apartment. In the dark, I hurried to his glass-roofed penthouse high above Washington Square, where he welcomed me in a brocade dressing gown, so different from the double-breasted Savile Row suits with padded shoulders and pinched-in waists he wore by day, which betrayed his nostalgia for the British way of life. In his sumptuous apartment, the air was thick with the scent of balsam and exotic fragrances brewed for him by his grandmother, and hypnotic with the atonal wailing of the Egyptian torch singer Oum Kalsoum, which seemed to send him into transports of delight. His tongueless, scar-faced manservant moved silently in and out tending to our needs. No secrets would find their way from here – some barbaric punishment had seen to that.

Omar was tall and dark, and drifted restlessly around the corridors of the UN, picking up his feet as though walking barefoot on hot desert sand. He moved with ease among the delegates, with an almost military constraint on his taut, disciplined body. His trim moustache accentuated the smoothness of his dark face and the piercing brilliance of his eyes. Here in the privacy of his lounge he was relaxed, moving to the music as he briefed me on the discussion about the contest and the contestants. Talking of the Congo tragedy, he compared the Belgians leaving the Congo to the British departure from Sudan. Even as the Union Jack was lowered on the lawn of Government House in Khartoum, the stinging smell of burning wafted over as the departing British officials made sure every record and file was destroyed, leaving the fledgling government without any methods or system of procedure.

He was a Nubian, and his personal trajectory was no less dramatic; just before independence, he had broken the rebellion of the army and ferreted out the mutineers in the jungles of Juba. His brief for their prosecution and the twenty subsequent executions is still prescribed reading for students of criminal law. His mentor in London, where

203

he had trained as a policeman and where he had been called to the bar, was Hartley Shawcross, who would be the lead British prosecutor at the Nuremberg War Crimes tribunal. At dawn, I would creep back to my apartment, feeling I had left the pages of *The Alexandria Quartet* and its mysterious hero, Nessim, laden with privileged insights in power politics.

By December I was exhausted, and took to my bed with pneumonia. A huge bouquet arrived from the office with a card from Eldon inscribed: 'With best wishes to Miss Weltschmerz [world-weary] for a speedy recovery.'

21

Bay of Pigs 1961

On my thirty-first birthday in January, in freezing temperatures and falling snow, the forty-three-year-old John F. Kennedy took the oath of office as the 35th President of the United States. It represented, in the words of Norman Mailer, who had been heavily engaged in the campaign, 'America living a beautiful dream of itself'. With his impassioned oratory Kennedy lifted the tone of governance from the old, post-European style of the warrior Eisenhower. He also appointed to the UN a most civilized and approachable man, Adlai Stevenson, who, bitterly disappointed in his failed candidacy as president or even secretary of state, had agreed to support the new administration at the UN as chief delegate, and before long the new dynamic of government filtered through and made itself felt.

Hopes among the delegates ran high when Stevenson was appointed; at last they felt, here was a liberal, renowned for the eloquence, wit and integrity that had been noted through two presidential campaigns. But although his attitude to Lumumba's death had not been quite what was wanted, he showed himself a great friend of the newly independent nations. I attended many functions where, in the intimacy of a small ambassadorial flat, he would sit comfortably on a pouf, eating native foods and acquainting himself utterly with African history and customs. His interest was found to be great, his attentions flattering: he received little gifts of tribal crafts and displayed them in the office of his delegation. Yet there was, and always remained, a pronounced personal antipathy that existed between him and the president, who never had the fullest confidence in his chief UN delegate.

Not long into his job, I sent a memo to my editor; a rumour was circulating around the bar in the delegates' lounge that Cuban émigrés were training in Guatemala and that a plot was being hatched to invade Cuba, replace Fidel Castro with their leader and re-establish a government friendly to the US. Devised by the Eisenhower administration, the plot committed Kennedy to proceed, reluctantly, it was said, while ultimately trying hard to distance himself from it. The plan was ill-conceived, and when indeed it took place was abysmally executed. The invading force, which included criminals condemned under the Battista regime, was unfit and badly prepared for the task. They had grossly underestimated the support the invasion would have from within Cuba, and the wily Castro, who had wind of the plan from Eastern-bloc agents, was fully prepared to repel the attack.

When the seven-ship armada dropped anchor in the Bay of Pigs, Castro's fully-fledged militia of thousands was lying in wait. The invaders were ambushed and routed. Of the nearly 2,000 US personnel captured, some were executed while others were imprisoned for thirty years. Kennedy was deeply shamed in the eyes of the world, despite asserting that the plot had been entirely hatched by the émigrés. The Soviets and their satellites and the Cuban delegation had a field day in the Security Council, and Stevenson was deeply embarrassed to fend off the verbal assaults.

By now, I was off enjoying *la dolce vita* in Rome, on a holiday I had long promised my mother, and from where I was to cross the Mediterranean to cover the trial of Adolf Eichmann in Jerusalem when he took the witness stand.

I had chosen the Hotel d'Inghilterra at the foot of the Spanish Steps for our rendezvous, for the romantic reason that Audrey Hepburn had recently made it her residence when filming *Roman Holiday*. It was elegantly old-fashioned and sumptuously appointed. The twin towers of the Trinita church overlooked the beautiful house, once inhabited by Keats and Shelley, and the Via Condotti, Rome's exclusive shopping street, was close by. Rome was a wonderful respite from the hothouse atmosphere of my New York existence. It was alive with exuberant living; the waters tumbled into fountains over cherubs and mermaids, beautiful people in dark glasses, bronzed, long-limbed, and clothed inventively, whizzed round on scooters. They were either mimicking the scenario of Fellini, or inspiring it.

My mother and I, too, were seduced into the social whirl on our first night together, at a party given by *Newsweek*'s bureau chief, Bill Pepper, and his wife Barbara, in their mansion on the Appian Way. I was fond of Bill. On a visit he made to New York during the Congo crisis, in the Epsteins' apartment where I was house-sitting, we shared our outrage at the politics of power, and the derisive way the Congo crisis was handled by what he called 'the tiny people'. Soon afterwards, he sent me *The Decisive Moment*, Cartier-Bresson's historic photographs of the world's tiny people, with its cover decorated by Matisse.

Their house was set back from the historic Roman road and was overhung by pines. In the soft evening air, the drone of cicadas provided the soundtrack and jasmine scented the air. In their marble hall, we were received by Barbara, a sculptor, extremely attractive in a fitted cream crochet dress, but on crutches with a broken leg. She was busy, coyly charming the princes of the Church, dressed in their robes and skull caps, their hands, when not holding glasses of champagne, tucked securely into their sleeves, by engaging them in animated banter. It was part of a campaign to obtain permission from the Church – which held the freehold – to add another storey to their house in the Trastevere. Judging by the drink-flushed faces of the cardinals, the response appeared to be promising. There were stars from the Cinecittà and other celebrities and aristocrats, milling around the elegant spacious halls partaking of exquisite Roman dishes. In the pervading climate, I suppose I was not surprised to see that even my mother was flirting uninhibitedly with a soft-tongued, silver-haired count. To my astonishment, they exchanged addresses and my mother invited him to Rectory Terrace.

On our tours of the city, however, my mother was unable to conceal her bad mood. She wondered why I was not married – was it because I was averse to men? – and whenever we sat down for coffee or a meal it ended with a discussion over tips. When it suited her, she was enormously generous, but she simply did not believe that either of us should leave gratuities for the waiter. She accused me of lavishly wasting my money and could not agree that this was misplaced frugality. It nearly spoiled what could have been an idyllic time together.

The stress continued to accompany us on our holiday on the Amalfi coast and in the hotel at Positano where the Peppers had suggested we spend time. I tried to humour her during the day, and after seeing her comfortably into bed I waited each evening to escape down to the sea with an admirer. Eventually, she, too was seduced by the little Mediterranean town tilting uphill from the shore, the narrow cobbled streets with their pastel houses and sloping rooftops flooded by the early spring sun. Our hotel was quiet, unpretentious, discreet and very beautiful. She enjoyed our excursion to the hilltop town of Ravello, favoured by recluse celebrities and feted by Richard Wagner (it became the setting for *Parsifal*), which we reached trundling uphill in a donkey cart, inhaling the scent of the lemons that weighed down the branches of the trees that lined the road. In the little village with its baroque church, we visited the Villa Cimbrone, poised on a ledge overlooking miles of the deepest indigo sea below, and watched diminutive white dots of sailboats floating dreamily past. I thought there could surely not be a more beguiling place on earth.

My mother wanted to see the house of Axel Munthe, a childhood hero. It was a boat-ride across the Bay of Naples from Sorrento to Capri, and a steep climb to the top of a hill. Here was the house of the eccentric Victorian Swede who, at the turn of the century, made it the home for his collection of Etruscan, Roman and Egyptian bits of sculpture and exotic plants. It had spectacular views, and we photographed each other leaning on the head of the Medusa, the bust of the Emperor Tiberius and the Egyptian Sphinx.

I was ready to end this idyll and continue my journey to Israel. I dispatched my mother on her annual trip to Munich to consult her doctors, and spent two days in Rome, in the hope of a briefing from Bill, who had covered the beginning of the Eichmann trial in Jerusalem. At the airport the next day, Bill finally returned my call and I discovered why I had been unable to reach him. He was furious that our editor had omitted to inform him that I would be replacing him in Jerusalem, which he felt was his territory. His anger was directed at our boss, but I had been placed in the middle and felt badly that my assignment could stir up such rage. I was afraid it might be the end of our friendship, but before he ended our conversation he graciously wished me good luck.

22

The Eichmann Trial 1961

In Tel Aviv, I booked into a small hotel by the beach and took a taxi to the home of my Israeli pianist friend, Nathan Mishory. At No. 130 Rothschild Boulevard, his mother opened the front door. Recognition replaced shock and she greeted me warmly, inviting me into the living room where the family were celebrating the end of Shabbat. They offered me wine and sweetmeats but there was a strange awkwardness, and I could not help noticing the meaningful looks which passed between them. Mrs Mishory had told me that Nathan was attending a concert down the road and, unnoticed by me, she slipped out to break the news of my arrival and pluck him out of the performance. Very soon, Nathan appeared, speechless and breathless. Silently, the family disappeared into a back room, leaving us alone. In the most tragic and touching walk of my life, Nathan accompanied me to my hotel. He began by telling me how, in the Debussy opera *Pelléas et Mélisande*, Mélisande had celebrated her illicit love for Pelléas by taking off her wedding ring and tossing it high into the air, from where it fell into a deep well. It was his way of telling me that on hearing of my arrival he, too, had taken off and nearly lost his wedding ring, which had been placed there two months ago on his wedding day.

My happiness for him was tinged with relief; he still seemed too much attached to me. He remained the person most attuned and sensitive to my needs who understood me and whom I understood best, and we talked many hours through the night. I did not meet his new wife; she was in New York for medical procedures.

Next day I left for Jerusalem. The journey as ever and always was moving beyond the describing of it; no one could travel along this road and remain unaffected. The trees, now grown, gave cool shade, the rusted hulls of armoured vehicles from the battle for Jerusalem still littered the highway. After an absence of nearly a decade, I was happy to be here, to feel at home, to feel I should never have left.

I learnt from talking to everyone I met that the capture and trial of Adolf Eichmann after years of dedicated hunt by the Simon Wiesenthal Holocaust Centre had convulsed Jerusalem. Every day, the *Jerusalem Post* unflinchingly printed the harrowing court testimony from witnesses and survivors, as they recounted the untold horrors instigated and carried out by the monster encased in glass before the court. Old festering wounds were newly disturbed and could never be healed. I could feel the depression everywhere on the streets, in the hotel, in taxis and shops.

The event of his abduction from Argentina in May 1960 had impacted on the world in triumph, but had also caused international controversy. Hauled before the Security Council, Israel's Foreign Minister Golda Meir could only fend off censure by asserting that the kidnap had been carried out by 'private individuals', not by the State of Israel. In the Knesset, unrestrained applause and a standing ovation greeted Prime Minister Ben-Gurion when he had made his announcement.

At dawn on 19 June, my eyes scrunched up against a blinding khamsin, I showed my credentials to a crack security guard standing sentinel under a cypress tree outside Beit Ha'am, the town hall where the trial was to take place. The wind swirled around, hot and unnerving, and was getting under my skin and into my pores.

Inside, I found a place among the two hundred and fifty writers and newspaper people charged with broadcasting the trial worldwide. The gallery was packed with skull-capped, side-whiskered Chasidim, brawny kibbutzniks in shorts and sandals and little old ladies in babushkas, rocking to and fro on the edge of their seats in traditional prayer movement. They had queued up from dawn in the Russian Compound to obtain entry to the trial. High up on a raised wooden dais sat the three judges: Moshe Landau of the Supreme Court of Israel, Judge Benjamin Halevy of the Jerusalem District Court and Judge Yitzhak Raveh of the Tel-Aviv District Court. The indictment was filed by Gideon Hausner, who headed the prosecution team.

Eichmann's day had come, and he was prepared. For weeks, I was told, he had sat, a faceless mask unmoved by the worst testimonies, impervious to the palpable smell of burning flesh evoked by witness after witness, each fighting for self-control. At 8.30 a.m., flanked by two guards, Adolf Eichmann bowed his way into the glass box and lowered himself into his seat facing the microphone. A shudder hissed through the auditorium.

He was semi-bald, wearing a neatly pressed suit; such a small, insignificant man, so shatteringly ordinary – 'The banality of evil', to use Hannah Arendt's phrase. Very little of his face appeared beneath his oversized black glasses and the earphones which covered his ears. Fidgety and nervous, he tried to shift into a position to adopt his well-rehearsed attitude. His mouth was working all the time and his tongue kept rolling round his toothless upper gums. Speaking into the microphone in a voice chillingly accented like Hitler's, he placed his hand on the New Testament. There were gasps in the court when he elected to swear by God. Was it to the God in the Psalm of David 'to whom vengeance belongs'? But, incredibly, by God he swore, repeating after his counsel, Robert Servatius: '*Ich schwoere zu sagen die Wahrheit, die ganze Wahrheit und nichts als die Wahrheit, so wahr mir Gott*' – the truth, the whole truth, and nothing but the truth. And it was by the people of the God of the Jews that he was to be tried, and by the spirit of my grandmothers, who had also invoked God on their way to the gas chambers.

Opposite him, the witness stand was silent now, haunted by the ghosts of those who had recounted the most shattering events ever to have filled the pages of human suffering. Eichmann looked straight past it and addressed himself directly to Servatius and the three judges. His sense of correctness seemed predominant in his psyche: whenever the guard on his right took his scribbled note to Servatius, he made a point of saying thank you; if the guard left too hurriedly, he called him back to express his thanks.

His language was clipped, with its Viennese inflexion and Nazi-clique jargon, and he seemed eager to get on with the business at hand. From the first moment the silence was filled by that voice, we all listened in stunned disbelief. He might have been going over the company accounts. Having established his fluency, his confidence increased and he was clearly at ease. Occasionally, deferring for permission from the court, he sat down and referred to a large pile of manila folders, from which he systematically searched out the one he required. Time had rolled back for Adolf Eichmann, twenty years had vanished, and he was quite, quite in his element. He was methodical and meticulous – in the same way as he had organized the attempted annihilation of the Jewish people.

Defence Counsel Servatius, dressed in a blue-green Italian-cut suit, his corpulent neck rolling over the collar of his tie-less shirt, conducted the cross examination. He claimed that the testimony was irrelevant, attacked the submitted documents on grounds of dubious authenticity, produced counter documents and ignored the agonizing evidence of the past several weeks. Eichmann was, he said, only following orders.

At the end of each day I was drained. Not even the companionship of colleagues at the bar of the King David Hotel could eradicate from my thoughts the events of the day and the person at the centre of it.

I heard that Eichmann's nightly routine was scribbling notes for the court to substantiate his plea of innocence according to the spirit of the law. There was a rumour that he was cracking up, although an electric cardiogram had proved otherwise. The defence had no wish to prolong the proceedings; their kitty was empty, according to Eichmann's assistant Wechterbruch. In fact, their blonde secretary admitted to me that they were really out of funds – she just about had her fare home. The trial continued each day in an atmosphere of unquestionable dignity, the etiquette respectful of best Anglo-Saxon procedure. But for us Jews, this was Pharaoh on the witness stand, and with it, 2,000 years of history were reversed, a reminder of the persecution and the helplessness of being hunted into exile and destroyed.

I was not alone in wanting the whole experience to end. The Israel Symphony Orchestra was impatiently awaiting the dismantling of the courthouse in order to harvest the microphone, and the post office needed to reclaim its sole telex machine from the building. Eventually, on 11 December that year, Adolf Eichmann was found guilty, his request for appeal was turned down and his plea for mercy to President Ben-Zvi rejected. He was hanged, cremated and his ashes dispersed over the Mediterranean Sea. At last he had the macabre satisfaction of realizing his proud boast: 'I will leap into my grave laughing because of the feeling that I have five million human beings on my conscience, which is a source of extraordinary satisfaction.'

My optimism and enjoyment of the country and its people returned when, as a guest of the government, I joined a Paris-based Japanese journalist on a trip to the Negev desert, travelling in a silver jeep with an armed convoy. We were to observe the construction of the flat road, dynamited out of the alluvial hills, which would serve as one of the major lines of communication from the Dead Sea at Sdom to the port of Eilat and the Far East. The work that day had come to a standstill in the 127 degree heat, the hottest day since there were Jewish settlements, and the men, sixty of them, were resting in the compound, listening to the monotonous wailing of Oum Kalsoum. The Israelis called it affectionately Tokyo Road, and it was almost complete.

On my return to Jerusalem, I fulfilled a promise to myself and drove to my kibbutz in Sasa, where I was received back as one of the family. For me, after seven years' absence, it still seemed one of the most exciting spots on earth. The children had turned into sturdy adolescents, the fruit trees I had helped to plant were heavy with cherries, apples and peaches, and the cyclamen and anemones, covered the mountains and valleys in a blanket of colour, leaving me wordless with wonder.

I returned to Jerusalem on my last evening for a final farewell. I had supper on the terrace of the King David Hotel, and as I looked across beyond the barbed wire, I wondered with yearning when I would be able to set foot in the City of David. For now, the red kefiyas of the Arab League peered out in triumphant possession, and I could only marvel at the sun glinting on the pink stone and the cypress trees waving in the evening breeze.

23

Ivory Coast 1961

Big changes had occurred when I returned to New York. In September Philip Graham, the hyperactive but charismatic publisher of *The Washington Post,* and a close friend of the president and his circle, had acquired *Newsweek* magazine and created a great deal of euphoria when he breezed through the office. He had installed his very own inspired troika of editors under Osborne Elliott: Kermit Lansner was a cultured former professor of philosophy, who could be heard in the late afternoons listening to Beethoven's last quartets in his office; Gordon Manning had a vast background in news management and an acute sense of humour. They soon earned the soubriquet of The Flying Wallendas, because of the daring and successful way they juggled news. Ben Bradlee from the Paris bureau, whose former neighbour and friend in Georgetown was President Kennedy, was transferred to *The Washington Post.*

Newsweek entered a new and dynamic era. No changes occurred in the attitude to or promotion of the female staff, however, but the new team were encouraging of my dedicated reporting and appreciative of the flow of information, my profiles of the big players in the news and my story suggestions, which were acknowledged as being resourceful and contributing to the immediacy and depth of published articles. I had also come to understand the political power-bloc structure and voting patterns and through my personal contacts could obtain at any time an interview for them with any UN or political figure.

The UN Assembly was nearing its end, but not before a wrangle over the passage of a resolution condemning the invasion of Cuba which took place at the ninety-nine-nation committee. Four resolutions were entering their final debate. I noticed the complacency among the Western nations and Latins filing into the committee room after dinner and various receptions, assured that the mildest, most anaemic of the resolutions would pass with a comfortable majority. But it was clear from the devious manoeuvres that the West could no longer speculate, even to the last, on the passage of their resolutions or the winning of their vote. The new countries of the world were stretching their muscles, and UN politics were becoming more unpredictable.

I sat for the next six hours in the press gallery, entertained with innumerable Arab proverbs and tribal anecdotes, startled by the loud invective and the ranting without context against Israel of the Saudi minister Ahmed Shukeiri, the threats and the unplanned features which were more entertaining than a Broadway show. The gallery was jam-packed and, interspersed with mink-wrapped ladies, equally represented by the pro-Stevensonians and the pro-Cubans who reacted with gasps of incredulity to the manoeuvring and haggling on the floor and who did not hesitate to root for their man, long and loud. It was a nasty meeting, full of personal vendettas. Zorin, the Russian delegate, fiercely attacked Adlai Stevenson. Communism, he said, produced real freedom and democracy, and was always thwarted by the West. No single delegation, he asserted, sustained the libellous accusations against the glorious Castro. Even the NATO countries had not fully supported the US. Stevenson defended the Cuban exiles in their 'right to choose'. He paid respect to their fight against the rule of the firing squad and ended by pronouncing the mantra which defined the US regarding the little island 90 miles from its southern shore: '[The] fortresses of tyranny may not fall at the first blow, but ultimately they will fall.' In defending the right to asylum, he quoted Karl Marx, who had sought freedom from oppression in England. The refugees, he said finally, are not 'the running dogs of imperialism'. He in his turn was applauded by his faction in the gallery.

The Cuban representative replied with a tribute to those fighting to retain the Cuban revolution, saying that the aspirations of the bands of pretenders trying to invade the Republic of Cuba were 'a bloody joke'. How can these puppets bring freedom to Cuba, he asked. He, too, received a wild ovation from the gallery and, it must be said, from the press.

At 2.26 a.m., two of the neutral nations which had remained

mostly passive, finally cast their vote. They had learnt the loopholes, and flexed their muscles to at least obstruct the policies of the Western world. In the last minutes, Sudan radically changed the resolution with an amendment, which required new instructions from respective governments and further debate the next day, and we could at last go home to bed.

The assembly finally came to an end, and I was able to spend my weekends in the country houses of my friends the Epsteins and my relatives in Mount Kisco. Days at the office often extended into drinks after work at the bar of the New Weston with the girls and writers in the office. My engrossing task was covering for my friend Gordon, a brilliant writer in foreign affairs, who had decided at the age of thirty-seven on yet another career change, to medicine. He had graduated from Harvard at sixteen, served in the army in Europe, then in the diplomatic corps as consul in Italy, and finally joined the CIA in South East Asia before becoming a writer. Switching to medicine was a daunting task which required a course in pre-medicine with undergraduates half his age, and daily attendance at lectures in Brooklyn College without attracting attention in the office. As in all the other tasks he set himself he succeeded here as well, and in the following year graduated to medical school in Philadelphia.

An invitation arrived in the last days of July 1961. It came directly from President Félix Houphouët-Boigny, requesting my presence at the celebration of the first year of Ivory Coast's independence. It was passed on to me by his chief delegate at the UN, Simon Ekra, and was summarily dismissed – *Newsweek* did not accept freebies and the occasion was not important enough to send a correspondent.

Everything changed when President Kennedy, aware of African nationalism as a political force, realised the urgent need by the US to support new leaders in the Third World as a way of combating and neutralizing communist influence.

So it came about that the attorney general was despatched to the independence ceremonies, and I along with him. I had little time to set everything in motion. I hurried to obtain my accreditation and insurance, and injections against yellow and all other fevers. I was handed a personal introduction to Robert Kennedy from Bill Bradlee, our Washington bureau chief, and from my UN friends I received letters to President Senghor of Senegal and Modibo Keita of Mali. I acquired a Baby Hermes typewriter, six reels of film and a few hundred dollars, with which to detour to Senegal and Mali on my way home. Bags were stuffed with air-cleaners, anti-snake-bite, DDT and my first full-length strapless gown since my college ball, and I set off for Paris on the first lap of my journey.

As never before in my Paris experience, I lived two nights in the four-star luxury of the Royal Monceau Hotel, with its classy history of residents, among others Eisenhower, Disney and Hemingway. From my room, furnished in the style of Louis XIV, I could see the Arc de Triomphe and at night dined amid marble-topped tables under crystal chandeliers.

At Le Bourget next day I boarded the VIP plane bound for Abidjan. Diamond-shaped red tags attached to my luggage set me aside for VIP attention and I sipped pink champagne and snacked on caviar canapés in the company of the Aga Khan, Mendès France and the president of Mauritania, who were sitting across the aisle. It was a far cry from the cross-channel ferries I used to frequent from Newhaven to Dieppe in steering class.

Sitting next to me was the young son of Houphouët-Boigny, returning from his studies in France, who entertained me with endearing bits of gossip about life in the family of the African leader. The air-conditioning offered a welcome contrast to the hot damp dripping airlessness I had left behind in New York. I was suddenly overwhelmed with the responsibility of representing *Newsweek* in Africa.

The bigger picture, which sent me on my way to Africa in the first place, was the recent and sudden cataclysmic collapse of France's two centuries of colonial rule and the birth of new nations formerly euphemistically named '*La France d'Outre Mer*' – 'Overseas France' – leaving them exposed to a frenetic competition between the great powers for influence and for access to their vast natural resources. After his tragic and unresolved humiliation in Algeria, President Charles de Gaulle realized that self-government could no longer be delayed. France retained all cultural and economic ties with their former colonies and with generous economic aid and all honours and respect conferred on their leaders on visits to Paris, it was clear to me now why France could always count on eleven votes on most issues in the UN.

When we landed, Abidjan was going wild on the eve of its great two days of celebration. The president, a small upright figure at the end of a red carpet, had come to greet his guests in person, while a brass band blasted out Viennese waltzes on the tarmac. Behind the surrounding fence, under a sky overcast with low black clouds, tam-tams beat out an eerier tune, while women in bright wax prints stood watching, and the waters of the lagoon, which nearly encircles the city, glinted in the remains of the light.

I was whisked off by a guide and driven to a skyscraper hostel vacated by civil servants for the visiting press. They handed me a little attaché case, a cornucopia containing a large bronze medal cast with the head of the president, an ivory paper knife, a timetable and invitations to every event, including meal tickets to restaurants. In my room, the bar was stacked with champagne, whiskey and more gifts of toiletries, and furnished with a telephone. Together with correspondents from *The New York Times*, the *Daily Express* and *Paris Match*, whom I met in the lobby, I was driven to a welcoming barbecue under the palm trees by the shore. A young boy was turning a whole sheep on a spit over charcoal embers, and I sat next to the host, the minister of information, with the result that my picture appeared on the front page of the local newspaper next morning. From then on, I was 'Miss *Newsweek*' to my colleagues and my hosts.

At the resplendent presidential palace next morning, Houphouët himself received the credentials of the invited guests. From the whole continent, from every nook and corner of Africa, they had come to celebrate yet another triumph over colonial supremacy. Here was the voting power in the UN, the nations who had to be wooed by East and West. Dressed in flowing tribal gold-embroidered pyjamas, djellabas, kente cloths and morning suits, they moved along slowly with patience and pride to shake the hands of the short man standing erect under a huge gilded glass globe chandelier. The fountains spurted water into a pool of bronze fish and the champagne flowed. Bobby Kennedy, who had been told to look out for me by our Washington bureau, took the opportunity to come over and invite me to the villa where he and his wife Ethel were staying for the week 'for a chat'.

I alone from the press was invited to a luncheon given by the mayor of Abidjan. I sat next to Tunisia's Information Minister

Masmoudi, a big player in Cold War politics. My colleagues had tried in vain to get close to him, and our conversation provided me with much inside information.

Down Abidjan's broad shaded avenues, with their sidewalk cafes and elegant boutiques displaying designer clothes, the cortège of limousines took the visitors to a march-past of the armed forces. The smartly turned-out columns of men and women on foot and on motorbikes could have been graduates from the French military academy Saint-Cyr. Houphouët stood to attention before a flag dipped in salute. Its inscription on the nation's colours read 'UNION DISCIPLINE TRAVAIL'.

Not surprisingly, the president had refused all interviews with the assembled press, but I had a deadline for my report and needed a quote for the magazine. So, I befriended a palace guard who told me where he would be and when. Sure enough, I was able to waylay the president and extract from him a comment of appreciation for Bobby's presence: 'After all,' he said wryly, 'he could have sent the vice president.'

That evening, I locked myself in my room to write my story. I typed 3,000 words, sifting out fact from the rumours which flourished among the guests at the feast. Then I ran to the post office to file my report, but the well-meaning but incompetent employee manning the telex scrambled my text and I had to start all over and type it out again under pressure to meet the deadline in New York. That night, I lost 2 kilograms in weight and pulled out three white hairs.

There was more to come, with a rustic outing to a picnic-banquet in the woods near the city presided over by the beautiful Therese, the president's wife. On the road, covered in red earth which had been sprayed with DDT, curious crowds were restrained behind barriers and leaned over to catch a glimpse of *'le petit frère du president'* – 'the president's little brother' – in his motorcade. On a platform, masked tribal dancers in straw skirts whisking horses' tails acted out legends, an extraordinary contrast with the sophistication of the guests. I used up all my rolls of film, overcoming the objections of the dancers, who feared I was taking away their souls.

At the long banqueting tables in the forest, local food arrived balanced on the heads of beautiful bare-breasted girls, to the delight and amazement of the 200 guests. A man on 12-foot stilts so enthused Bobby and Ethel, that they insisted he should come to America. He declined, saying he needed to attend to his crops. The party ended with a local saxophonist struggling through 'The Star-spangled Banner'.

That night, as a fireworks display lit up the sky over the entire city, a feast took place in the palace gardens. Everybody was turned out in evening gowns and white tuxedos and I wore my $28 ballgown from Macy's. The tables heaved with a buffet of delicacies flown in from Paris. I looked on in amazement as the former French administrators fell over each other in a most undignified scrum to fill their plates.

The celebrations ended with a spectacular parade, a march-past of Ivorian athletes, who were wildly applauded. Although Bobby seemed attuned to the relaxed protocol of Africa, he appeared on the stands in cutaway and top hat. It was his only sartorial error. When a crowd of excited Ivorians broke through the police cordon, and were being beaten back into line, Bobby calmly walked into the melee and started pumping hands. In the excitement, a small boy fell out of an acacia tree in his attempt to get near their special guest, but luckily was unhurt.

It was known in administrative circles that in my reporting at the UN, and especially on account of my fluency in French I had gained the trust of the African delegates and an understanding of their politics, for there could have been no other reason for my summons the next day to the villa of the local beer baron where the Kennedys and their entourage were staying. That the US administration could usefully quiz an inexperienced young reporter for information unavailable to their advanced systems of spying intrigued me. Bobby, surrounded by his retinue, sat relaxed in the lounge and did not get up when I entered. He was slight in build but looked muscular, with his pale blue eyes and shock of dark hair which he kept pushing out of his face. He was genial and chatty over coffee. Bobby's right-hand man, G. Mennen Williams, came swiftly to the point: in view of the large diplomatic presence of Eastern bloc countries in neighbouring Conakry (Guinea) and Bamako (Mali), who of my African contacts embraced communist ideals? My African contacts, despite their confidence in me, had more sophistication than to tell me their strategy in the Cold War and the scramble for its enormous natural resources. But in my simplistic way, I left them a little reassured; instead of naming any names, I told them that the Russians had sent aid in the form of snowploughs to Guinea and that the French remained on their plinths and were unlikely to be knocked down. More problematic, I felt, would be the risk of unrest among the forty ethnic groups which constituted the Ivory Coast and the need to achieve a common base for unity among the six major tribes.

At dawn next day, I joined a crew from *Paris Match* travelling to Yamoussoukrou, the president's ancestral home. Three miles into the bush, I had a glimpse into the occult world that seemed to begin where the city ended, the demons residing deep in the rituals of the animism that has remained with all but the urban population. When the men left the jeep to take pictures inside the dense woods that seethed with life, the driver begged me not to abandon him to these demonic forces. Unlike me, he said, he was not registered and would disappear without trace.

A little half-moon of people stood by the gate of the president's bungalow as our car drove up, with that static quietude of the African which seem to confuse existence with eternity. A woman suckled her baby; next to her, two musicians guarded the gate syncopating a plaintive note on the ram's horn with a beat on the drum. Opposite, little children were placing crudely carved ex-votos by the clammy banks of a huge pond, which lay so still under the menacing sky. I saw a crocodile thrashing the surface of the water before disappearing again below. A man in a palm-leaf straw hat was scanning the surface, shuddering. The villagers of Yamoussoukro, he told me, were at the mercy of the crocodiles, who had to be appeased with facsimiles of children, and all they could do was to invoke the ancestral spirits to keep them safe.

Policemen in khaki opened the low gates. In the courtyard we passed three generations of Houphouët's family and mounted the step to the bungalow. The president, dressed in a white silk suit, greeted us with enormous courtesy. He apologized for his wife's absence ('*Ma femme est très fatiguée*' – 'My wife is very tired') and invited us to accompany him to mass. In the white church with its lace-patterned stone walls, among the simmering excitement of the villagers, he knelt in silent devotion in his pew in front of the altar. A bespectacled young man in shirtsleeves played an untuned organ and two little black angels in sneakers tapped their feet to the rhythm while serving mass. To what image of a God Houphouët devoted his prayers remains a mystery. Having wrenched his kingdom from the white man, had he also inherited his God?

Prayers over, a smile of infinite kindness playing around his lips, he waved to the cheering crowd, '*Bao*,' he said, 'I am coming.' A young man turned to me and asked me whether he talked this way in Abidjan.

We returned to the bungalow and awaited his return. Inside, the room covered the whole area of the building. It was cool and dark with a decor reminiscent of the chateaux of France. Giant moths and salamanders were crawling up the plastered walls in the gaps between the Gobelins tapestries. The floor was covered in Moroccan carpets and crystal chandeliers hung from the ceiling. A gilded elephant and a marble Venus stood in the middle of the room. Beside the entrance door was the huge head in pure shining gold of Pokou, Queen of the Baoulé. Her lips were twisted in the agony of a gasp and a perpetual scream seemed to issue from her mouth. The president explained that she had saved her people, the Baoulé, by throwing her child into a crocodile-infested river when escaping her pursuers, a sacrifice which allowed her people to cross to safety when driven from the land of the Ashanti in the neighbouring kingdom of Ghana. It was clear Queen Pokou was close to the heart of Houphouët. He was seeking through her to restore to the Baoulé (one sixth of the population) a sense of their heritage, by grafting into his legacy a direct descendant of the queen, a mysterious little girl who had attended all celebrations seated on his wife's knees, which had caused much speculation.

Outside, the persistent sound of the tam-tams and the horn were still tapping on my nerves and made it difficult to hear the quiet voice of the president. He was relaxed and seemed happy. Yamoussoukrou was his Tara. He came here, he said, to ponder on any difficulties confronting him, and when he made his decisions here, they were all good.

In soft tones he responded to my questions with lengthy anecdotes about his mother, a habit which reputedly disconcerted French Prime Minister Guy Mollet when, in the gathering of the Council of

Ministers, Houphouët would digress endlessly with her wisdom. But he always resumed the main line of his discourse; his rootedness in the land, his peasant's intuition. Behind the strongly defined eyebrows, his brain was acute and unmuddled, the monotony of his voice perfectly controlled and almost hypnotic. At times it was difficult to hear against the enervating sound of the tam-tam which penetrated the room. Seeing my discomfort, the president explained that the message of the beat was essential for his villagers: 'be tenacious', it said, or *'j'y pense, donc j'y demeure'* – 'I think, therefore I persist.'

Houphouët was practising medicine in Dakar in 1944 when a delegation of fellow tribal chiefs summoned him to serve his country. Mourning the loss of his mother, his ten-year-old child and his only brother in the space of a year, he finally succumbed to the call. He organized the trade unions, abolished forced labour, and controlled the tribes. Called to the parliament in Paris with other African representatives, he absorbed the strategy and learnt the rules of the political game, with which he subsequently confronted his masters. He explained to me that he had chosen the elephant as the symbol of his people because the elephant is kind and hard working, but be careful not to wound him, for then he becomes fierce and violent and charges. As regards Africa, he was prophetic: he foresaw a crisis so terrible that 'we will be sorry colonization is over. And then those who come to our help as the real friends of our people will be our friends for always.'

It was time to attend the next ceremony, the Festival of the Sacrificial which was to take place across the compound near the eucalyptus tree, where many had died, sacrificed to their gods. I parted with a feeling of great admiration for this man who had brought independence and stature to his people, declined bloodshed of black or white, and still came to his village to settle disputes and land claims. When he came among them, brown tribal robes and sandals had replaced the white silk suit and Italian shoes. A path opened up among the women to receive him in their best *pagnes* and the men wriggled their toes and stretched their muscles in preparation for the continuous dances that were to begin in the afternoon. There was an invocation at the tree, and then the president walked back to his bungalow, stopping at the entrance to wave goodbye to me.

I was deeply moved when Simon Ekra, the UN delegate, brought me a farewell gift of a specially made wax print dress, of the kind worn by the women of Abidjan; it was another measure of African hospitality towards strangers, which I had experienced throughout my days in the Ivory Coast. I left for Dakar with a great feeling of warmth and attachment to this part of the continent. It is an enormously rich country, with water in plenty, trees and lush vegetation, coffee, cocoa and minerals, yet one could feel a great undirected energy, a pall of restive lethargy, where French artisans teach ancient native crafts of carving to the population and men are frightened to be left alone in the forest for fear of being eaten.

My travelling companion on the airplane to Dakar was the financial adviser to President Senghor. He had been a contemporary of mine in Paris as a student. At first, I declined his invitation to his house, and with the help of his driver looked in vain for an available hotel room. Not finding one, I ended up knocking on the door of his magnificent home, where he received me with delight and an 'I told you so!' The heat was blistering, but the house was airy, its outer walls of lace-patterned stone producing a flow of air. In the cool of the evening, his servants in attendance, we dined and talked and he told me most of what I needed to know about his country and its finances. In my bedroom that night, I had an accident leaning on the washbasin, which crashed to the floor. My host heard the commotion and appeared too soon on the scene to rescue me, as though he had anticipated the disaster, which left me no alternative but to spend the rest of the night in his room.

Next morning, he escorted me round his city. I looked with wonder at the women; their very walk proclaimed their pride in being the most beautiful women on the continent. They were tall, large-boned and stately and held their heads high. Their headgear accentuated the purity of their features and matched the colours of their full-length drapes.

On the instructions of my host, I took the ferry from the city centre to the tiny off-shore island of Gorée. It is only a twenty-minute ride, but it extends centuries into the dark ages of slavery, when hundreds of thousands of Africans in shackles were dispatched from there, the cellar with the Door of No Return into the unspeakable horror of the transit ships that took them to America. I descended between two winding staircases into a gloomy dank chamber. I could hear the mournful beating of the waves against the outside wall. A shaft of blinding light lit up a crudely fashioned hole, just big enough to push through a man, woman or child.

It was a terrifying reminder of the human toll, the greed and cruelty of the nations of Africans who sold their people to the highest bidders and sent them on their journey of terrible humiliation, suffering and death. Those who survived were the ancestors of my friends walking the streets of New York.

24

Death of Dag Hammarskjöld 1962

One crisp, clear, mellow autumn Monday morning, I was watching the workmen at the UN running around with coils of wire, installing the communications which would supply the 16th Session beginning that day, when an event occurred which dwarfed all others.

I was summoned to the press section; word had come to the twentieth floor at noon from Sture Linner in Leopoldville to Under Secretary General Ralph Bunche that a plane, thought to be that of the secretary general, had lost radio contact and wreckage had been spotted from the air. Could it be...? The news spread like wildfire. One by one the men and women from the press hurried in; we trooped from wire service to wire service, from the Associated Press on the fourth floor back to Reuters, to Agence France-Press and United Press Information on the third, trying to glean information. But it was on the twentieth floor, where the UN had its private cable line, that the scene was most poignant. Here, the under secretaries, among them the closest friends and collaborators of the enigmatic Dag Hammarskjöld, were poring over each letter as it was spat out, straining to see, hoping against hope. At 11.55 p.m., Reuters reported out of Ndola in Northern Rhodesia: investigators had reached the wreck and identified the bodies of the twelve dead. The secretary general was among them.

Hammarskjöld had been on his way to Ndola in a desperate attempt to negotiate a peaceful resolution with the fleeing Tshombe, in the belief that he could secure an end to the secession of Katanga on the strength of the entry into Elisabethville by UN forces. For some reason, the prohibition against night flights in Africa had been waived, which gave credence to the conspiracy theories.

226

As newsmen moved to their typewriters to break the news to the world, delegates started crawling into the delegates' lounge in stunned, slow motion. Through the glass windows the jagged outline of Manhattan's skyscrapers looked remote. In the landscaped gardens that reach down to the river, petals were falling from late flowering roses and workmen were gathering the fallen leaves. A coal barge glided soundlessly past up river. It was a pleasant and reassuring sight that contrasted with the surreal happenings inside the tall glass building. In the press room, the wrinkled, white-maned dean of the press corps, Max Baer from the *Neue Zürcher Zeitung,* tore out sheet after sheet from his typewriter, leaned his head on his hand and gave up, sighing 'I can't do it.' Hammarskjöld always saluted him on his birthday. In the secretariat, girls were carrying coffee trays with tears streaming down their faces. The UN flag now flew at half mast; all the other flags were lowered.

We were briefed in the basement conference room by the three under secretaries. Sitting at the huge round table used for committee business, Under Secretary Tovares went through the formalities in a choked voice, ending with: 'This is a tragic loss for the United Nations, for the cause of peace everywhere and for humanity.' Adlai Stevenson's message was brief and defined the man and his Herculean struggle: 'He was imbued with the spirit of the law and the law was the Charter.' In a reversal of roles, our usual sources began to interrogate the press for news; not wishing to show how little information was available, they collared us to find out what other delegates were thinking.

Secretary of State Dean Rusk led the signing of the book of condolences on the thirty-eighth floor. The Russians and their satellites were conspicuously absent from the line-up. They speedily defined their position: 'We Russians attack Hammarskjöld over the conference table; you imperialists, you assassinate him.' The Soviet colleague echoed with schadenfreude: 'If he had stepped down as so many nations had wanted him to, this wouldn't have happened!'

As the jittery world organization took stock of this event, national positions were taken and discussions with regard to appointing a successor began to be bandied about along predictable lines. It would take a long debate and much recrimination before a solution would be found. Nobody doubted that the plane had been sabotaged and an assassination intended. By whom, and for what purpose, remained a subject for conjecture and was never to be resolved with satisfaction.

Discussion now centred around the very future survival of the United Nations, the model of its constitution and on a successor to satisfy the East, the West and the neutrals. From his collaborators in the secretariat, the only comment was that there could never again be a man such as Hammarskjöld, with his genius and utter dedication and all the complex suggestions circulating were regarded as a series of boxed contingencies, one hanging on the other.

Barely two hours after the confirmation of his death, the chaos was making itself felt. So precipitous had been the decision to make this trip, that no deputy had been appointed, no sealed envelope left with instructions to carry on for him or sign letters and cheques. Ironically, it fell to the delicately poised under secretaries from Russia, the US and the neutrals to form a ready-made troika.

The Security Council met informally that night, and drafted a message to which the Soviets associated themselves with the condolences only, omitting to endorse the political capabilities of the late secretary general. We in the press gaped at their bad taste, but it seemed to me that to do so would be sheer hypocrisy.

Late into the night, delegates hung around the bar. Omar Adeel of the Sudan delegation slumped into an armchair in a corner of the lounge, the little table in front of him stacked with empty whiskey glasses. He had lost a personal friend. But I kept my distance, knowing that if I wanted insider information, I would have to journey to the Village that night, because sitting next to him was Omar Loutfi of the Arab League.

Next day, the assembly was forty minutes late in starting. The president stood up next to the empty seat beside him; the intake of breath was audible. After four minutes, it adjourned. Ostensibly, it was as a token of condolence that no business was transacted. In bald reality, everyone needed time and instructions from their governments before beginning the debate. And in the city, the name of Hammarskjöld was on the lips of every city official and every schoolchild. Every rabbi, beginning the poignant Kol Nidre service on the eve of Yom Kippur, made reference to his memory.

There was none of the excitement that usually sparked the opening day of the General Assembly. Delegates had arrived singly and had gone directly to the chamber. Mongi Slim the Tunisian, aspiring to high office, Habib Bourguiba, Adlai Stevenson in a shiny dark grey suit, Zorin looking composed, serene and less bad tempered than usual. Only Sir Patrick Dean of England wore a black tie, and the Ghanaian dandy Kenneth Dadzie had one stuffed into his pocket from where it peered out. When Israel's Foreign Minister Golda Meir arrived with a little old lady, her sister, on her arm, she was asked for her pass by the guards. She was very gracious about it and had a wry look on her face as she proceeded upwards on the rolling escalator.

After much behind-the-scenes activity, a ballot was held for presidency of the assembly, and the winner, Mongi Slim, a small, ambitious and vociferous Tunisian, was unanimously elected to the post, the first African to be so. He had prepared his speech, and had a trick with his voice, so that it could drop in compassion or rise in accusation. When introducing the eulogies, he brought the Swedish ambassador Mrs Roessel to the rostrum with words which brought sobs to his audience. When the eulogies were done, he used his latter voice to summarily launch an attack on the French, the Portuguese and the South Africans. This was Mongi, allegedly the peacemaker, fulfilling his tacit promise to the Afro-Asians, and he instantly received an angry response. The next day I challenged him on this. In his nasal voice, and rolling his 'r's in his adopted French, he defended his acceptance speech, saying he was fully in his rights in the spirit of the resolutions in what he had said.

There was a celebratory reception in honour of President Kennedy that Friday, brought to the rostrum of the UN by the tragic death of Hammarskjöld, and standing next to him in the receiving line of UN executives was Mongi Slim. I watched Golda Meir stopping to reminisce with Kennedy about their previous meeting in Boston. As she moved forward in the line and stretched out her hand to Mongi Slim, he abruptly turned his whole body away, his hands anchored by his side. It was a subtle gesture, unnoticed by most, but unstatesmanlike and untenable in his capacity as the newly elected presiding entity over ninety-nine nations, who had pledged in his acceptance speech to 'endeavour to preside over your work with all the necessary impartiality and in strict fulfilment of the rules'. *Newsweek,* first in reporting this snub, created a stir. Slim's candidacy as successor to Dag Hammarskjöld was never mentioned again.

When I discussed the event a few days later with Mrs Meir she said, 'I wondered what he was going to do. But I thought that even if the words choked him, he would have to say something in his role as president of the assembly.' I had gone to find out from the foreign minister of Israel what her reaction was to this most undiplomatic slight. She was very restrained: 'We've been used to their rudeness in the last thirteen years,' she said, 'But after his acceptance speech I thought that he would try to overcome this tendency. After all, he is not acting as a Tunisian; he is the presiding entity over ninety-nine nations.'

Golda Meir had received me in a large, sun-filled apartment, high up in Exeter House Hotel. Below, Central Park South looked like a model toy city with tiny mechanical cars catching the sunlight. Packets of cigarettes and boxes of matches were strewn around and newspapers covered the chairs. She spoke quietly, her oversized features crinkling up into deep ridges around her nose, and at times her eyes would light up with a smile. In the event of Slim's becoming secretary general, she said, Israel would be cut off from the secretariat. She added: 'How impossible it would be to discuss our problems with a member of a nation sworn to destroy us. The uncertain peace in the Middle East would be gravely compromised. We would not protest. But we would act as the circumstances dictated.' U Thant, on the other hand, who headed the Burmese delegation, and was the first Afro-Asian statesman to pay an official visit to Israel, would be acceptable to her country, she said.

Of the eighteen items on the agenda, the most important was the review of the Charter. It represented the United Nations' most desperate fight for its life in its entire history, with the Russians pursuing their insistence on the troika, and the newly independent countries feeling the Charter had lost its efficacy. The most contentious debate of all would be the abolition of the veto, which, in its present form, represented a paralysis of all executive action. It also involved a split in the Western Alliance, with Western European powers no longer considering the US as leaders in all political initiative. Other major matters under discussion were the status of Berlin and the admission of Red China to the UN.

But first, the necessity for a replacement of the secretary general had become crucial. No one wanted to take the risk of jeopardizing an early appointment, since the Congo was once again on the point of exploding over the Katanga succession. Bomboko, convinced that a ceasefire with Katanga would endorse its right to statehood, insisted that jungle-trained Congolese forces were best placed to attack Katanga on its western border, if only they would be provided with the jets, transports and equipment to bring Katanga into submission. They would prefer to do this through the United Nations, since the US and the USSR were in agreement on this issue; for this to succeed, however, France and the UK must be persuaded to withhold their veto. Instant executive mandate was required.

Discussion, debate and bargaining took place in caucuses behind closed doors. The UN was turning on itself in a tedious process full of petty disputes and points of order. Since the withdrawal of both Mongi Slim and Irish Frederick Boland from the running, U Thant had become the only compromise choice, and it remained for him to make his position clear and to state under which conditions he would accept. The method of his election, whether by the Security Council or General Assembly was in contention, but since no government wanted to be responsible for rejecting a possible solution in view of the calamity that would ensue, U Thant was finally appointed in November in the Security Council to fill the unfinished term of office as temporary secretary general of the UN. The General Assembly could again proceed with its business.

A great camaraderie had evolved among like-minded correspondents of all nationalities during these anxious and engrossing days and nights. Often, we pooled information and pointed each other to new leads. Having more access to sources than some foreign correspondents, it was a matter of course for me to pass on material surplus to *Newsweek*'s needs to colleagues and to receive insights from their areas of interest. Sometimes, after a turbulent session, after everyone had filed or broadcast their copy, we would end up at Jewish author and Holocaust survivor Elie Wiesel's flat on Riverside Drive. He was reporting for Tel Aviv newspaper *Yedioth Ahronoth*. We were joined by Tommy Lapid of *Maariv* and Shmuel Almog of Kol Yisrael. The interior of the apartment was green, the same green as everywhere in Upper Manhattan, and sparsely furnished. He cooked spaghetti and served us red wine by candlelight, and afterwards, as we sat cross-legged on the floor in a circle, came the singing.

Elie started it, his voice tense and deep, his dark eyes shut, as he led and transported us in the old Yiddish songs of his youth, before it was taken from him. His singing expressed the agony and the abomination of all he had experienced and when he sang '*S'brent, Bruederlein, s'brent*', he left me beyond tears.

As a child in his shtetl in Transylvania, he had been steeped in the study of the Talmud and the mysticism of the Cabal; in the death camps of Auschwitz and Buchenwald he discovered absolute evil. Before his eyes, the black clouds of smoke rose from the ovens where his mother and beloved little sister had been thrown. He had witnessed the hanging of a child, a little angel in chains, and his own father's agonizing death. He searched for but could not find the God of his faith and, like Christ, cried out for an explanation. To François Mauriac, who befriended him in his Parisian days, Wiesel was '*l'enfant juif crucifié*'.

Elie brought to my apartment a present of his first book, *Night*, but I found myself unable to read it and hid it deep in a corner where it would not stare at me reproachfully and remind me of its heart-stopping content. He had waited ten years to write it. Even now, when we knew each other, he had not resolved his quarrel with God or with man. Nor had he regained his desire to live, or restored his belief in humanity, history, literature or religion. Even among friends, he rejected all intimacy.

Once, he took me to a Hasidic Jewish celebration in Brooklyn. The large hall was packed with men in black gowns and fur-trimmed hats. I stayed at the back as Elie made his way to the podium, where he was received like a long-lost child by the rabbis, who were knocking back vodka from small glasses. Elie took one and sipped it slowly. He was instantly reproached by the rebbe: 'Is this how you drink in Vishnitz?' he mocked him, laughingly. Elie hesitatingly took up the challenge for the honour of his past and kept up with the refilled drinks. He had no intimation then of his redemption of sorts, of a family of his own, a large and admired body of work and his intervention wherever in the world cruelty and injustice caused pain and destruction. His dedication would finally be recognized with his award of the Nobel Peace Prize in 1986.

In New York in the autumn, there was a surge of social life. It seemed more invitations than ever came from the delegations to tea dances, cocktail parties, birthday celebrations and independence day festivities, and they were hard to refuse. One engaging encounter at a party was followed up by others, in the open and stylish way typical of New Yorkers. An English accent and a good job was an open invitation to the hospitable salons and the interesting people who drifted in and out of parties and made a connection. At my friend's house, we discussed the world with Norman Mailer who, then between wives, was dating my friend. Miles Davis's brooding appearances at gatherings defied all decorum, but his was a powerful presence when he entered the room, and one merely ignored his language, which was dense with swear words. One time, at the home of the heir to chain stores Huntington Hartford, I danced with a beautiful Italian. We talked about opera and art but somehow I fielded his personal questions and wanted to leave this acquaintance there. Next morning in the office, a swan created from lilies of the valley was delivered to my desk, with a legend taken from *Lohengrin* and challenging me to turn him once more into a prince.

I had met Ved Mehta, Indian staff writer for *The New Yorker*, through Katherine Halton and when she left for home, I took over escorting him to his social engagements. Without sight from an early age, Mehta miraculously navigated himself round New York, but liked to be accompanied to literary parties, where he was the darling of hostesses. He was witty and engaging and, perhaps relying on my physical descriptions of people, wrote with extraordinary insight. I became very friendly too with Rene Farmer, the ex-wife of Art Farmer and a photographer from Uruguay, who for no particular reason spent much time at the UN. She ruled in Harlem, and drew me into her husband's world of jazz players, among whom she was still queen.

I rearranged my one-room apartment, now furnished with gifts crafted by my departing friend Ellen Ochi of a black and red Calderlike mobile and a black lacquered coffee table, and added some bookshelves. Tired of trawling the sales racks at Bergdorf Goodman, I decided once again to make my own dresses. I hired a sewing machine for one month, and with exquisite remnants from the French couture houses which I discovered in a shop on Broadway and 56th Street, I cut out on my floor and sewed my new wardrobe from the leftovers from royalty.

It finally dawned on me that my telephone was being bugged, presumably by the FBI, when I noticed the crude, intermittent but repetitive bleeps, some sort of electronic intercept which punctuated my calls. More mysteriously, at a Pakistani party, I heard a repetition of a conversation which had taken place in my flat. This situation required caution and additional cushions to silence the phone when I had company. No wonder my Russian friend Vadim Bogoslovsky always enthusiastically accepted invitations to parties at my flat, but never showed up. Invariably, I would find his business card in my post box next morning, apologizing that when he had arrived he had found the party over. I had met Vadim often, stalking parties with the younger generation diplomats, watching, listening, his hands clasped behind his back, never on the dance floor. His role in the shadowy ways of the communists, was minder of Soviet Under Secretary Suslov. On the day that he asked me for lunch, he told me he had accidentally admitted to being half-Jewish in an interview with *The Jewish Daily Forward*, a local Long Island newspaper, and begged me to use all my influence to prevent *Newsweek* from publishing this revelation. His request was serious, because, remarkably, his job was at stake. No arm-bending with my editors was required; the matter was too insignificant to publish, a fact which he attributed entirely to my intervention. His gratitude knew no bounds – it was as typical as it was absurd of the clumsy cunning of the KGB machinery, in which my new-found friend was undoubtedly an operator. In the end he had risked nothing, nor did he gain anything, but *Newsweek* gained a great deal. We met weekly for lunch, never at the same restaurant, when he was and remained a channel of information, a vital hotline from the thirty-eighth floor and from the Kremlin itself. This was to prove invaluable in the dramatic happenings to come.

In January I was asked by Roberto Holden, leader of the larger of the rival Angolan independence movements, to go underground in Angola to record and report the resistance war against the Portuguese, who maintained their harsh and anachronistic colonial grasp. Disillusioned by the failure in the Security Council to make progress on the issue, Holden's group had decided to obtain the self-determination on their own.

He proposed a four-hundred-square-metre area for an on-scene report in northern Angola, where his nationalist forces operated out of forest villages, harassing and demoralizing the Portuguese military, destroying crops, mining installations and transportation networks.

His highly disciplined organization would provide my passport and an escort on my entire night-time ten-hour trip from Leopoldville to the border. Carriers would take care of the equipment on the walks through tall grass and across streams from village to village. Mango, banana and pineapple trees would provide food, and fresh palm wine, drink.

In passing on the request, I pointed out to Eldon that the prospect was not as risky as it sounded and that a very interesting story would emerge, provided that necessary precautions were taken, and I was willing to go unless someone else wanted to. I was told that the marches would be paced to the endurance of their 'guest', and the river crossings were spanned by bridges made from logs interlaced with vine. I would require a sleeping bag, water purifier tablets, basic medications and two pairs of shoes. Portuguese raids were known well in advance through the grapevine, and with prior warning there was always time to beat a retreat and take cover in the forests. Eldon was very interested and was quite willing to send me – but no company would insure me and *Newsweek* refused to send me without cover. Instead, I embarked on another awfully big adventure.

25

Yugoslavia 1962

I was tempted by my colleagues from the Yugoslav media and diplomats to explore Yugoslavia on my spring vacation. Their country, like they themselves, sounded welcoming and friendly and I was attracted to the people and their history, the natural beauty of the land and the tolerable face of communism, where many ethnic groups lived harmoniously as one under the benign despotism of Tito who, alone, had stood up against Stalin.

When I told my sister of my plans, she asked me to stop over in London and stay with her to reconnect with her children. I could combine my visit with having my long-neglected teeth fixed on the NHS. I accepted her invitation, and asked her to arrange an appointment for me with her local dentist, Mr Booth. She also decided to have a cocktail party for my colleagues from New York who would be in London at the time.

I arrived, exhausted, from a late press night at the office, laden with gifts for the children and presents of champagne and sweets sent to me on the airplane by my friends. It was a strange mix that evening in Hampstead Garden Suburb and, on sherry and cakes, it really was not a success. My sister's friends and neighbours had little in common with the worldly sophisticates from New York, who included Hella Pick of the *Guardian*, Ved Mehta, who was in Marylebone researching a series of articles on the theologians for *The New Yorker*, and staff from the London bureau. When the evening was over, I asked my sister for her car keys to take Ved to the Tube station. She declined, so he and I set out together to Golders Green on foot.

Next morning, I sat down at the breakfast table in her kitchen to write my thank you notes. I had occupied my niece Harriet's bedroom and evidently, according to my sister's inspection, had left it untidy, my underwear scattered all over. Deeply offended by what she considered a pollution of her daughter's space, my sister had second thoughts about having offered me hospitality, and wanted no more of it. She exploded in anger and asked me to leave. Her outburst seemed quite irrational, without attempt at mediation by her husband Martin, who observed it all in silence standing in a corner. She clearly regretted inviting me and had had enough.

I had but one thought: to escape from the whole experience, to catch a plane to Paris and forget about the dentist. Instead, my conscience dictated to me not to waste NHS time. I ordered a taxi, packed my suitcase with the offending clothing items, drove to a hotel in Bedford Square, and doubled back to the suburban practice of Mr Booth. Only it wasn't Mr Booth who opened the door to invite me into his surgery. It was his locum practitioner, filling in three weeks for him.

The practice was in a red-brick corner house on a shopping parade in northern suburbia. I sat in the waiting room alongside a thin, pale, prim woman with a tight grey bun and a fearsome frown. Next to her, sat an intimidated-looking silent ten-year-old. After the child went in, it was a long time before the door opened again. The dentist returned his pale-faced young patient to his mother and apologized for the delay. I had to wait again before he came back for me; he told me that the boy was traumatized and had vomited all over the chair in terror of his mother. Some remedial psychotherapy had been required and the chair had needed to be cleaned up.

After he had finished with me, he insisted that the inlays he had prepared required a return visit, and the next day as we chatted he told me he had qualified in medicine and he was acting as locum in his previous discipline for Mr Booth while awaiting the results of his exam qualifying him to practise medicine in America. This was a necessary qualification for America, where he wanted to pursue his intended medical speciality in psychiatry. I left my card with him and said, out of politeness, that I would be glad to assist him if he needed help in New York. He had no card to give me but told me his name was Todes. Cecil Todes.

In Paris, a visit to my old friend Anne Girdlestone gave me a lingering yearning for the comfortable regulated life, French-style. And yet, during the weekend spent in their Normandy *domaine*, there was a hint of unfulfilled dreams and desires. For the moment, she had given up all her professional aspirations, and as the wife of an industrialist and dedicated mother to her two young sons, she seemed happy enough.

Afterwards, I set out for Trieste, to catch a steamer that would take me down the Dalmatian coast. It was a chilly night when I joined a steady stream of passengers boarding the Orient Express at the Gare de Lyon. An air of mystery and anticipation surrounded the trailers stacked high with pillows and blankets, which were rolling up and down the endless platform emptying their loads into carriages. They had exciting, exotic markings: Istanbul, Zagreb, Trieste, Milano and Belgrade. I found mine and climbed up the vertical steps, shoved my suitcase inside and dragged it to Berth 32. To my horror, a short man in a brown velvet jacket sat on the opposite bunk, with very little distance separating him from me. I could smell his breath as our foreheads nearly touched. Mumbling some pretext, I dragged my luggage into an adjoining compartment and awaited an attendant, hoping to change my ticket. When no one came, I climbed down to an office marked *Renseignements* – Information – and asked if there was some mistake. A snooty official said that there wasn't but '*vous n'avez rien à craindre*' – 'You have nothing to fear.' I told him I was not afraid and declined a derisively offered transfer to a ladies only carriage. Knowing how humiliating this would be, I slunk back to my new berth. Snickering remarks followed me down the platform.

An attendant came to make up six beds. I was sitting crouched on the bottom berth with my head bent, when a snub-nosed youngster of nineteen put his face through the door. 'We are five,' he said and asked to see my ticket. I pulled it out slowly, hoping that by the time my charm had seeped into his insolent bones he would have accepted my claim. It must have worked, because he peered at my ticket, mistook the year for the number of the seat and nodded. I suspected he could barely read.

He passed the word to the other faces which appeared in the compartment to take up their berth for the night. There was a ripple of excitement. Do I play *pelote*? Do I sing? Do I go to sleep early? I assured them that I did none of these things and moved into the corridor to let them settle in, smack into the stare of the sinister man from No. 32, who was clearly looking at me and thinking: 'Okay, smart girl, so this is better than me?' It was.

My bedroom mates that night were five members of the French football team, en route to a match in Rijeka. There was Bebe the Pole, a typesetter, and Pierrot, at twenty-five, older by four years. I didn't learn his occupation but he told me his birth sign was Virgo. Yves bagged the bottom berth next to me. He had short light-brown hair and warm, grave blue eyes that seemed to have been scooped out of their sockets and left there. Their manager, a gentle, unathletic-looking little man with a clipboard and a querulous voice, quickly took stock of the situation. Yves snores, Bebe talks in his sleep, but apart from that he assured me they were harmless. I had looked forward to going to the dining car, but how could I with five growling stomachs begging me to bring them back the leftovers from my meal? Two of my berth mates, the one with wavy hair and the jazziest of them all, Jeannot, vanished to visit a shop girl from Prisunic, leaving the rest of us to chat and eventually to turn to the wall of our bunks and sleep.

At morning light, the train whistled its way through the steep green hills rising out of the bay of Venice. The water looked a brilliant turquoise under the morning sky and there was a taste of snow on the air from the Dolomites.

Milling crowds thronged the squares of Trieste as I made my way to the Hotel Milano. It was May Day, and the townsfolk were carrying placards, chanting slogans and punching the air. Once the pride of the Hapsburgs, the city was charmless now, its grand palazzos peeling and bullet-marked. The air was magnificent though, the chestnut trees were in full bloom and the wind nipped the skin off my face. How different it must have been when James Joyce was in residence, incubating the miraculous and enigmatic *Ulysses*. Dinner at the hotel was served on a stained tablecloth by one rushed young man. The clientele at the other tables were quite openly talking about me, and tried to start a conversation. They looked ugly and unhappy. My ignoring their advances caused noisy raucous laughter and the smacking of lips. Clearly the emancipation of women had not filtered through to *Mitteleuropa.*

Next day I boarded a small coastal steamer. Fellow passengers included two ladies from Southern Rhodesia, an Englishman, captain of the ski team, and a retired Air Force officer who sported a camera, binoculars and had no sense of humour.

Unexpectedly, Lois, a colleague from the nation department, was awaiting me in the two-tiered bunk which we were to share. She must have consulted the same travel agency as me. My luggage arrived on a wheelbarrow, hand-drawn by two Italian longshoremen. I was introduced to some of the crew: Jeko, the radio operator and Luka, the second engineer, a young man wearing a short beard and a St Christopher on a gold chain round his neck, who wanted to know the price of the antelope jacket I was wearing. Captain Kanonis was elusive. He had a bony weathered face and a froth of white hair on each side of his face. He spoke little English and appeared to be leaving the running of the ship to his young officers.

Our first stop in Yugoslavia was a little town called Pula, where a policeman boarded the ship and cleared us. I was guided round the Roman arches and columns of the huge amphitheatre which defines the city, creating layers and layers of historic events visible in its streets. In the evening, looking for a little light entertainment, Lois and I went to a local dive, the Riviera Hotel. We were instantly the centre of attraction for the men in the dance hall, who claimed us as dance partners. The three sets which we were expected to complete with each one seemed endless. My first partner was a tense and trembling youth who was jealous because I looked at other men. Next came a properly trained male ballet dancer, who, finding a modern bebop girl like me, showed off all his choreographic skills. I could see the cook and the kitchen maid glued to the window of the dance hall, gaping. Sweat dripped from my forehead.

When we arrived back on board, the second officer invited us both for a nightcap. I first took to him because he gallantly rose to our defence when the radio engineer and the first mate teased us mercilessly about our performance at the Riviera; sensing my distress, with its combined ingredients of German affronted correctness, British Victorian prudery, Jewish blood and Czech melancholy, he would not let the others say that our Romeos were pimps. His name was Tino. He was my height, slim and black-haired, his thirty-four-year-old face deeply tanned. His blue eyes were of an indescribable brightness, and I instantly felt attracted to his sensitivity, his simplicity, his support and the strength of his convictions when talking about his country and its people.

Our second stop was the ship's home base in Rijeka. Keeping a promise I made to my football team to cheer them on, I went to see them lose against the much heftier looking players from Bulgaria. It was fun sitting up on the tribune in bright sunshine among a sea of handsome faces in the stadium which nestled high above the coastline. I seemed to be the only female present and, dressed in my pink suit, attracted as much attention as the game itself. Very occasionally, the crowd rallied to the side of the febrile French who put up, I thought, a credible show. Sadly, I saw Yves, my berth mate from the Orient Express, being carried wounded and lifeless from the field and blamed myself for having been a bad mascot.

We stopped next in Sibenik, with its beautiful harbour embraced by the town, and climbed to its mediaeval cathedral. The climate was mellow, the people friendly, helpful and welcoming and the sea sublime. After every outing to some monument depicting the history of civilization, there was a warm welcome back to the ship and her crew, with a few glasses of slivovitz (plum brandy) and a meal of *cevapcici* (spicy meatballs) and *blitva* (a sort of Swiss fondu).

Nothing disturbed the peaceful running of the ship, except when Luka insisted on showing me the engine room in the bowels of the ship. Wanting to impress me, he moved the central lever to 'Stop'. Instantly, I could hear a change in the purring of the engine. Within seconds, a reprimand came down from the captain, via the first engineer and addressed to me: I may look but I must not touch. I was in a spot, and not about to grass on my young friend. Instead, I explained the situation to Tino who again came to my rescue. I think he must have expected some reward on the bridge that night when he tried, unsuccessfully, to seduce me.

It was when we got to Split, a dreamy place, that it happened. I had visited the town and the Diocletian's Palace and had returned to the ship with a feeling of anticipation. After dinner, I joined Tino and the first engineer and we talked of the sea and ships. The boat was not due to sail until midnight, when Tino's watch started, and though he should have gone to sleep till then, at around eight o'clock he suggested instead that we go for a walk, urging me to fetch a coat. Lois was fast asleep in our bunk. I put on my gold slippers and my Aquascutum coat and together we left the ship, walking side by side, hands in our pockets. He asked me whether I wanted to go into town or up on the hill to the monument. Yugoslavia is full of monuments, and they are all beautiful, so we walked up and came to a windy promontory where a huge glass-walled tower beamed out a light in memory of all dead seamen. There was a bas-relief that I could not make out in the darkness and some cactus leaves scored with names of lovers, which made Tino angry. He adroitly steered the conversation to an island, called Mariana where lovers go, but I replied that we were too old for such trysts.

And so we walked and smoked, and turned back to a dark spot where the waves pounded the rocks. He sat me down and told me about his childhood, born out of wedlock to an Italian father and a Yugoslav mother. As I sat shivering on the rugged stone he lifted me up. 'You are cold,' he said, and then he pulled me into his arms and kissed me. '*Un solo*,' he said, the key phrase of the evening, '*Un solo bacio!*' – 'Only one kiss!' I went through my routine of how it was wrong and bad, considering he was married. But it was so nice to be kissed by him; rarely had I felt so much pleasure. And as we continued down the hill, we walked pressed against each other until we reached the little town. He was known here, a regular visitor, but he did not seem to care about being seen; he kissed me in the darkness and in the light and he kissed me with people passing by.

Singing the one Dalmatian song I had learnt, we walked through Split with its brand new apartments. 'Is it only rich people who live here?' I asked and he replied diplomatically that it was a mixture. I wanted to go back to see the magnificent statue of the fighting Cardinal Ninsky in the square outside the palace. It was badly placed and lit only by the moon which had come through the clouds. But it had the feel of a Michelangelo statue, with a power and a tenderness in the fibre of its limbs and a Mosaic strength.

Then we went to the park and sat on a bench and he was beginning to suffer, and I stopped his caresses though I didn't want to stop and it was cruel and bad. I tried to explain what 'betray' means, that both he and I were 'betraying' someone. He did not know the word but understood it at last. 'I know it is bad. I know I'm married. But right now I want one thing. Only one thing.'

Poor Tino. He had to wait a week to have what he wanted, and by then he had all but given up. Twice he had gone to his midnight watch, once waylaying me as I trotted around after Lois on our constitutional, making me feel perfectly ridiculous as I emerged from the shadows. So we stayed and talked and when his watch came on, he asked the first mate to stay on watch for an extra half hour so he could be with me, but that did not achieve his aim either.

Quietly, the ship chugged hypnotically over the blue water. We left the Adriatic Sea for the Ionian and its myriad islands floated by. We passed the menacing mountains and stopped in Montenegro. When we docked at Corfu, I had to make a decision: should I rejoin the ship on its return journey from Piraeus or await another? My feeling of relief at leaving the charged atmosphere was tinged with regret. I asked Captain Kanonis, whose last voyage it was before his retirement to his island of KrK, to decide for me. He said I should make the return journey with them and booked my passage as far as Dubrovnik.

I stayed four days on the island at the Hotel Astir. Corfu was probably the most conquered and invaded space in all history, from Ulysses through to Napoleon and finally the British. I hired a bicycle and rode for hours along dusty paths. Cypress trees lined my way, which took me through olive groves in the midst of harvest. I passed old men sitting outside tavernas by the roadside, drinking coffee and playing backgammon. Occasionally, a shaky hand would flourish a stick in the air in greeting. More often, there were just bland stares, looking on in wonder as I pedalled past. Deep-scented trees and clusters of the mauve flowers of the Judas tree hung over my path.

In Corfu town, I drank lemonade in the esplanade, which had a very English feel about it. On the green, youngsters were practising for their annual cricket match, which had taken over the psyche and the passion of the islanders. I visited the iconic white church and the impregnable ramparts, but instead of studying the culture and the island's multi-phased history, I went to the beauty parlour in

243

town, hoping to improve my appearance. I could not wait for my ship to anchor in port.

Tino was asleep when I boarded. But around noon, deep in conversation with an English doctor near the bridge, I saw the door on deck open with a great noise and there he was, his face radiant with pleasure. He clasped my hand so long and so painfully that the diamond of my ring, which had slid around, was cutting into my flesh. He simply looked into my eyes and could say absolutely nothing. In the evening, I joined him on the bridge before the end of his watch and asked him for a drink so that we could talk, but there were a lot of English people at the bar so we had to maintain some formality. Somehow, we stumbled into Tino's cabin. After so many frustrated attempts, we were here together at last, despite my scruples and moral qualms. It felt strange, and the conversation was awkward. Even then, as he began to kiss me, we were interrupted by Dinko, the second mate who, without knocking, had come to show off a handbag he had bought for his wife in Athens. Soon after, in walked Luka, all three men looking resplendent in their uniforms. Tino called them The Three Musketeers, and I nominated him d'Artagnan. And soon it was time for d'Artagnan to go into battle on the bridge and steer the ship safely through the night, and I returned to my bunk.

Next afternoon, I kept him company while he was counting the inventory of the lifeboats, wearing a sweat shirt and straw hat. He told me that he had arranged for the chief steward to turn out his cabin and scrub it clean for me. And that night, Tino had what he wanted. We lay down together in his cabin in the darkness and the engine made a pretty humming sound and it was better than the best. In the end, it was so simple; we made love until we were exhausted, and when he went up to his watch I waited for his return – and the next night and the next. Until three nights later, I left him standing on the dock at Dubrovnik, both of us turning away from the tears.

It was not the first time in my transient life that I was leaving behind a person for whom I had intense feeling. Once again, I had brazenly overdone it, immersed myself too deeply in some overstated romantic notion. It was a brief encounter, between boats, a fierce attraction, knowing I was prepared for the outcome and could cope.

And of course I could. Except this once, away from the self-importance and posturing of the diplomats and politicians I encountered in my glitzy existence, I had the crazy notion that he was the kind of man I could spend my life with, knowing of course I never could or would, because with real people like this young sailor one only connects in passing at sea.

Ten minutes before my bus left for Sarajevo, I penned a letter to Tino: 'I must say goodbye to you, to Dalmatia, to the sea, the hills with the Cyprus trees, barking dogs, whistling trains, shouting children ... this town full of echoes of historical and other events. I shall miss it for my particular echoes, and send you my love.' I would never know how he felt about our experience, which would perhaps soon be repeated on the next voyage with another impressionable young woman.

I sleepwalked round the ancient seaport of Dubrovnik, with its walls and beautiful old dwellings. At No. 3 Ulica Zudioska, three narrow stone-flagged streets away from Arvaede Square, I had noticed, written above a Gothic arch on the first floor of the stone front of the narrow house, a modest Hebrew phrase: 'God Bless You As You Enter.' It was in the confines of the ancient ghetto, the home of the Dubrovnik Jewish community, the oldest, together with Split, in Yugoslavia, built in the early fifteenth century. I walked up a flight of steps and entered the synagogue. It had a deserted, sad, dusty look, as though no one prayed there anymore. But in its emptiness, it bore witness to the doom-ridden cycle of persecution and toleration which befell the Jews here as everywhere, and had maintained itself on basic survival. Three arches divided the *bima*, the elevated platform from which the Torah is read, which was draped in faded velvet. The place for women was in a raised gallery behind high wooden grilles. They even had their separate entrance.

I started on my journey by bus to Sarajevo. It took nine hours through the lovely wooded lands of Herzegovina, which reminded me of the forests in Bavaria. We made frequent stops in perfectly beautiful little towns full of sunshine and laughing children. Only the facilities were apocryphal. When we needed, we were led to the most foul-smelling holes in the ground that ever fertilized the earth and lean-to shacks bizarrely made out of marble by a dignified

245

gentleman. In Sarajevo, with two hours to spend, I walked across the small pedestrian humpback Latin Bridge over the River Miljacka and faced the corner of the street where the fatal shooting of Archduke Franz Ferdinand and his pregnant wife on 28 June 1914 precipitated the First World War. I was cold, tired and apprehensive about my sleeping quarters on the train on which I was travelling to Belgrade. They did at least ask my sex when I booked, which was a promising sign. The station was a huge unlit marble structure. Gypsies were camping in the central hall, consuming three-course meals out of newspapers on their trunks. Outside, a three-lane highway led up to the station, and there was a huge fountain with water-sprouting frogs.

I arrived in Belgrade in the evening. The taxi driver took me through a grey, concrete cityscape that looked like the set of the film *Metropolis*. The chairs on the kerb outside my hotel were stacked for the night, and the man at the desk seemed not to understand that I was hungry and looking for a meal. I must have been the only client in that eerie place. I was undressed and in bed when there was a knock on the door. A man's voice said something in Croat and, feeling tired, frightened and persecuted, I yelled at him to go away. He continued, his voice raised. Finally, silence descended. When I unlocked the door in the morning to leave, a tray laden with congealed scrambled eggs, bread, cheese and fruit was sitting on the floor outside my room.

I flew to Athens that day and teamed up with my mother at the Hilton Hotel. In the shadow of the Acropolis I regained some calm. After a few days we set out for a tiny, unspoilt island called Spetses. We stopped over at Hydra, where Leonard Cohen had spent his hippy year and which he had described so fondly, and everyone was still playing the guitar. Our fellow traveller on the hydrofoil was a silver-haired amiable man who dropped us off on his way to his very own adjoining island. He introduced himself as Stavros Niarchos, and would later turn out to be a shipping tycoon. The hotel was basic but restful, disturbed one day by the sounds of a screaming child trying to stop her mother chasing her pet rabbit round the garden for dinner. The barman in our hotel merely shrugged his shoulders.

We returned to the mainland, sailed from Piraeus and crossed the Mediterranean to Bari in an unseaworthy little craft. This much I had learnt from Tino: the lifeboats, encrusted and immobilized by many layers of paint, could only result in disaster when they were needed.

My mother and I parted in Venice, as she continued her journey to Munich for her annual body review with her German lady doctor and I made my way back to New York.

Part Four

Cecil

26

Cecil 1962

The letter was waiting for me when I arrived back in New York. It was in my mail box among a stack of bills, crested invitations and advertisements. The sender was Cecil Todes, my dentist in London, and started 'Dear Miss Loebl', adding that he nearly began 'Hi Lili' but he had decided to 'cut the corn'. He wondered whether the Yugoslav men had affected me and informed me that he had passed his exam and was arriving in New York in the first week of June. He sounded very excited and had given my address to the hospitals to which he had applied for jobs, and he wanted me to inquire about the visa situation. In a postscript he asked me to look for accommodation; an alleyway would do, but I was not 'to displace the cat'.

I loathed being back and my heart and my thoughts were anywhere but Madison Avenue. But I felt he needed help, although his flippant tone and the gauche, insinuating wording in his letters struck a wrong chord and I found it difficult to overcome the separation in my mind between his professional role in a long white coat and the familiarity (calling me 'honey') of the private persona.

I contacted the dean's office at Mount Sinai for clarification about the visa. They confidently saw no problem in converting it once he had been hired by an institution. I wrote back, congratulating him on the ECFMG, which sounded more like a dodgy international organization than a professional qualification and said that after my bird's eye view of England from a dentist's chair I thought coming to America was probably a good thing.

I apologized that my one-room flat would be uncomfortable for two and suggested we find a cheap room in the area when I knew the date of his arrival or, alternatively, I could park myself out on another cat and leave him the alley. I told him my schedule at *Newsweek* – Tuesday through Saturday, Friday all day and half the night – and said he should call me on Plaza 2–500, extension 356.

When he finally wrote me his date of arrival, I thought it best to vacate my flat to give him breathing space so I went to spend the weekend with my aunt in Mount Kisco. I filled the fridge with food, advised him on the use of the shower, wrote down the name of my neighbours and gave him detailed instructions on how to get here in a taxi that took seven minutes from the air terminal. He was to enter the red outer door and look for my name among the listing of tenants, above which he would find a little envelope with two keys on it. One would open the front door of the house, the other the door to my apartment. I also wrote down my aunt's phone number in the country before leaving town.

I was in the bath when my aunt called me to the phone; a man with an English accent wanted to speak to me. I dressed, made my apologies and to my surprise, rushed to catch the next train to the city.

My apartment in E 58th Street was one long room extending to a kitchen at the end, with folding doors and a bathroom on the side. It had a sofa bed covered in blue, a couch from the Red Cross warehouse, a couple of armchairs and Ellen's beautiful lacquered table. I was also storing paintings left over from Jose Maria's New York exhibition, three of which were on the wall.

He was inspecting these when I arrived, peering through large horn-rimmed glasses, which gave him a goofy look. He was taller than I remembered him and slim, dressed in black drainpipe chinos, the kind the hippies wore in London, and a brown corduroy jacket over a polo shirt. I realized that I knew very little about this man who had descended on me. From some vernacular references I assumed he was Jewish, from his vowels that he was South African. That he had recently ended a three-year affair with an actress who had gone off to marry a Canadian businessman on the rebound remained an unspoken secret which only surfaced later. The testimonials which arrived for him, signed by various prominent consultants with double-barrelled names, were in fulsome praise of his skill in gynaecology, and spoke highly of his talent as a surgeon, both from a medical and a social point of view, and of his management of patients and his interest in their care. He had been outstanding at New End Hospital, his last appointment before coming to America. I was reminded of the needy small boy he had so sympathetically helped beyond fixing his teeth.

It was getting late, nearly too late to ring round the local hotels to resolve the lodging problem. We were discussing this, when, from his perch on the arm of the sofa bed where he was sitting, he suddenly bent down and interrupted me with a kiss. I had not expected this and was taken by surprise. Yet, somehow it seemed inevitable – why otherwise had I rushed home when I heard his voice? Without his glasses, his eyes were a soft dark brown near my face and soon we were both lying on the sofa. It was difficult to adjust my mind and cross the bridge over the divide; the white-coated man who had drilled my teeth was now passionately wandering all over my face with his lips. I wondered if he felt sex was indispensable to assure him his lodging for the night, or whether he had really felt attracted to me while my mouth was open wide. It seemed pointless to send him away, but it was strictly a compromise; I was not willing, or ready, to enter into another dramatic situation and, under protest, he spent the night on the sofa by the window.

And so I allowed Cecil to interrupt my life with this diversion he created, and reassembled it in a new direction to include him.

We spent his first day, my day off work, sightseeing in New York, but the next day I had to go back to work and leave him to his own resources. On my way home in the evening, I ran into him on First Avenue; he was carrying a bunch of yellow chrysanthemums for the table with the evening meal he had prepared for me. I was deeply moved, though I hated chrysanthemums, especially yellow ones. From then on, sleeping across the room from each other seemed pointless and so he installed himself on a cot we borrowed from my neighbour Alice, and we spent our nights close together. The words of Polly in Kurt Weill's *Threepenny Opera* when first she takes on Mack the Knife whirled round my mind: '*Ja da muss man sich doch einfach hinlegen, ja da kann man doch nich kalt und herzlos sein*' – (You just have to lie down, you can't be cold and heartless) He had really moved in now.

Cecil's first interview was at Hillside Hospital, a classy psychiatric in-patient institution with a progressive treatment and training programme in Queens. He was offered the job as psychiatric intern on the spot, but had to convert his visitor status to a student visa. The six weeks' waiting was a testing time and nearly broke his morale. Finally, he started work on 1 August 1963, on a year's contract.

The beginning of the General Assembly meant new personnel to be interviewed and ongoing issues to be reported. I decided to simplify my life. Instead of listening to a two-hour militant tirade of Soviet Foreign Minister Gromyko on the subject of Cuba and Berlin, I handed my editors a twenty-five-page text of the lengthy speech obtained from the press attaché. But I had to find an opportunity to pass on an invitation personally to Gromyko to lunch with my bosses, and managed to waylay him emerging from a luncheon with President Kennedy. I experienced one of those Gilbert and Sullivan episodes. 'Will they eat me with salt and pepper?' he wanted to know, to which I responded with something witty about them not being cannibals. Gromyko's new chief delegate, Federenko, who was standing beside him, then interceded with words which crudely sounded like '*dynaminsky magazinsky*'. This was rewarded by Gromyko with a request to have the invitation in writing.

I did my best to include Cecil in my life, my invitations, and my outings with friends. I cooked meals and made room in my closet for his modest possessions, shifted the beds around, and introduced him to the American version of unreality. At first, I believed that our affair and his stay was of short duration. By the time his visa finally came through and he started work at the hospital, his moods and his love-making became a priority for me. The tenderness and delight when we were together were unspoken; there was no end in our wanting each other, although *Newsweek* inevitably got in the way.

I began to realize how troubled Cecil was and how all the initial bravado was a cover for the rumbling depression he had experienced in his early days in London as a Commonwealth student, initially lodging with his brother and his wife in a semi-detached flat in Willesden. Then, in the middle of some curative treatment he had sought, his therapist Dr Dembowitz died suddenly and along with him a discussion with Cecil about the absurdity of his shotgun marriage to a Yugoslav woman he had met at the Lyceum Dance Hall. It lasted six weeks, caused his father's heart attack and cost him his mother's inheritance in exchange for a divorce settlement.

His second venture into trying to make sense of things was even more catastrophic; it was a powerful and damaging interpretation by a maverick genius, Patrick de Mare, in which he made him responsible in a devastatingly cruel and irresponsible analytic sort of way for his mother's death when he was seven years old. This instilled in him a deep and troubling sense of guilt which remained with him always. I hoped I could blow away the loneliness in which he had taken refuge and live only in the confidence of our intimacy by sharing his silly Jewish jokes and the anecdotes of his family circle, which seemed the only attachment he had brought out of Africa.

At *Newsweek*, meanwhile, Eldon had been transferred to the London bureau and British politics, leaving Arnaud in charge. This radically changed the atmosphere in the department. Arnaud truculently challenged my every report and queried my suggestions, even my expense account. On one occasion, when I was entertaining two Soviet ministers for lunch at Quo Vadis, primarily to sound them out on the possibility of a permanent visa for our correspondent Patrick O'Grady, the amount on my credit card was high. These gentlemen had consumed two bottles of vodka, and the desired result had been obtained, at a price.

We were a close-knit community in the foreign department, and the elders in the business, the veteran writers, were very protective and paternal in their outlook for me and were not at all convinced about the sudden appearance in my life of a live-in lover.

When I stopped to think about it, Cecil must have felt quite remote from the superficial encounters which filled my life. What he really loved was music, for which he had a profound appreciation, and theatre, in which he had immersed himself in London. At receptions and parties, in the Starlight Roof of the Waldorf, or the ballroom in the Plaza, he cringed when I was seized from his side by some smooth foreigners or African potentate. So, when I felt *Newsweek* was getting in the way, I began to limit outings to these frivolities.

Weekends were a time for getting to know each other, and were exclusive to him. Sometimes we rented a car to go to the shore, where we spent the night in the shingled hotels, New England style. On our first venture, we stopped at the Captain's Lodge Inn in Stratford, Connecticut. We argued about whether we should sign in as Dr and Mrs Loebl, but he would have none of it, and so I became Mrs Todes for the night. He refused to help with the driving, though he was a much safer driver; he insisted on this because it was I who was paying the bill and over this, too, we argued. He was a powerful swimmer and loved to dive into the huge waves of the Atlantic, ploughing dramatically through them; it reminded him of Cape Town and Muizenberg and how much he missed the sun and the sea.

Though I restricted myself now to working hours, there was a lot going on after the resumed session of the General Assembly broke up. Through my sources, I learnt that Dr Martin Luther King had requested to speak on the floor of the UN's Committee of Twenty-four when the subject of apartheid came up. I knew that consultation on themes related to the debate were not new in the committee, which listens for hours to petitioners on their cause. This, however, was more volatile: the appearance of the leader of the anti-segregation movement would put racial problems into the nerve centre of the world parliament with unknown consequences. I sent a memo to the editor of the nations department.

Dr Martin Luther King never appeared before the committee. He was prevented from doing so by the highest authority in the land, to whom news had been filtered through our Washington bureau. I heard that Bobby Kennedy himself had manipulated this embargo. The reasoning, I was told, when I expressed my feeling of betrayal, was that for a leading black personality to enter the debate on racial segregation could create an automatic psychological link-up in the minds of the Afro-Asian block, and set a precedent for future US malcontents to air their views. In 1963 America had yet to confront its own apartheid.

Once again in September, the post of president for the 17th Session of the General Assembly came up, a high and coveted position for any government, with its power of controlling the agenda and manoeuvring the vote. The choice had been made, it was only a matter of putting ballots in the box. The remaining contenders were

Pakistan's Zafrullah Khan and the tiny loquacious, plump former president of the World Federation of Buddhists, Professor Gunapala Malalasekera, Ceylon's ambassador to Canada. Then, one afternoon in August, there was a frenzied call from the Ceylon Embassy to eight foreign embassies in Ottawa, begging them to return unopened a document they would be receiving in the mail.

Our curious ambassadors found a five-page text, bearing the name and title of Malalasekera on its printed stationery. It was explosive in its condemnation of the 'military overlords of the Pentagon' and of a 'solid NATO voting block'. It also condemned the steamroller tactics of the Afro-Asians and declared a conspiracy and misinformation on key votes cast. All hell broke loose at this 'mischievous document'. In the delegates' lounge, Zafrullah Khan sat contentedly stroking his beard; he had bagged the presidency. Conspiracy theories abounded: some thought this may have been a personal vendetta by someone in the Ceylon Embassy who hated Malalasekera; alternatively, the Pakistanis had paid someone to eliminate the running contender.

I was alone in obtaining the dread document, at midnight, at a secret rendezvous. As the only member of the UN press corps in possession of a copy, I was asked to name my price. For *Newsweek* it was a pleasant scoop, in an article slugged 'Out of the Bag' it trumped even *The New York Times*, which published the story three days after we appeared with it and all the British press picked it up and rewrote it at length. As a result of my exposure, Malalasekera's diplomatic career was in ruins. In Cold War politics, the Russians, whose candidate he was, were furious. There was no acknowledgment for my role in it – my name had been removed from the article 'for my protection'. I felt once again the disadvantage of not being a man. It was typical of their policy about women that they appointed Peter Webb from London as the titular head of the UN bureau.

But soon I was to find myself in an irresistible tide of events which threatened momentarily the very survival of the civilized world.

27

Miami 1962

The fallout from the Bay of Pigs adventure had continued. On instructions from Bobby Kennedy, for whom it had become a personal crusade, the CIA had tried and failed to destabilize – with poisoned cigars and Mafia hitmen – the Castro regime. Of primary concern was the fate of the 1,113 participants in the invasion, and how to obtain their release.

Over the past weeks, negotiations had been ongoing through intermediaries to exchange the prisoners (whom the US wanted) for bulldozers (which Castro needed) without appearing to involve the US government in the process. The man chosen for this task was James Donovan, and I asked my editor if I might accompany him on the first lap of their journey from Havana to Miami if and when this exchange took place.

In distance, it was 90 miles; in red tape, it was unending. Knowing how capricious was the way of Fidel, I would have to move fast on the tip-off. First, I needed clearance from the State Department in Washington (our bureau worked on that), then I had to obtain permission from Immigration and Naturalization in New York, with affidavits describing my assignment and of course landing rights in Havana. I discussed this at the bar with the Cuban ambassador, Garcia-Inchaustegui, and followed it up with a calculatedly pleasingly worded request: 'If and when negotiations between Premier Castro and Mr Donovan are brought to a close and implemented, I should like to cover the return of the Bay of Pigs invaders from Havana.' I added that I was a British subject and had been covering UN affairs for *Newsweek*. A cable was sent to Fidel Castro by our editor-in-chief, Oz Elliot, along with a letter requesting my entry visa to Cuba.

Events moved fast. The bulldozers had been assembled and were ready to roll and Donovan was on his way to Havana. By now it was late October. At the end of the weekly editorial conference, Arnaud strolled over to my desk and told me that it had been suggested that I go to Miami to cover the arrival of the prisoners without further delay. Within an hour, I had bought a small suitcase, a pair of comfortable shoes, borrowed a typewriter, money, and had booked an airline ticket. I dug out some cotton dresses and my swimsuit, scribbled a note for Cecil and set out for the airport. Our paths must have crossed on the Freeway, when Cecil was on his way home from the hospital.

Miami was overheated with frenzied excitement. Rumour had spread that all 1,113 prisoners and many of their relatives were due any moment, and though it was evening, the Cuban refugee community were out in the streets in high expectation. A cabbie on his first job, and a stranger in Miami, finally dropped me at the McAllister Hotel. Outside my air-conditioned room, neon lights flashed, advertising the local palaces of millionaires – the Fontainebleau, the Copacabana – and below, the palm-fringed boulevard stretched for miles along the sandy shore by the marina, where huge yachts were cradled and rocking in the evening breeze.

I changed out of my dripping clothes and headed downtown. In the bars, crowded with Cubans, I received all the information I needed for my report, setting the scene for my piece on 'Cuba Today', which I sent off to New York. Arnaud cabled back that he wanted more, and changed the premise of what he wanted. In one bar, a group of young men I was drinking with beckoned me to follow them through cavernous cellars underground. It was the hub of their monitoring service, and they persuaded me to come back tomorrow when they would have important information for me.

Donovan arrived on the afternoon flight from Havana. He limped off the steps of the Pan Am plane at Miami airport to applause, wearing a rumpled navy silk suit and clutching a stained zippered brief. He was alone, except for a token prisoner released on credit. It rapidly emerged that he had been outwitted and outdone by Castro. His talks had not been helped by a painful allergic reaction in his bottom which tormented him throughout his complex negotiations.

Without the availability of a *sitzbad* of warm water where he could sit and alleviate his suffering, or indeed hot water for shaving, the circumstances had not been propitious to outwit Castro, even if he had been shrewd enough.

The outcome of his dealings, he told us, would now depend on Castro, whom he had to handle with kid gloves in order not to jeopardize the success of the mission. He insisted that negotiations had not broken down and that they depended on the maximum amount of money and goods that the Cuban Families Committee could muster, hoping to endorse the myth that the US government was in no way involved in contributions. The wily Doctor Castro had already changed the shopping list from bulldozers to medical supplies and baby food, and Donovan was prepared to return with us within forty-eight hours to finalize the deal.

When I finally tracked him down to a hotel where he was staying under an assumed name, Donovan told me he considered the return of the prisoners 'a moral obligation', and felt he could accomplish more skilfully what diplomacy had failed to do as a 'a metadiplomat'. In a two-hour interview, during which he was in constant telephonic contact with his campaign manager and with Senator Javits, his running mate for political office, he confided to me that his dealings with the mercurial doctor would fill a book. He had had no contact with the prisoners, but tensions had been high; the execution of six counter-revolutionaries had taken place within his hearing and there had been a firing on a hotel in Havana by students.

I did not much trust James Donovan; he seemed basically cold, uncaring and opportunistic. He described how he was constantly accompanied by heavily armed guards in his residence in a villa, and how he watched himself on TV on every news bulletin, which affirmed the perceived opinion that 'Donovan had arrived in Havana to serve as a decoy to the American invasion'.

By the end of the week, nothing had occurred. The deal seemed ultimately to be fizzling out and my hopes of seeing the Palace of the Revolution faded. Castro raised his price to $62 million and kept people dangling on the line, raising futile hopes. The snags hit by Donovan were no longer connected with the merchandise. What Castro really wanted was an admission of guilt to complicity in the invasion, in the form of an overt Washington contribution to the ransom. Ultimately, his interest was not so much in obtaining supplies, his sights were set on maximum propaganda receipts. Since Washington was unlikely to openly associate itself with the transaction, the deal was doomed to collapse. For me, it also put in doubt the good faith of Donovan. It was not until just before Christmas of that year, after a much greater crisis was over, that the prisoners were quietly exchanged for the sum of $53 million dollars, food and medicine, paid for by private donations.

Meantime, in the cellar of a downtown Miami bar, the real drama evolved. A group of young Cubans handed me documents containing information about the extent and purpose of Soviet activity on the island of Cuba during the past month. I could not believe my ears as they told me about the covert Soviet takeover of the island, with bases in every province, and gave me proof of Soviet military 'technicians' who had taken command of the 300,000 Cuban soldiers, who were now under the command of Russian generals. These documents and photographs depicted eighty-seven ships docking in Cuban ports and unloading strategic nuclear missiles, including two consignments of medium range ballistic missiles installed on nine sites, with a range of 2,400 miles and an arsenal of forty launchers. They pinpointed where the installations for the firing of guided missiles were being constructed, and disclosed very precise data concerning the most important military bases obtained by their intelligence. They were able to confirm that 800,000 tons of armaments had been sent to Cuba by Soviet Russia and its satellites in recent months.

The reported U–2 overflight in May had discovered the installation of some of the SA–2 missiles and had been followed by a warning to Khrushchev by President Kennedy at the General Assembly the previous month against placing offensive weapons in Cuba. He had publicly received assurances from Gromyko himself that the situation in Cuba was well in control, suggesting that there was nothing to worry about. It was now evident that most of the installations and missile sites were placed underground in farms and haciendas, schools and fields, undetectable by air. Their information not only detailed every province where these activities were being spread about, but listed the ports from where the equipment and material was disembarked.

261

Worst of all, a guided missile launching pad closest to the Panama Canal had been installed adjacent to Guantanamo. Khrushchev, stalled in his objective to create a viable economy and a model socialist community as an example for the whole of Latin America, had decided instead to build missile bases in Cuba to train against the United States.

I filed all this information to our foreign department, cable after cable, every aspect of the situation that had been asked for and more. I had reported the scene in Havana, located the skyscraper where the Soviet High command had taken over the offices, and described the atmosphere in Cuba in the grip of the Soviets. I had encountered some of the 200 anti-Castro organization who were sitting and waiting for the homecoming of their men.

It was Friday, and I was hot and exhausted and felt that something really important was about to occur which I wanted to avoid. I took advantage of the proximity of a small British off-shore island and sailed in a creaky small boat to Bimini. I landed in a time warp, with little boys in knee-length flannel shorts and women knitting on benches in the park. I bought some duty-free cigarettes, a bottle of Joy perfume and waited for the return trip. The sea was rough, I was ill all the way, and when I was not throwing up over the side of the boat, I lay on the floor wishing I were dead.

The next day I hurried back to New York. It was the 20 October 1962.

28

The Cuban Missile Crisis 1962

The office rang early on Monday morning, my day off. Arnaud's voice was tense and full of foreboding; all news channels had carried an alert from the White House: The president would go on air at seven that evening with a message of momentous significance for the very future of the nation, and maybe the world. I was to go immediately to the UN to find out what the president would say. My instinct was to tell Arnaud what I thought: that the information on which the president was acting was the same I had unearthed in Miami. Only later, at a high-level editorial conference, did it emerge that my cables had been filed away in the cabinet without being read.

Within their small groups, the delegates communicated to each other that something was afoot in the saga of David and Goliath. No one seemed to know that in the past week secret meetings at the highest level of US government had discovered the development of a perilous situation.

Cecil and I had looked forward to a poker game, which he loved to play, and dinner at Denise's flat in the Village. We met on the steps of the UN after a feverish day. Manhattan was becalmed; a spectral shroud hovered over the empty streets. An occasional yellow cab broke the silence and the steam gushed out of the empty sidewalks from the underworld.

We did not play poker that Monday night. Instead, at 7 p.m., we learnt that the world was on the brink of a nuclear war.

Speaking in his gritty, strangulated voice, President Kennedy announced that as a result of stepped up surveillance on the island of Cuba in the past week, unmistakeable evidence had established that offensive missile sites were in place. Their purpose: none other than to provide a nuclear strike capability against the Western hemisphere. He outlined a seven-stage action plan, including a quarantine of the island to prevent deliveries of offensive weapons and a demand for the immediate dismantling of missile sites and the withdrawal of all missiles. What sent shivers down our collective spine was the pledge: 'It shall be the policy of this nation to regard any nuclear missile launched from Cuba ... as an attack by the Soviet Union on the US, requiring a full retaliatory response.'

The president called on Khrushchev to halt and eliminate this 'clandestine, reckless and provocative threat to world peace and ... to abandon this course of world domination ... and move the world back from the abyss of destruction'. He warned of 'many months of sacrifice and self-discipline ... full of hazards ahead'. Implicit in his statement was that if the US attacked Soviet troops in Cuba, it would inevitably lead to thermonuclear war.

New Yorkers responded with controlled panic. Gristedes, the supermarket on First Avenue, was filled with people hauling loaded trolleys of food supplies to their cars. My brother, on business in Boston, phoned and asked me whether he should head for home. Cecil was trying to calm his patients, while not at all immune to worry himself.

At the UN, Vadim Bogoslowsky, paying me back for saving his job, kept up-to-date information flowing at clandestine meetings in restaurants around town. He revealed the hidden agenda over the blockade, and the content of the letters flying back and forth on 24 October from Khrushchev to Kennedy, and again of the two letters of 26 October, in which Khrushchev offered to conditionally withdraw Soviet missiles if the US pledged not to invade Cuba and removed their missiles from Turkey. It was the fragile beginning of a denouement. This was followed on 27 October by a reply from President Kennedy, in which he pledged not to invade and to end the blockade, on condition that the USSR immediately withdraw its missiles from Cuba. Some clandestine verbal assurances about US missiles in Turkey were also in the package.

Living in the vortex of the crisis was a twelve-hour unmissable commitment for my colleagues and me, who were drawing on every reserve of energy. There was no time for domestic tasks, and clothes had to be recycled from the bottom of the laundry basket. In the office, there was much blame attached to the fact that no one had bothered to read my cables from Miami. Kermit Lansner, the executive editor, called me into the office, shook me by the hand and expressed the gratitude of all the editors for my good work, which had set the magazine ahead of the competition. How could they show me their appreciation? I replied that I just wanted to be left in peace to head the UN bureau, and try again to enter Cuba.

The Security Council met amid heated discussion on the Thursday evening. Adlai Stevenson defended the US position in rousing rhetoric. He threw the gauntlet at Soviet Ambassador Zorin's denials: 'Answer simply whether or not Cuban missiles were in Cuba. Yes or no?', he challenged him. 'Don't wait for the translation – yes or no?' Zorin advised him that he would have to wait for his answer, to which Stevenson famously replied 'I am prepared to wait for my answer until hell freezes over', which apparently regained him some respect from President Kennedy.

Once again, Bogoslowsky passed on the crucial deliberations from the thirty-eighth floor in time for our week's deadline: U Thant was preparing to go to Havana to act as intermediary. The crisis had brought together the world's pundits from the press and writers, and an intelligent, informed and exciting group of people joined UN correspondents at headquarters wanting to accompany him. The initiative had been taken by Pierre Huss of the Hearst Headlines corporation, and a KLM plane was pledged and ready. Once again, I packed my small suitcase in readiness.

Correspondents from *Borba* and *The Times* received the immediate go-ahead from their editors. Zero hour was approaching, but no OK given. The US government and the Soviet Union cabled their consent. Even the Cubans were willing, provided passport numbers and other particulars were given through the Czech Embassy in Washington. *Life* magazine's chief correspondent obtained a collective visa and tax clearance. Time was running out. Cuba's ambassador wished me good luck and 'God bless you'.

Then came the coup de grâce: U Thant became frightened of a media scrum and declined to let us witness his moment in history.

In the event, the Burmese did well on his peace mission and

injected the organization with a brand new imperative, although I learnt later that when he left for Havana that Sunday, the crisis had already been settled in the exchange of letters between Kennedy and Khrushchev, and that his intervention would have been useless without these. Nonetheless, negotiating directly with heads of state had never been in the remit of Dag Hammarskjöld and U Thant was applauded.

Cecil was pleased with his appointment at Hillside. He respected the director, Dr Robbins, who practiced milieu therapy, a holistic approach in which the doctor reacts to and adapts a variety of life situations in an entirely new multi-disciplinary therapeutic environment. He shared his ideas on the treatment of patients and the dynamics of the community and made friends with young colleagues and support staff. For the first time in his medical progression, he had found his métier and his muse, with whom he shared an inside view of patients' needs. He had a room at the hospital at his disposal, and except when he was on call, could live in or out as he wished.

He began now to enjoy New York life. His selection of plays to see and concerts to hear was always exciting. It was my first experience of The Fringe, Shakespeare in the Park, of Broadway, and of *The Rite of Spring* performed in the open-air Shea Stadium. Conducted by Stravinsky himself, the discordant language with its brutal harmonic clashes and driving rhythms was dazzling in the outdoors. We saw Zero Mostel in *The Producers*, and heard Billie Holiday and Ella Fitzgerald in the clubs around town. Once, on an outing to the Blue Note in Greenwich Village with Ved, we went to hear Blossom Dearie. She sang in a small high-pitched voice and delivered her songs with a girlish coyness as she accompanied herself on the piano. The audience greatly loved her. Not Ved. He waited to the end of a song, then got up from the table and marched to the piano to confront her on her singing. I was used to Ved's aggressive response, but this time he had misjudged her adoring audience, two of whom jumped up and were about to punch him in the face when we dragged him away to the door marked *EXIT*. We went to baseball games and ice hockey matches. We were invited to the Long Island home of our senior editor, Otto Friedrich, whose picture gallery of Grosz cartoons delighted Cecil, and to Indian biriyani feasts with Kusum Lall, one of the researchers in the office, and her man Anand. We spent weekends with the Epsteins in Connecticut and savoured the relaxed and sumptuous easy-going leisure hours, which Americans know so well how to provide. Cecil warmed to the unstinting hospitality extended to friends of friends, their willingness from the first press of the hearty handshake, which translated into an illusion that it meant friendship for life, and their respect freely accorded for professional achievement instead of the hereditary privilege to which we in Britain were accustomed.

In getting used to sharing my life with him and pitching my work to his free time, I found we both had to adapt, not always successfully, to our diverse cultural systems. He had broken away from an enclosed family-bound Jewish South African society, part colonial English, part Litvak shtetl, but still clung to both. Sometimes it did not work. At times, I felt uncertain about my feelings for him and when things became a little difficult someone else appeared on my scene. In a crisis of doubt and uncertainty in my commitment, I fell for him.

His name was Martin. My brother who was in town took me along to a party, and over the course of the evening, Martin entirely captured my romantic fancy, and I obviously his. Everything about him was familiar: tales of his solitary exile during the war spent as a shepherd boy in the Pyrenees writing poetry; his education in France and his life in Israel; a marriage which was about to break up over the difficulties with a disabled child. He left with my telephone number. I invited him to dinner. Cecil sensed the atmosphere between us and acted like a frightened rabbit caught in bright headlights. Martin was Central Europe – he talked poetry and literature. He sent me red roses and chocolates, and the next time he came, Cecil was at Hillside and he spent the night. It certainly was not a sexual attraction for me; Martin made some powerful connection with my past and flattered me. He left New York soon after.

I realized how much I must have offended and hurt Cecil because I told him the truth, which he refused to acknowledge, even when for a little while I withheld myself from him. But it did not register with him and he acted as through a fog. He came less frequently to the flat, which suited me because it really was too small for two. But as the months went by, it was forgotten, both of us being immersed in our work and our outings.

In spring, I was commissioned to write a defining article on the Congo for *The New Republic* magazine which irritated him, and he constantly interrupted me because he resented my working in the evenings when he came home from the hospital. When a cover story on Israel was scheduled, I volunteered my services in assisting Amos Elon, *Newsweek's* stringer, in Jerusalem to combine it with an extended holiday. The agenda was a movement in the direction of Arab unity and the threat it posed to Israel. I was invited to sit in on a meeting of the Mixed Armistice Commission taking place on the Syrian border and assess the chain reaction in Jordan triggered by revolt in Yemen; the plan to divide the Dead Sea with a stone wall in order to secure the water level on the Arab side; and finally the fifteenth anniversary celebrations of the creation of the State of Israel.

I think Cecil had an inkling, but the reason for my visit was unsaid between us. I left him comfortably installed in the apartment and left to take my flight to Paris. Two days later, I would travel by train to Marseille, where on 22 April I would join the SS *Jerusalem* bound for Haifa.

29

Betrayal 1963

A bouquet of blood-red carnations awaited me in my cabin on board ship, accompanied by a telegram in French full of wistful longing from Cecil. Our moments before departure had been clumsy, Cecil wordless and withdrawn and me babbling nervously, seeking refuge in absurdities. I had found myself, with a merciful seat between us, next to a religious Jew with side locks and a wide-brimmed hat who blessed everything before he touched it. He addressed a prayer to the carton of food which was put in front of him, then held it up and examined every item in it. He opened his can of coffee, which exploded in a fine shower of sticky gluey dew over everyone in sight.

I checked my luggage at the Gare de Lyon, and set out on the metro to our office in the rue de Berri. It was the same Paris as always: low-hanging clouds and the musty rotten smell of the metro with its blue and white enamel station indicators and its superlative speed and efficiency. A new young man in the office called Yorrick Blumenthal took me to lunch at a bistro round the corner. I visited an acquaintance who lived in a mansion on the Champs-Elysées, and after cocktails at Fouquet's and trawling for presents in the rue St Honoré, he accompanied me to the train station. Once again I was in a couchette with five men, but I was too tired to care and ignored the enveloping smell of garlic and general filth and slept till dawn, when I left my snoring companions to their lecherous dreams. Outside, the green fields edged in cypresses were bathed in golden light under drifting clouds. Avignon passed, illuminated by the dawn glow. I watched as we sped through van Gogh country and stopped briefly at Arles. In my accustomed fickle way, this now replaced all other countries of choice for which I harboured the deepest desire to live forever.

In Marseille, I dispatched my luggage to the boat and went in search of Patrick McGrady, a local *Newsweek* correspondent, deeply engrossed in a story on the French legionnaires. I stopped short of knocking on his door at the grand Hôtel de Noailles when I saw a pair of high-heeled shoes outside. Eventually, he drove me in his hired Peugeot along the Corniche in the sunny bustle of the morning. With the mistral blowing in our faces, we bought some espadrilles at the market and had a breakfast of croissants, fresh baguettes with pate and rosé wine in a dockers' cafe, alongside the men with their blue overalls and wine-coloured cheeks.

Patrick left me on board the SS *Jerusalem* and I watched us being tugged out to sea; in my cabin, I found a summons from the chief purser. My baggage, he said, was being moved and I was to report to the first class dining room. In my new accommodations I found myself surrounded by outrageous luxury, with my own bath, a sea view and utter peace.

My fellow passengers were young people from Corsica, Algeria, Argentina, Poland and Sweden, none too emotional or professionally Jewish, just going to see if they wanted to make their home in Israel. The captain, whom I immediately fell for in a platonic way, summoned me to sit next to him at his table. He was a short man with a Players Please beard and dark brown eyes, reared in the British Merchant Navy, where he must have acquired his delicious sense of humour. To those who expressed an incredulous 'What, a real Jewish captain?' he retorted, 'You know, ma'am, there are real Jewish prostitutes, too.'

It was not difficult to take to this life on the Mediterranean, and I surrendered to every moment of it with pure pleasure. New York and *Newsweek* seemed like a distant nightmare, and all I wished for was to share this moment with Cecil, whom I missed terribly. On deck at dawn, the sea was like an animated lake under the reflected rainbow against the backdrop of passing islands.

I had my hair styled by an Egyptian coiffeur, and, tanned by the sun, was greeted with gasps of admiration by my fellow diners. On *erev Shabbat*, the officers played hosts to the guests, and grace was said before a ceremonial dinner, with fine wines and sumptuous desserts. From the synagogue in the hold, the men returned impeccably dressed in white shirts, and afterwards there was dancing on deck round the pool, muted because of the mourning for the late President Ben-Zvi, who had died recently. The evening ended with a nightcap and a heated political debate in the captain's quarters. I was well immunized against the amorous advances of the officers and could only think of Cecil, and wrote to him that I would like to have him there with me, sharing the indulgence which had always eluded us shifting beds around in the limited confines of E 58th Street.

In Tel Aviv, my idyll ended as I went to work. I picked up my mail from Cecil and cables from the office at *Haaretz* newspaper where *Newsweek*'s stringer Amos Elon was based, and was informed of the planned take-out on Israel. I zoomed around the country, gathering information from government officials. Golda Meir was in hospital, so I talked to her deputy, Abba Eban, and to Shimon Peres, her protégé, whom I knew from New York. I concluded from these and other conversations with Gideon Raphael, Israel's ambassador to the UN, and the US ambassador to Israel, that the threat of the envisaged tripartite union of Arab states seemed as ephemeral as ever, in view of the diversity and the backwardness of social structures, with little back-up to implement the slogans with their enticements. Nevertheless, whatever the fault line in the Arab firmament, the unexpressed feeling was that Israel was sitting on a powder keg which could explode any time; the pronouncement that preceded any policy statement in the Arab vocabulary was always the destruction of Israel.

I was driven to the HQ of the UN High Commission, where a changeover of commissioner was taking place. The resplendent pile in Jerusalem stone, base of the former British Governor, was a mansion high on a hill accessible only through a stretch of no-man's-land overlooking the new and the old city, a beautiful and strange place to be. The UN expert ensconced in the flower-filled mansion expressed his admiration for the agile young Hashemite King of Jordan and voiced the belief that, if left alone, Israelis and Jordanians would get on famously.

The Knesset where I attended a debate was a drab, semi-circular ground floor chamber in a four-tiered structure in the middle of town. I watched the short stocky figure of Ben-Gurion take his seat.

When invited to do so by acting President Luz, he jumped to the rostrum, tugging sheets of paper out of his pocket, and delivered a forty-minute policy speech. He was in a solemn mood, and the members of the Knesset listened subdued to how Russian and Czech arms were pouring into Egypt and German scientists were helping Nasser to build jet aircraft and rockets that could reach Israeli cities. His voice was atonal, rising on occasion to a piercing shriek when he added that, without a shadow of a doubt, the Arab countries were contemplating an attack. Few people sat in the auditorium; his statement was on the wires around the world even before he started. Unsurprisingly, in July of that year he finally resigned his leadership of the country which he had steered to nationhood and victory in two wars. Weary and disillusioned with party politics, he retired to the tranquility of his desert kibbutz.

In the meantime, despite prevailing Israeli doubts that Arabs could function under a joint military command, a new wave of nationalism was sweeping the Middle East, with the announcement of a federal union linking Egypt, Syria and Iraq, threatening Israel from both north and south. It was estimated that an attack was only two years away, by which time Israel would be hard put to match submarine for submarine, rocket for rocket. The bitterness expressed in government circles stemmed from the fact that while Nasser was being pampered by the great powers, Israel found herself more and more geographically isolated.

The military parade along the shore in Haifa to celebrate Independence Day, which I observed from a perch in an army truck, was intended to boost morale and proceeded without a hitch, with an awesome display of air power and a tightly disciplined march-past of the army. Watchful eyes scanned the shadows of every wind-chased cloud, from the Judean Hills right down to the Red Sea shore, in an attempt to avoid the present situation being shattered. 'If we lost another war,' one veteran told me, 'It would be our last.'

I met Martin on my last Saturday in Israel, in a little whitewashed church with a spire in the Arab village of Abu Gosh a few miles out of Jerusalem, acting out a great romantic B-movie fantasy. It was the venue for secular Jews wanting to avoid the strictures and the tedium of the rules imposed by the zealots who rule the Holy City and bring it to paralysis on the Sabbath.

272

I had arrived before him. We sat a while side by side, while the organist bravely bellowed out a Bach toccata. Then, on a grassy slope outside, he unpacked the avocado sandwiches prepared for us by his wife. My sense of revulsion was instant; what was I was doing here with another woman's man, eating her bread and adding no doubt to her misery with their disabled child? Gaby Stein, to whom I had confessed my impulsive action over lunch at the Hebrew University, had warned me against this encounter. It was then that I realized that I had broken a deep but unarticulated bond with Cecil, and had dealt him a blow from which I hoped we both would recover.

Meantime, I faced the illicit car journey through the deserted streets of Jerusalem, bewildered and confused. The very silence of the ancient streets seemed to rebuke me. Martin was more terrified of the street patrols of the Haredim catching him driving than of being discovered by his mother, who lived on our route.

I think we tried, and failed, to make some sense of our encounter. We parted, each one of us pursuing our separate realities. By this time it was too late; Cecil's letters, full of loving allusions and missing me concealed his depression in banter. Spending the weekend in the apartment, he had been invited by my friends to their homes and on outings to the beach; he had gone to a poetry reading in the Armory and to the theatre to see Virginia Woolf. He also reported that I had forgotten to sign my rental cheque and that the landlord was pursuing him.

Drenched in remorse and trailing a worsening bronchitis, I beat a retreat to the desert. Beersheba had changed from a one-horse town to a lively multicultural community. The Desert Inn, opulently decorated with exotic ceramic tiles and hand-woven fabrics, was my oasis, where I could breathe in clear dry air and bathe in the brilliant sun. Drinking my cocktails on a camel-covered bar stool on my first evening, a convention of Israeli tax collectors burst into song with the kind of spontaneity and exuberance which cheered me. I was driven to Dimona and told to avert my eyes from the secret government structure in the distance behind the high wires. I hitchhiked to Masada and received an offer of marriage from both of the soldiers driving the truck. Then I returned to Jerusalem to bid farewell to my friends. At the port in Haifa, there was a great gathering of people I had met, and of colleagues from the press to see me off on the Greek ship. From Martin for some reason, I had parted in the service room in the Dan Hotel in Tel Aviv.

In Italy, once again I met my mother; both of us were troubled. I was tired of travel and remorseful about Cecil, from whom I was now unreachable as I was on the move. In his last letter to me in Israel, I had an inkling something was not right when he ended his letter with the mention of a social worker he had taken to the beach in a Ford he had bought for $150 from Shlomo Bondy, my friend from Sasa. As for my mother, I had failed to realize how sad she was. Still young, dynamic and feminine, but naive and trusting, she had always been guided by my father, had always been charming and feminine for him and was feeling her fifteen years alone. I wanted to tell her about Cecil, and confide in her my self-doubt and my self-inflicted troubles, but felt she was unreceptive, though I suspected she understood more than she pretended; instead, she erected a solid wall around herself which made me shrink away from sharing my experiences with her. The only way I could tell her about Cecil was in terms of 'a man with big ears for whom I am buying a present'. The few times I tried to tell her things to be close and intimate with her, things seemed always distorted and came out twisted, and became interpreted through a way of life she thought was hers, entrenched in a different era, from which she had been snatched.

And so, what Cecil described in his letters as 'The Baedeker Way' – Florence, Siena and Rome – no longer held any charm for me. My mind was elsewhere, and the cloying smell of incense and the sad gilded virgins irritated me, as did the hordes of tourists spilling out of coaches and trouping around. My mother and I both avoided talking of our pain; we merely talked of the banality of life on the trot. And when we parted, she for home and I for Nice, we had failed to find a bridge into understanding.

I made my way to Marseille, with a stop-over in Nice for rest and recuperation. On the Italian border, the death of Pope John XXIII was announced. In Nice, I visited the van Santens in their beach-front apartment. Bram was entertaining his fantasies through his binoculars; they were trained on the bikini-clad girls stretched out on the beach, oiled and offering themselves to the sun like the Aztec virgins to their sacrificial knives. By the time I arrived in Paris, I was shaking with fever and spent the remaining four days of my odyssey in my hotel bedroom with a raging fever. I sent a brief cable to Cecil, announcing my flight and time of arrival at Idlewild and asked him to come and meet me.

He came in his newly acquired Ford, and when we reached my apartment, he told me coldly and deliberately that he had found someone else.

30

Reconciliation 1963

There was no script for what occurred on that Sunday night in the empty flat: the sobbing; the recrimination; why had I left New York and stayed away four weeks? I veered between anger at his capitulation, and self-hatred for chasing after a chimera. His letters had been full of love and care. He had asked me to come back to him, and I did. The distance had made me aware of his meaning in my life and, despite the issues between us, I would not have liked to live without him. I should have realized that right or wrong, I really was in love with this man and now he was gone and nothing else really mattered. I missed him stretched out next to me and railed against the revenge and the punishment he meted out to me. And it was my unattainable ambition to make it up to him.

I should have known that in New York a single, professional man, unattached even temporarily, was too good to leave alone. There were too few to go round. Even our friends the Jelins had presumptuously consigned our relationship to the dustbin, and had taken it upon themselves to appoint Alice's sister Martha as a candidate replacement for me, the attempt, recorded in a letter to me in Israel, taking place in an outing to Fire Island.

I had lost 15 kilograms during my travels and was drained and tired from both my bronchitis and the misunderstanding with my mother. I went to work in a blur next morning, oblivious to the extreme August heat and damp. Here too, the atmosphere in no way lifted my spirits; the head researcher was hysterical over Arnaud's leaving and acted like a drill sergeant with 'her girls'. I found myself sick of diplomats, politicians and Africans, and was dreading my attendance by command at a joint leaving party at Eldon's flat for

276

him and Arnaud with all the brass and their wives. Knowing how they loathed each other, I should have liked to avoid it at all costs.

Then came a tragedy of the most profound kind, which affected the whole organization. Phil Graham, the charismatic publisher of *Newsweek* and *The Washington Post*, had been committed to psychiatric clinic Chestnut Lodge after a long period of irrational manic behaviour which translated into an uncontrollable passion for a young Australian employee in the Paris bureau. On a weekend remission to their home after a reconciliation with his wife Kay, he had retired to their bathroom, propped a .28 gauge gun (the plan had been to go bird-hunting) against his head and pulled the trigger. He had been a power base in the land, with influence ranging from the White House to local politics. There was panic in the organization, its future uncertain in the hands of his widow Kay Graham, who, in the event, emerged from under his shadow with a steely agenda.

I, meanwhile, bruised and battered, carried my misery around with me, staying in the flat, wallowing in sentiment and listening endlessly to Edith Piaf. While it was my ambition to erase what had transpired, I found that my grief and self-hatred were tinged at times with fury. Nothing in the letters between Cecil and myself had indicated anything but loyalty and love for each other, and he must have been aware of my disillusion with Martin and the Israeli situation. I felt he could have held on to me, instead of being so vengeful and without restraint in his punishment.

I weighed all my options. As usual in such circumstances in the past, I wanted to take flight. But the stock in which I had invested proved worthless in the economic crash. In any case, my precipitous letter of resignation from *Newsweek* was torn up by the editor. Instead, my colleagues closed ranks around me and determinedly forced me to take part in their social lives. The attitude of my colleagues at work and my friends at the UN was that only a rotten person could treat me in such a way, and they insisted that I had had a lucky escape and was much better off without him.

I attended the Jewish wedding of a junior writer in the office. It took place in a temple in the Bronx, and I attended along with my friend Kusum Lall, who wore a sari embroidered with 24-carat gold, adorned with rubies and pearls and emeralds and constituting her dowry. Dwight Martin, *Newsweek*'s senior editor, also came; he said he liked the groom because he had once challenged him in outrage for being patronizing towards Inuits in an article. A veteran of every war arena, he was all-American and tall, with thick gold-coloured hair bouncing off his boyish face; an admirer of Mencken, he dominated every scene in all circumstances, with an air of authority and reckless outrageousness where nothing or no one was sacrosanct. But beneath the clowning, there was a deeply loyal, kind human being who always sustained his friends. Here, looking bizarre in a white satin yarmulke, his long legs spilling out into the aisle, he engaged the doyenne of the gathering, a ninety-year-old lady from Vilna, in a Yiddish conversation made up from the bastardized German he had learnt on assignment in Berlin. The guests were sequined, bosoms dripping out over too-tight gowns, the staging and lighting effects spectacularly garish.

Afterwards, munching kosher egg rolls, Dwight loudly insisted they contained prawns and pork. As part of his perverse humour, on our way home, he dragged Kusum and me to the Bauhaus on 86th Street in German Town, which was known to have been the hang-out in the thirties and forties of Hitler acolytes and home of the *Bund* in jackboots. We sat on the Tyrolean chairs chugging Steinhägers and mugs of Würzburger Hofbräu, toasted Cecil with every drink and watched men and women in dirndls and lederhosen dancing the *Shuhplattler* and waltzes. Twice I tried to flee and twice I was captured and hauled back by Dwight. I became maudlin. Accompanied by his booming descant, I sang louder and shriller all the *schlagers* and kitsch songs from my youth. We began with 'Was kann der Sigismund dafuer', and continued with 'Am Golf von Biscaya'. I don't think the present company had heard anything like it since 'Sieg heil' rocked these halls. And when tiny Kusum danced the ländler cradled in Dwight's bear-like arms, they wouldn't go home. I recalled nothing more as we three tripped out of there. All I could think of was another Sunday dealt with, and without pain.

Cecil's interview for a post as fellow at Harvard had been successful, and he graduated from Hillside Hospital, adding yet another scrolled parchment to his cache. I had been invited to the ceremony for the departing residents and the cocktail party that followed. No sign of the social worker. Cecil looked downcast; he must have felt the wrench from the comfortable situation, the friendship he had forged with his fellow doctors, and was confused in the situation we had created for ourselves. On his way to Boston, he came to say goodbye, his dark eyes clouded with longing. It was not the best omen for taking up his appointment.

The social worker must have followed him to Boston. On that first Friday, I was returning from Jones Beach on the Southern State Parkway, when a convertible sneaked up and crashed into the car in front of me. There was a mighty conflagration and the car concertinaed. I found myself lying on the grass next to my overturned car. Fire fighters came to douse the first car and floodlights illuminated the scene, a growing number of people massing around and gawking. I withheld my name and place of work from the police. Any mention of an accident involving *Newsweek* personnel would have been all over the first editions of the *News* and the *New York Daily Mirror*. The photographers were no threat, they only took shots of the dead, and I wasn't hurt, merely shocked. Nevertheless, when they insisted on taking me to Bellevue Hospital, the first person I rang to rescue me was Cecil. It was bedlam in the ER, and on the ward women were running around with slit wrists, bleeding and soiled with diarrhoea. I was told Cecil had gone away for the weekend.

Soon after, inevitably, it was all over with the social worker; she disappeared off the radar and was never mentioned again, and our correspondence resumed. It started with a phone call; the distrust was there between us but worse than that was his disillusion with his new surroundings. His room was too small and had to be shared with another resident. I deconstructed a meeting I had attended with the philosopher Martin Buber in response to his accusation that I was too passionate and, between the bookshelves and the bourbon bottle I began to sleep again.

Our relationship resumed against all prevailing advice, when I emerged at weekends from the small shuttle on the tarmac at the airfield at Logan. Cecil always waited for me and, the first time, there was awkwardness between us. His insensitivity in not disclosing what plans he had for us for the weekend did not help my confidence, and so it always came as a surprise when we toured the beautiful autumnal countryside. But slowly, in the spectacular beauty of the landscape of New England and Maine, we seemed to find our way back to each other.

I savoured the respite from the sterile existence in which I had to function professionally, the posturing and the politics and the public personalities. Here, under a watery blue sky, the maple trees lining the highways, dense with leaves in every conceivable shade of yellow, the beaches were now ours alone. The gravel crunched under our bare feet; we threw pebbles into the shallow water at low tide and picked up driftwood pounded into weird shapes by the waves. It was warm enough to eat our lobsters outside, on tables laden with blueberry muffins and olive bread and iced water. Removed from the frenetic social life of the city, we talked about Cecil's family, his older brother Vic, a radiologist whose brilliance he admired and envied and his much admired older sister Hodda. He told me about his age-old friendship with Sydney, married to a young French woman orphaned in the Holocaust, who not long ago had lost a child from a previous marriage to leukaemia and how he had gone to Paris to give blood during his last days. On our return to Boston, we haunted a local Italian pastry shop for crunchy confections, especially for the addictive canola. These rarely survived the walk back to his male-only hospital billet. I shared the night with him in a cubby-size room with a bare light bulb and a narrow bed, the coarse fibres of the horsehair mattress digging into my spine, and making risky sprints to the bathroom across the corridor hoping to remain undetected.

Initially, Cecil moaned and complained. Many of his patients at the Boston City Hospital were local drunks, chained to their iron bedsteads under police guard. His accommodation on call was terrible. But slowly, he began to feel more at ease in the elegant university campus, and enjoyed the high standard of seminars on his chosen field of paediatric psychiatry. The dean of the faculty was very caring about his young Fellows; he befriended Cecil and always included me on social occasions. Cecil slowly became integrated into the social life of the Harvard community and was much in demand for the tennis games in which he excelled.

At work, we were gearing up to the General Assembly and my assignment at the UN was as a listening post. The evening before a pre-Assembly invitation to lunch with Secretary General U Thant, I was coming home from the dry-cleaner with my clothes slung over my shoulder when I was knocked semi-unconscious. My purse was snatched and my report on the briefing was impaired. But the secretary general welcomed me with his accustomed grace and during lunch I absorbed the message that he had a function to fulfil. Limited by the constraints of being a dummy in the game of power politics, he emerged as an ambitious man with not too resilient a mind but a clear one. He seemed to have sliced out his empire as a father figure to the underdeveloped countries, to which he expressed his total commitment. His elected position depended on the four powers. He had none of the exquisite finesse of personal diplomacy practised by the sophisticated Dag Hammarskjöld, and his political goals were limited to the development of the Third World.

To his great credit, the stability of the secretariat was assured after the chaotic and frenetic reaction that followed the death of his predecessor. The input of the UN in regional conflict had been successful and the unity of the Congo had been largely restored with UN assistance. Most important of all, he initiated the signing by the other three powers of a treaty banning nuclear testing in the atmosphere, in outer space and under water. It was a colossal step forward.

There was much excitement and expectation when it was learnt that President Kennedy was to attend the General Assembly. His charisma was still ablaze from his June 'Ich bin ein Berliner' speech, in which he had condemned the Berlin Wall and exhorted the communist East Germans to dismantle it. Americans and their allies looked forward to his appearance before them.

It was a familiar scene, my fourth session on the job: the blue uniformed security guards and clusters of policemen gathered outside the iron gates, the flags snapping in the icy wind and the great motorcade whipping in through the secretariat gate and stopping in front of the revolving door of the General Assembly building. Roped off in the melee of the press and camera-wielding delegates and ambassadors, we had no intimation that this would be the last appearance among us of this sprightly young president who leapt out of his limo into the greeting hands of Adlai Stevenson and U Thant. Spontaneous applause greeted him. He was tall, smiling and elegant in a severe black suit. He entered the elevators, and we took our places in the press booths above the Assembly. There was a long wait; it was explained to us later that the president's back had required a massage.

His speech, with a modulated overview of the state of world events, expressed confidence in the UN and in its progression towards peace in the world and affirmed the support of Americans of the organization. He was applauded, as was his rousing appeal to all conflicted nations, in Berlin, Laos, Angola, South Africa and the Congo.

Two months later, he would be gunned down by an assassin's bullet.

31

The Death of the President 1963

On 22 November 1963, just after half past one, I was on my lunch break at Ohrbach's department store. A barely audible newsflash from UPI interrupted the music: three shots had been fired at the presidential motorcade in Dallas. The president had been hit. Before I could drop my purchases and reach the exit, a second bulletin followed with the news that 'Kennedy has been wounded, perhaps fatally'. I raced up Fifth Avenue and ran the eight blocks across town to 42nd Street, trying to avoid collision with stunned New Yorkers sleepwalking round the streets.

On the steps of the UN, the overriding concern among the delegates who nudged up to me was whether the gunman was black. Stunned and incredulous, I joined my colleagues in the press section, glued to the TV. The facts that emerged from the confusion were slight and unconfirmed. The exchanges and circuits were crippled with overload and were blacked out. Even Ben Bradlee, our Washington bureau chief, had a dead phone line. As the sparse, muddled and contradictory information filtered through from Dallas, we supported each other in the hope that with the available medical skill and the speed of surgical intervention, he could be saved.

But it was short-lived. The president was pronounced dead at 2 p.m. (1 p.m. Dallas time). By his side was his traumatized wife; his trusted staff surrounded him. There had never really been any possibility that he could survive; the assassin's bullets had penetrated his head and shot off the side of his face.

The carnage was not restricted to the president; next to him Governor John Connelly was also hit, but recovered quickly from his wounds. Confronted with a threat to national security, conspiracy

283

theories abounded; there were fears of a terrorist plot from outside, and an internal strike from the radical right, who made no secret of their distrust of and antagonism towards Kennedy. There was also concern for the young family of the adored leader and for the future of the country. On the pronouncement of his death leadership had already passed into the hands of his Texan vice president, Lyndon Johnson.

Not since Pearl Harbour had the United States experienced such a disaster, and not since Lincoln had America lost an elected president to an assassin's bullet. How deeply Kennedy was loved showed in the outpourings of emotion by a people who seemed to have felt a personal bereavement, who were now fearful and apprehensive, uncertain about what was to come. I recalled how, only weeks ago, from the roster of the packed General Assembly, young, handsome and agile, stabbing the index finger of his right hand to accentuate a deeply felt point in his address, he had spoken of the progress of peace and prosperity in the world and reiterated his uncompromising stand on equal rights for blacks. And how, on my visit to the White House as a guest of his press secretary, Pierre Salinger, he had stopped to exchange warm words with me on his way through the Rose Garden back to the Oval Office which Pierre and I had just vacated, apologizing for reclaiming his workplace. Now this era, and his dream of a new Camelot, had disappeared forever in the banal trauma cubicle of Parkland Memorial Hospital.

At the UN, the international community proceeded with the utmost decorum. The collective behaviour transcended political and regional positions and was scrupulously upheld. Even the Russians murmured their condolences. I heard Adlai Stevenson utter eloquently as no one else could: 'We shall bear the grief of his death until the day of ours.' A pervasive convulsion now seized the country, dominated the collective psyche and paralyzed every niche of life. Even the Boston Symphony Orchestra had switched from a scheduled Handel concerto to the slow movement of the *Eroica*.

Finding Kennedy's murderer had to be done swiftly; the fear of a conspiracy which was transfixing the Texans, always less than enthusiastic about his liberal stand, had to be laid to rest. By evening, the evidence became clear: a lone ex-marine called Lee Harvey Oswald, a drifter with both communist and right-wing pedigree, had fired the two shots from a mail-order gun from a window of the Book Depository in a well-planned and orchestrated execution. He had escaped, subsequently killed a policeman in his flight and was finally captured leaving a cinema.

The Kennedy family behaved with their accustomed regal stamina and poise. In the absence of the president's cabinet (they were over Honolulu on a flight to Japan), far from Washington, Bobby took charge of handling the official and family disaster. But it was Jacqueline, her pink suit stained in his blood and spattered with his brains, who towered in grief over her dead husband like, in a Greek tragedy, the Trojan queen Andromache over her beloved Hector. She never left his side, insisted on the priest giving the last rights to his spirit already departed and objected to the post-mortem required by Texas law, overruling the medical examiner who refused at first to release the body without it. She arranged for only his trusted aides to be close to the coffin and rejected the offer of the marine guard of honour to be the pall bearers on landing in Washington. For the dramatic swearing-in of the bewildered Lyndon Johnson on Aircraft 26000, she refused to change into the pristine white suit her aide had laid out for her. It was her last act of defiance against the Fates. Her role as president's wife now passed to Lady Bird Johnson. As First Lady, she had ceased to exist.

My work at the UN was completed, with all the comments and reactions reported. It was the nation department and the Washington bureau who handled the snuffing out of one regime and the installation of another, in an unrepeatable week in journalism. I helped to process the copy in the office and prepare the magazine for publication through the night. At dawn, I took a shuttle to Boston, where Cecil was waiting for me.

We had not much appetite for travel; instead, we drove round the old parts of post-colonial Boston, saw the flags fluttering at half mast and retreated early to a shingled white-painted hotel outside the city to watch TV and devour *The Boston Globe* and the *Record American.* The whole world seemed to be in mourning for Kennedy. At home, there were memorial services in Westminster Cathedral, St Paul's and at Windsor Castle. Laurence Olivier interrupted a performance at the

Old Vic and had the audience stand up while the band played The Star-spangled Banner'. The Soviet radio played dirges and Gromyko, the great hard-man was reported leaving the US legation in tears. The universal outpourings of grief surprised us. All the world leaders, even those in political contention with Kennedy, announced that attending the funeral in Washington was their priority.

Along with the rest of America, suspended in time and fixed on the unravelling of the aftermath of the assassination, we stayed up most of the night, watching events on TV from our hotel bed, overwhelmed, conscious of having lived through an earth-shaking event that could not be surpassed. We saw the handover of one administration to the next; the preparations for the interment of the president; the lying in state in the Capitol and the millions of stupefied Americans filing past the catafalque. There were glimpses throughout of executive decisions which had to be made to accommodate the unprecedented arrival in Washington of every world leader – an emperor, kings and queens, presidents, prime ministers, dukes and princes. There were few absentees. Their accommodation and protocol at short notice was a gargantuan task for officials, who had trivial problems such as finding a bed long enough for General de Gaulle.

Just as we thought nothing more startling could possibly occur, our disbelief was once again stretched to the limit, as the unthinkable played itself out before our eyes.

At eleven o'clock, the screen switched to Dallas City Jail, where they were bringing out Oswald. He looked bemused but insolent. He was handcuffed to a plain-clothes policeman as he stepped out of a shabby dark brown prison elevator into a vaulted basement garage for transfer to the county jail. A tightly packed crowd of the media milled around him, popping flashbulbs and sticking microphones in his face. There appeared to be a total lack of order and no sight of security staff.

No one noticed the podgy little man in a business suit and a fedora hat who muscled his way through the throng, positioning himself on Oswald's left side, until we heard him shouting 'You killed the president, you rat!' At the same instant, Jack Ruby, a Dallas nightclub owner, drew a revolver from his hip pocket and fired point blank into Oswald, hitting him in the middle of his body. Oswald fell to the ground instantly, tugging at the officer to whom he was chained.

Not implausibly, we assumed we had strayed with the handset onto the scene of some wild western and a distorted perception of reality set in. Even the yelling and the commotion which followed left us perplexed. The TV announcer stumbled through some attempt at a report. His consternation reflected the national psyche; this simply could not have happened.

But it did, and with it vanished forever an acceptable explanation for the killing of Kennedy, whilst conspiracy theories about the possible involvement of more sinister forces abounded and conjecture on how the police in Dallas could have so misjudged the security arrangements of their extraordinary prisoner grew. In the end it all became academic, because Lee Harvey Oswald never recovered from his abdominal wounds and died two days later.

The decommissioned Victorian morgue of Boston City Hospital was an unconventional setting in which to view the most solemn pageant in American history. Yet here we were on that Monday morning of Kennedy's funeral, invited by Cecil's colleague, Costas Papadopolopulous, a young psychiatrist from Athens. He had claimed the place that had housed corpses, square and white-tiled with a floor slanting to a central drain, in preference to the narrow cubicles and straw mattresses assigned to young doctors on call. He had hired a large TV set and comfortable chairs for his guests, and provided a spread of minted meat balls, souvlaki, meze and sweetmeats to sustain us through the most spectacular event in history. Choreographed in large measure by Jacqueline Kennedy, who had modified the centuries-old protocol wherever she was willing to compromise, the ceremony kept us transfixed from the moment the coffin left the Capitol till it arrived at St Martin's Church.

There was no equal to the drama of the pain and the agony emanating from the tragic figure of the widow, her tear-stained face obscured by a veil straight out of a Goya painting. Flanked by her children, by white-gloved, blue-uniformed infantrymen of the Old Guard and by brother-in-law Bobby, she waited for the procession to pass by. Six matched pairs of horses drew the carriage, followed by one solitary riderless giant of a sleek black horse with a pair of boots reversed on the stirrups, and then Jacqueline began her stubborn march on foot, heading the procession of family limousines. To the mournful stutter of a muffled drum-beat, and under the spotlight of a bewildered world, she strode with determination behind the coffin, accompanying her husband on his last journey.

It heralded the end of an age of style and sophistication not previously experienced in US government. From the moment little John John raised his right hand in salute, to the last kiss of the flag draping the coffin in St Michael's Church, where Caroline reached under the flag to be closer to her daddy, we were glued to the screen, the souvlaki choked by tears.

32

Murder 1963

The following weekend, Cecil's past exploded around him and threatened to terminally disrupt our life together. It was Thanksgiving, and we had decided he would come to New York and spend the long weekend together with friends in Connecticut. After the gloom of the past week, and a dumbing down at the UN, I felt in a celebratory mood. I took time off work, rented a car from a firm on 82nd Street and parked it in the basement garage of the UN, walked home hugging huge brown paper bags stuffed with groceries, and prepared a meal of his favourite foods.

Everything was ready and I was dressed and perfumed, the sparkling Mateus rosé wine was nicely chilled. And then the phone rang. It was Cecil calling from Boston. At first I did not quite grasp what he was saying: on returning to his place in Boston, he had found his actress ex-lover Gwen sitting on his doorstep and he wanted to show her New York this weekend, so would I leave the keys to the car I had rented with the parking attendant for him. I blanked out, stuttered something incoherent, but could not get round the words. In the end I must have capitulated, because after that, he hung up. I hurled all the food I had prepared into a black bin bag and threw away the ruins of a bouquet of freesias, his favourite flowers. I called up some friends who all but said 'I told you so', and tried to invent all kinds of diversion with which to entertain me. But I just ached my way through this preposterous situation, remained where I was and went into mourning.

I tried to figure out how he had stumbled into such a situation, not of his making, and allowed himself to be so disloyal and unfaithful. He had rejected this woman after a long cohabitation, either before

289

or after his meeting with me, had welcomed her disappearance from his life, yet here she popped up, and he did not face her down. There was a hint of revenge in this carousel of betrayal, in which I was not entirely blameless. But now we were too deeply involved for him to tolerate so shabby a turn.

She timed her reappearance and staged this melodrama aptly. Cecil was searching for meaning to his past and groping for his future. He seemed overwhelmed by his ghosts. Beneath his wry throwaway lines and affectionate banter was a deep sense of unresolved loss; while he had happily treated the Jewish adolescents at Hillside, with whom he emphasized, he shuddered at having to handle with physical force and medication the alcoholics in the underbelly of Boston. He did not understand these patients and felt helpless in making any impact on their condition. He blamed all his miseries on his mother's death, which he felt left him unprepared, aged seven and alone in the world. He was ineluctably moving in the direction of making psychoanalysis, a discipline in which he felt he could achieve a personal resolution, but did not know how to go about it. Obtaining a US visa and a licence was fraught with difficulties and had many obstacles. In any case, I sometimes felt that although he was enticed by the wide-open, generous and hospitable Americans, he preferred cricket to baseball and the interiority of the English, insulated against themselves, which resonated with him and his Edwardian upbringing. And then there was me and those brief nights of my madness in bed last autumn when I turned my face firmly to the wall, rejecting his embraces and his love-making, and he barely objected.

Meanwhile, he had built inside himself a mausoleum in which the joint tenants were Gwen and his ex-wife Lydia, whom he had married because he had wanted to, who must have fulfilled some function in his life but about whom he only remembered the annoyance and the loss of respect from his family. He had sent Gwen away because, he had told me when I asked him, 'Things weren't right between us, it wasn't possible.' But Gwen was now another addition to the mausoleum and presented him perhaps with some sort of reprieve. For the moment, she was back, and holding all the cards.

By Monday, though, Gwen was gone; they must have talked of the possibility of her leaving her well-heeled husband, although she never would have done, in the knowledge that Cecil again would reject her. So how had she found out where Cecil was and why had she come after all this time to summon up the demons which now engulfed him? From the compressed tone of his voice on the phone, it sounded as though he had sunk into a self-indulgent depression from which he relied on me to bail him out. I reacted in the only existential way I knew how: I penned a missive, a sort of outpouring of frustration and a farewell enactment of what our love affair had taught me about him.

Whenever the complexities of my life became unmanageable, I consulted the diminutive German-Jewish GP, Doctor Schiff. Her crowded practice was on the West Side, and her remedy, as always in the past, was a dose of vitamin B 12, which she injected with verve and conviction into every one of her young women patients living and loving in New York.

It certainly cushioned me against the next calamity. Together with the entire office staff, I went to a farewell party for Dwight Martin, one of my mentors at *Newsweek*. Editors and writers, researchers and reporters were gathered at the Jaeger House, a vast old-time restaurant on Lexington Avenue at 85th Street. We all regretted his leaving – he had legitimacy and authority and was entertaining. The atmosphere was relaxed, the drinks flowed and the food kept coming. Filmore Calhoun, another mentor, entertained us with a hilarious ballad, enumerating Martin's exploits – some unprintable – and his eventful coverage of events in Korea and Singapore, and in Tokyo. None of his achievements was spared Calhoun's acerbic rhymes. Everyone was dancing and socializing, and there was no awareness of the sinister undertow and the tragedy that was unravelling.

A trainee researcher, uninvited presumably because of rank, had crashed the party and seemed to be making herself available to any and all of the senior editors, especially Arnaud de Borchgrave. Next morning, she was found dead, naked in her bed; her body, smeared all over with Vaseline, was strapped head to ankles to that of her flatmate, indicating that some bizarre perversity was involved in her gruesome killing. I did not know Janice, but I shuddered at the violent end of an obviously profoundly disturbed girl who only hours before had danced and drunk in our midst. All of us who had been at the party were under scrutiny. But the chief suspect turned out to be our very own Arnaud de Borchgrave, who was the last person to be overheard talking with Janice on the telephone and who featured prominently in a diary found near her body.

First at my desk the following morning, I had been dumbfounded when de Borchgrave called me in to the empty foreign department and told me of Janice's murder. I was in his office when they arrested him. Two burly homicide detectives barged into the newsroom, demanding in loud voices that could be heard all over the floor to know where he could be found. And as the staff trooped in one by one to begin an orderly day's work, they were nonplussed to see our boss being led away by the police.

We learnt that he had been put in a holding cage in the precinct until the next morning, when he was released through the intervention of a former politician friend. We were all interrogated individually for our version of the events of the night before, but it was Arnaud they visited in the office for months afterwards, continuing their inquiries, without, however, finding a single charge against him that would hold. The atmosphere at work in those fraught days became intolerable.

We were all uneasy in the presence of our own colleagues, and the climate of doubt and suspicion hanging over each one of us was suffocating. It was presumed that the killer had been at the party the night before, and could therefore be anyone sitting at the next desk. We eyed each other with fear and a feeling of distrust was pervasive throughout the entire magazine. We avoided our former drinking companions and lunched alone. The police hunt was urgent and intense, prodded on by Janice's celebrity uncle Philip Wylie, a prolific bestselling writer who was personally involved in trying to find the murderer. Many months later, an Afro-Carribean man was framed and jailed and later released without secure evidence against him, and the crime was never satisfactorily resolved.

The double murder rocked Manhattan. Sex and violence created its own salacious momentum and the tabloids revelled in the exposure. They splashed it in detail on their front pages, exploiting it in all its lurid description. Worse still, one red-top newspaper published the in-house directory of female employees, listing addresses and phone numbers with callous disregard for the consequences to us. It did not take long before we were pestered with relish day and night by every pervert and crank, who rang us at home and camped outside our front doors with lascivious taunts and threats. It was too much to bear. We were offered security escorts, but I had had enough.

My lease was close to expiry and, as in the past, I chose the glorious anonymity and convenience of hotel living. This time, I chose the Beekman Tower Hotel, a classy abode on First Avenue, next to the UN. I packed my cases and dismantled my flat and with it my history of the past three years. I piled my furniture outside the house and locked the door behind me. My Garcia Llort paintings came with me, but the historic sofa, the cot-bed Alice had lent us when Cecil moved in and Ellen's table ended up on the kerb outside on E 58th Street. They did not linger there; when I rushed back to retrieve my favourite nightdress, I found the entire contents of my flat had vanished. Like the scene of the slaughter in Racine's *Bajacet*: '*Tout est rentré dans son calme habituel* – Everything has returned to its usual calm.'

While Cecil was regaining his equilibrium, I attended the ritual diplomatic receptions which went head to head in the season, celebrating independence or an anniversary of a rebellion, or the visit of a head of state, or even a christening of a family addition, or merely a reminder of their existence. Moving around a flower-decorated ballroom with music discreetly playing, a champagne glass that was never empty in one hand and a canapé in the other, was a relaxed way to engage with stimulating people from every country in the world while gaining useful insights. It was not an unpleasant pastime for the dark winter months. Slowly, even the crisis at *Newsweek* became history and we returned to our normal lives.

The 18th Session in September trundled along after Kennedy's assassination, and nearly came to confrontation with the Afro-Asians, the weightiest single cohesive bloc in the UN. Their historic conference at Addis Ababa in the spring resulted in a defiant pledge to liberate the remaining enslaved countries, particularly South Africa, from colonialism. Their words were vituperative, their obligations enormous. All this was happening despite their prevailing concern about the discontent and strife which erupted in open violence in their countries, where few of them had been spared political foment, described by *Le Monde* as the '*psychose de complot* – conspiracy psychosis'. Independence had come perhaps too easily and too swiftly. Looking at the map in my diary for the year 1960, a huge green swathe spanned the colonial territories from Algeria down to Angola reaching to the heart of the continent, excluding only Nigeria, Ghana and Guinea, designating French West and Equatorial Africa. Two years later, there were thirteen independent states with deep-rooted tribal divisions, each with their assured seat and their vote here on the East River in the forum of nations, with all the rights and trappings that accompanied their status. At a September press conference, Ivory Coast leader Houphouët-Boigny, whose regime was one of those threatened, described the fiery manifestations of the political awakening of the masses and the widespread discontent as the 'wind of madness sweeping through Africa in the storms of decolonization'. The euphoria that followed the expectations of independence was short-lived. African workers were let down by their leaders, watching corruption distort the texture of government.

It was to the credit of Adlai Stevenson, who canvassed patiently and brilliantly with the delegates 'not to raise the dust of mutual recrimination, and that strong action was more effective than strong words'. He personally fronted the Committee on Racial Discrimination, humbly requesting a chance to work out 'our problems'. As a result of the quiet diplomacy he advocated, the Afro-Asian votes merely obtained a ban on arms shipments to South Africa, avoiding their expulsion, and removed a threat for a reconvening of a special session after the Christmas break, as in past years. Everyone heaved a sigh of relief. Once again, Adlai Stevenson's genuine understanding for the emerging nations had brought its rewards. He was sustained in the belief he had confided in me one day over dinner, that 'one day, Miss Loebl, we shall all be brown'.

Lyndon Johnson's debut appearance at the end-of-term session of the General Assembly was heavily attended; nearly a thousand delegates from 113 countries (Kenya and Zanzibar were the fledglings admitted the day before) filled the hall. His great height towered over the secretary general as he strode to the chair so recently and vibrantly occupied by his assassinated predecessor. He was tanned by the Texas sun, crackling with the taut, restrained energy regained since his tentative state at his inauguration on Air Force One. His address was delivered in phraseology not so different from Kennedy, and the warm, loud and lengthy standing ovation he received on arriving and leaving seemed to reflect an awareness of a certain grandeur about the man who had pledged continuation of the Kennedy policy. When he finished his speech, he was escorted by a barricade of UN guards and secret servicemen to an adjoining lounge, where in a sheath of sunlight from the giant windows he exchanged a hearty handshake with each one of the 113 heads of delegations.

He had delighted the Russians, whose Ambassador Fedorenko, an old sparring partner of mine, told me he was impressed by this quiet, restrained and solid man who had delivered a very positive speech on the theme of 'peace to all our countries', noticeable for its absence of any of the threats or strong warnings which Kennedy used to inject. In fact, all controversial points had been avoided and an end to the Cold War emphasized.

Sir Patrick Dean, the British representative, was more patronizing, conceding that Johnson's speech had been workmanlike and 'an excellent bit of craftsmanship'. The Africans appreciated his courage on subjects controversial in this country and the Asians were pleased with his lofty and comprehensible message. It was a satisfactory end to a mediocre session, remarkable mainly for the death of a president, the melting of the Cold War and the signing of the Test Ban Treaty.

The old guard had changed; this was my third president and I began to think about my career. At the age of thirty-three, I had stumbled by fluke, through my languages and my British training, into a man's world, and had spent six unplanned years in most unexpectedly sustained excitement. I had developed a passion for the political process, observed the pirouetting around issues by politicians and had developed an intuition for deconstructing the game-playing, from the deadly serious to the opportunistic. I had learnt to puncture pomposity and convey with increasing assurance its underlying meaning. My recognition was reflected in the friendship and trust of the people I worked with, both at the UN and the office. However, while I was invited to go on TV and write for other publications, my incursion into a man's world would never be rewarded with promotion. It was the unchallengeable policy of Kay Graham that women writers were not tolerated on her magazine. Yet it was me whom she entrusted with introducing Donald, the heir presumptive to her publishing empire, down from Harvard, to the UN and its workings. He shook hands with key personnel with the utmost respect and courtesy, displaying the exquisite manners I so admired in young Americans.

Tentatively, Cecil and I set about mending our relationship. We were too attuned to each other and too much in love to remain apart for long. His relief was palpable at having been made to face up to his past and genuinely leave it behind, and he came out of the experience remarkably renewed as he joined me in the intense rounds of social life with friends and family. We went to the theatre, jazz clubs and ice hockey matches. We both felt right to be together again. In Boston, he took me to a one-woman show performed by Lotte Lenya. One of her acts portrayed her at the end of her telephone in Nazi Germany, speaking to a close friend who was no longer allowed to visit her. Her understanding and support of this surrender, and the excuses she provided for her friend, even attempting to console her, resonated unbearably. Up there in the stalls of the Boston theatre, I could not contain my tears as I relived the experiences of my childhood that I had set aside.

That winter, I was invited by the Israeli ambassador to a special gala, an American theatre tribute for the Habima company, whose production of *The Dybbuk* Cecil and I had seen. It was a supper dance; the guests were stars from Hollywood, theatre directors, composers, performers and politicians and I made an extra effort to match the occasion. In a black sleeveless Valentino dress, I crossed the threshold of the shimmering Starlight Roof at the Waldorf Astoria. Abruptly, the band stopped mid-number and restarted with 'Hi Lili, Hi Lo'. In a corner of the ballroom, my old friend Raymond Cohen from our days at the Arizona Hotel was beaming at me from the piano on the bandstand, waving his great hands in my direction. Everyone looked up and stared at me. I recognized Danny Kaye and Theodore Bikel, Martha Graham and Julie Harris, Serge Koussevitsky, Fredric March and Jacques Lipchitz, and took my seat among them. I waited for Ray to finish his session and we walked home together with much to talk about, just like in the old days.

33

Wedding 1964

At Christmas, Cecil and I retreated to the seclusion of a sumptuous flat on First Avenue, lent to me by a colleague, and over roast turkey drumsticks from the deli we chewed over the events of the past and our plans for the future.

I was restless and wanted a change from six intense and eventful years which had surpassed any job expectations. Tempted when there was a vacancy in the Jerusalem office, I had bought the latest model Olivetti portable typewriter in preparation. Cecil's appointment at Harvard would end in the summer and he was under pressure now to decide on his direction in medicine. Through my State Department connections, we had tried and failed by every means to obtain Cecil's Green Card. Even then, he was required to qualify in state board exams in order to practise in any US hospital, and although he had no qualms about passing these, he had had his fill of exams. He felt that his future was to be in paediatric psychiatry. The seminars at Harvard had been enlightening, and had resonated profoundly with his experience of childhood. He had studied and closely identified with the works of Winnicott and Bowlby and thought he could combine this discipline with a training in psychoanalysis.

His invitation to interview as a candidate for the Institute of Psychoanalysis in London came in mid-February, and I decided to take an early Easter vacation, go with him and introduce him to my family. We both felt that once his future was assured, I could set to work on mine.

On our second day in a hotel in Dorset Square, Cecil rose early to attend his interview in New Cavendish Street. He was apprehensive and excited; everything rested on the outcome. While he awaited the decision of the admissions committee, we headed north, passing in the train from King's Cross all the familiar landscapes of my itinerant life.

It had been a long time since I last rang the doorbell of our house in Rectory Terrace. My mother, alone now, received Cecil with her customary grace, but confided in me her doubts, voiced by her friend Mrs Freedman, about the propriety of bringing a man home without being officially engaged. She also pleaded with me that if I was going to be married, the wedding should take place in America; she had no appetite for arranging a third wedding in her home. Cecil's sleeping quarters were in the room on the half landing and I had to wait for the sound of my mother's heavy breathing signalling that she was asleep before tiptoeing down the three steps to join him.

Back in London, we stayed in Bloomsbury, opposite the boarding house of the Madigans where I used to live, but we were too preoccupied with Cecil's results to forage round in my past. Apprehensively, he presented himself before the board. I was in our hotel room when he returned with the news of his acceptance. He crushed me in his embrace, and trembling with excitement asked me if I would have him now.

For three mindless days of optimism about the future and with feelings of sheer delight, we flew to Paris. In the ancient Hotel Saint André des Arts, at a corner between the Boul'Mich and St Germain, I shared my well-trodden past with my husband-to-be. We slept in a tiny room under the eaves of this mediaeval hostelry, where the bed took up most of the space, and surfaced into the late afternoon hubbub of the market in the rue de Buci, where we selected our supper from the cornucopia of fresh produce. We chose ties for Cecil at Dior, soft leather gloves in the Galleries Lafayette and slim, gold-rimmed spectacles at Lussac. The severe dark horn-rimmed ones were cast into the river and floated away under the bridges of the Seine. I think we both felt for the first time that coming to Europe was coming home.

There was one more hurdle to cross. Rejected by the renowned analyst of his choice, he was referred to and accepted by Dr Lothair Rubinstein for his psychoanalysis training. Such were the stringent rules of the analytic cabal, that approval for entering into marriage had to be obtained before beginning the course and was known to be generally discouraged. It was a tribute to the old-style perspective, the pragmatism and humanity of this man that he gave his consent. It also made me aware of the phenomenal significance he was to have in Cecil's life. His early discipline in neurology in Vienna and his broad experience of psychological medicine was reassuring, and he seemed a safe personality to influence the first years of married life. Tragically, seven years later during a session of an International Psychoanalytic Conference in a Hapsburg Palace in Vienna, Dr Rubinstein died in Cecil's arms. It was Cecil who, having tried and failed to revive his analyst with the kiss of life, had to pronounce him dead to the stunned assembly.

Back in London, between performances at the Old Vic of *Hobson's Choice* and the First World War show *Oh, What a Lovely War!*, we met Cecil's future supervisors and past tutors in psychotherapy, who initiated me into a bewildering world where everything means something. Clearly, they had high regard for Cecil and introduced him to Anna Freud after a lecture at the Maudsley, where, in a hall packed to the rafters with eminent men of medicine, she delivered her vision of the mental welfare of children. She presented her arguments in a clear, high-pitched, almost hypnotic voice. When it was over, she mingled with her audience in the hall and spoke words of encouragement to Cecil.

On our return to New York, news of my engagement spread like a forest fire, and the invitations followed in abundance. Our chairman, Fritz Beebe, a kind benevolent supporter of mine, held a reception for us in his home. In Boston, the dean gave a garden party attended by the many friends and colleagues Cecil had gathered around him. In my sober moments, I confronted the future with trepidation. Cecil was undergoing possibly the most expensive training in any syllabus. For the next six years in the NHS, he would have to earn enough to finance the required five-times-a-week analysis, Institute fees and supervision – not to mention the three children who were to make up our family, as they had his and mine. Even the gruelling extra night jobs he took on at the hospital in Boston would merely be a small contribution. I calculated that we had exactly enough funds to live on for two months, after making a down payment on a flat.

Cecil did not share my worries, confident that with his experience and training he would instantly find a hospital job. We both asked our parents for money; my mother kept her promise of financial help, but from Cecil's father came the reply that the coffers were empty, Cecil having already borrowed money to buy a car.

I therefore seized the opportunity to add to our supply of money. My Aunt Antonie and Uncle Fritz were over from Texas, depending on the kindness of friends in their helplessness for their transportation needs, and were thrilled to bring to my apartment a former Bamberger, Heini Fleischmann. He had shepherded them around the city and they now presented him to me as a successful man of property, a safe pair of hands with whom they had invested some savings, and they gave me their full encouragement to do the same. I remembered him from my childhood, though he was not part of our social circle. His family was respected and he seemed eager and willing to augment my savings by a lucrative short-term investment in a spectacular development project on Staten Island in which he was involved. The returns would be huge and would come soon.

And so I sat down, under the approving gaze of my aunt and uncle, and wrote a cheque in the amount of $2,000, nearly emptying my account. As a bonus and a symptom of complete madness, I entrusted him with a sapphire stone which my friend Yakov Aviad from the Israeli Consulate had bought for me in Mexico. This he said he would have mounted by a fine jeweller whom I could not possibly afford. I was so enthused that I phoned Cecil and suggested that he too invest with this man.

Time passed, and I waited in anticipation of instant wealth. Instead, there were only brief communications, containing promises and eventually excuses. Finally, the announcement came that Fleischmann was bankrupt, but that the money would be paid in April. It never was, then or ever; the sapphire was returned to me in some tawdry setting and Fleischmann was never seen again.

I penned my resignation to the editor-in-chief at *Newsweek*, requesting to be considered for a possible opening in the London bureau. The reply came back that there was no vacancy in the office, but as they did not want to lose me, they would employ me to replace staff and fill in on vacations. On the parental front, the letters introducing ourselves and receiving good wishes and regrets flew back and forth from Newcastle and Johannesburg. No one of either family was available to be with us on our wedding day, with the only exception being my cousin Werner Loval, who was serving as Ambassador to Mexico, who had found some official pretext to come to New York.

Cecil had searched for family ties in a telephone directory in Boston and discovered Samuel Todes, a distant cousin, professor of philosophy at Massachusetts Institute of Technology. He introduced us to his father, David Todes, now retired from teaching in Rochester New York. We met him in the Biltmore Hotel on a snow-laden day in mid-winter. He was good-looking still, with a mass of silver hair, and he recounted to us his extraordinary tale. As a young man in Lithuania, he was sent to study Hebrew, Arabic and English at a gymnasium in Tel Aviv so that his parents could avoid the statutory payment for two Russian children's education. On his return home, the Cossacks were plundering the communities; aged just sixteen, he was put on the Trans-Siberian Railway to Vladivostok, en route to America to join relatives. Lying about his age, he joined the Jewish Brigade in Canada to fight the war for the British in Egypt. He was severely wounded in battle and was in danger of losing a leg, when he was rescued from the surgeons by an aristocratic Scottish nurse who took an interest in this handsome young Jewish boy. One day while convalescing, the nurse summoned him to meet an important person, asking him to dress in his best fatigues. In the hospital lobby, T.E. Lawrence was waiting for him. He took him away, taught him to ride camels and educated him about the desert and its natives. And that was how in 1919, Uncle David Todes delivered the British bribe of gold to the sheiks at Aqaba, in order to secure their allegiance. He described Lawrence as a darkly brooding person, who yet commanded his respect and eventually his trust. The bribe contributed to the history of the Middle East, and the British generals rewarded his participation with the offer of a commission in the far away Indian army which he declined, returning instead to New York to marry his sweetheart.

I now dealt with the complexity of organizing a wedding in between reporting on fraught discussions at the UN about the urgent need of a UN military presence in Cyprus and arguments over who was to pay for it. Work piled up, including an interview with Foreign

Minister Abba Eban. I saw little of Cecil, except to celebrate Passover with our friends the Jelins and their new baby, and Easter in Wantagh with Senior Editor Otto Friedrich and his wife, hunting coloured eggs with their four children in their garden at the end of Long Island. On Cecil's thirty-third birthday, I travelled to Boston laden with a satirical album illustrating our life together with clippings and photos, a mohair sweater I had knitted for him, a Barbra Streisand record and a brand new tennis racket.

Cecil worked to the last minute and arrived in New York the day before the wedding, with a Harvard armchair, and a gold ring he had beautifully fashioned for me himself in the dental laboratory of the university.

We exchanged vows under a gnarled old apple tree in the Friedrichs' garden. I wore a short white jacquard dress copied from Balenciaga by my friend Mimi. Kusum Lall had woven a canopy of marguerites and cornflowers in familiar Hindu tradition, which served as a chuppah for our ceremony. Everyone at *Newsweek* and all the friends I had made over the years loyally made the trek to the end of Long Island, and all of Cecil's close colleagues from Harvard trooped down to join in. The maverick rabbi who had agreed to conduct the unorthodox outdoor ceremony was a nephew of Kurt Weill, and Elie Wiesel and Yakov Aviad stood up for Cecil. Otto Friedrich had designated himself as the father of the bride and officially delivered me into Cecil's hands, all his children formed my escort to the table covered with a red cloth which served as an altar. Afterwards, we danced late into the night to a band made up of students from Columbia University. The tables groaned with the food I had helped Otto's wife Priscilla to prepare and store away in the cavernous freezers over the past few weekends, and the drink flowed.

We spent that night across the water on Fire Island in our friend's wooden beach house. The next day, we completed the formalities, made a round of visits, obtained our licence from the courthouse in downtown Manhattan and closed down the apartment. I had declined to make a wedding list for which everyone had asked me, and we could only select some of the many presents that arrived to be contained in our trunks. The remainder were set outside the apartment door for the janitor.

The chair, Mrs Hull's carpet and my Garcia Llort painting were carefully wrapped and ready to go, but when the taxi came to take us to the boat, Cecil had disappeared. Much later, he returned and explained as though it was the most natural thing in the world that he had stood in line to cash in his accumulated Green Stamps.

As the skyline of Manhattan receded into the distance Cecil and I entered our flower-filled cabin on board the *France*, setting sail to London and a whole new life together. We would face the many challenges of married life, have a family of three children, celebrate Cecil's brilliant career and deal with his eventual debilitating illness.

But that's another story.